Regulating Readers

Regulating Readers

Gender and Literary Criticism
in the Eighteenth-Century Novel

Ellen Gardiner

Newark: University of Delaware Press
London: Associated University Presses

© 1999 by Associated University Presses, Inc.

All rights reserved. Authorization to photocopy items for internal or personal use, or the internal or personal use of specific clients, is granted by the copyright owner, provided that a base fee of $10.00, plus eight cents per page, per copy is paid directly to the Copyright Clearance Center, 222 Rosewood Drive, Danvers, Massachusetts 01923. [0-87413-695-4/99 $10.00 + 8¢ pp, pc.]
Other than as indicated in the foregoing, this book may not be reproduced, in whole or in part, in any form (except as permitted by Sections 107 and 108 of the U.S. Copyright Law, and except for brief quotes appearing in reviews in the public press).

Associated University Presses
440 Forsgate Drive
Cranbury, NJ 08512

Associated University Presses
16 Barter Street
London WC1A 2AH, England

Associated University Presses
P.O. Box 338, Port Credit
Mississauga, Ontario
Canada L5G 4L8

The paper used in this publication meets the requirements of the American National Standard for Permanence of Paper for Printed Library Materials Z39.48–1984.

Library of Congress Cataloging-in-Publication Data

Gardiner, Ellen.
    Regulating readers : gender and literary criticism in the eighteenth-century novel / Ellen Gardiner.
       p. cm.
    Includes bibliographical references and index.
    ISBN 0-87413-695-4 (alk. paper)
    1. English fiction—18th century—History and criticism. 2. Authors and readers—England—History—18th century. 3. Didactic fiction, English—History and criticism. 4. Criticism—Great Britain—History—18th century. 5. Fiction—History and criticism—Theory, etc. 6. Gender identity in literature. 7. Reader-response criticism. 8. Sex role in literature. I. Title.
PR858.A79G37   1999
823'.509—dc21
                                                                               99-23072
                                                                                     CIP

PRINTED IN THE UNITED STATES OF AMERICA

Contents

Acknowledgements	7
1. Introduction	11
2. A Will to Read: Intellectual Property and Critical Practice in *Clarissa*	38
3. No Jury of his Peers: Reading *Tom Jones*	63
4. Writing Men Reading in *The Female Quixote*	89
5. Friendship, Equality, and Interpretation in *The Cry*	110
6. Privacy, Privilege and "Poaching" in Austen's *Mansfield Park*	134
Notes	152
Works Cited	182
Index	192

Acknowledgments

I OWE A GREAT MANY PEOPLE MANY THANKS FOR THEIR HELP AND SUPport. Those who offered suggestions and comments during the earliest stages of this study's genesis include: Thomas E. Maresca, Michael Sprinker, Rose Zimbardo, Linda Frost, Bonnie Hain, Michael Bernard-Donals, Kevin Railey, Dean Casales, Taisha Abraham, and Helen Cooper. Many of my colleagues at the University of Mississippi have also read and offered comments on various chapters: Doug Robinson, Karen Raber, Ann Fisher-Wirth, and Jay Watson. I'd like to express especial thanks to Mary Stuckey, who read the entire manuscript and praised me for what I did well, to Deborah Barker, who read the entire manuscript and helped me to focus its argument, and to Debra Rae Cohen, who also read the whole thing and helped me to correct my mistakes and tighten my prose.

To my parents, I owe thanks for loving me and providing me with support and encouragement as I have pursued my goals. I am also grateful to my husband, Greg Shelnutt, who reads everything I write, asks questions, and keeps me on my toes—which sometimes results in my stepping on his. His love and support keep me productive. Speaking of which, I am grateful for my daughter Emily, who has helped me learn how to make the most of my time. Finally, I would like to thank my aunts Kathleen and Mary McKay, to whom this book is dedicated, for taking me to the library every Saturday and for being such powerful role models as educators and women.

The William Andrews Clark Library, the University of Mississippi's Graduate School, and the Department of English all helped to subsidize this study. I would like to thank in particular the librarians of the Clark Library for their help and hospitality during my summer fellowship in 1991.

A portion of Chapter 4 was first published in *Studies in the Novel* 28 (Spring 1996): 1–11. A part of Chapter 6 first appeared in copyright © Devoney Looser (ed.), *Jane Austen and the Discourses of Feminism* (New York: St. Martin's Press, 1995; Houndsmills: Macmillan, 1998). Reprinted with permission of St. Martin's Press, Incorporated and Macmillan Press, Ltd.

Many thanks, as well, to Donald C. Mell and the outside reader for the University of Delaware Press, but especially to editors Christine Retz, Melody Sadighi, Brian M. Haskell, art director Ellen Kazar, and everyone else involved in the production process at Associated University Presses. I couldn't have done it without you.

Regulating Readers

1
Introduction

THIS BOOK TRACES THE RISE OF THE NOVEL-AS-CRITICISM; IT EXAMINES how fiction helped to shape professional critical practices and to define the role and function of the professional critic in the eighteenth century. Twentieth-century scholars have hitherto traced the rise of professional criticism only to mid-eighteenth-century periodicals.[1] It was here, in this more overtly polemical arena, that the new professional critic, "whose unenviable task it [was] to render an account of all new books,"[2] was said to be embroiled in a battle to shape audience's tastes and to form a literary canon.

Linda Zionkowski has argued persuasively that mid-eighteenth-century novelists were also engaged in a debate that centered on the formation of a literary canon, that they, too, "participated in shaping social, political and aesthetic beliefs."[3] In this book, I take her argument one step further when I recognize these novelistic practices as inherently equivalent to the work of the new professional critic. As part of the struggle for power within the field of letters, the battle for critical authority and professional status became part of aesthetic representations of eighteenth-century "life" in literature, and thus, an integral part of the novel.

As Frank Donoghue has shown, the eighteenth-century transformation of the conditions of literary production, most notably the ways in which the book trade "increasingly transformed readers into [a] social group capable of conferring fame upon authors," precipitated "a crisis among aspiring authors."[4] Novelists from midcentury on bristled at the idea that the new professional critic—often, in the early years of criticism, a political hack—would have the power and authority to judge their work, and so responded by representing their characters as metaphoric readers or critics. I argue that Samuel Richardson, Henry Fielding, Charlotte Lennox, Sarah Fielding (with Jane Collier), and Jane Austen appropriate, interrogate, and transform the spectator-as-reader trope first developed in Addison and Steele's *The Spectator* and Eliza Haywood's

The Female Spectator as they jockey for critical authority in their novels. Their various figures of the ideal critic all embody traits, such as a moral objectivity and a private sensibility, that were first described and delineated in these two periodicals. Each author creates a different spectatorlike persona to reveal these traits, suggesting through these personae the importance and degree to which class, gender, and education determine their critical perspective. All of the novelists included in this study represent the majority of their characters as unskilled or inadequate spectator/readers, and suggest that the best critic is an alter ego of the author him or herself.

For professional reasons, then, Samuel Richardson, Henry Fielding, Charlotte Lennox, Sarah Fielding and Jane Collier, and Jane Austen each attempt to construct and then to valorize an idiosyncratic version of a proper, moral critic whose judgments will have authority over other readers whose judgments, in turn, will have none. This latter type of reader may fall into one of two categories: 1) the privatized reader (often a woman) who interprets or judges properly, but who has no desire to make that interpretation or judgment public, or 2) a would-be professional critic who makes public judgments or interpretations that are morally, emotionally, politically, or intellectually suspect. For each type of reader depicted, the degree to which his or her character is linked to feminine discourse or qualities significantly determines the level of readerly authority he or she will achieve in the public space of literary print culture.

In reading the novels of women alongside those of men, I follow the lead of such eighteenth-century specialists as Ruth Perry, Catherine Gallagher, and Mitzi Meyers,[5] all of whom have traced women's roles in the development of fiction in that century, all of whom have revealed the ways in which women who were respected members of the eighteenth-century canon created powerful, authorial subjectivities for themselves. This study amplifies these critics' important work on eighteenth-century women and professional authorship through its focus on novelists as practitioners of the branch of literary production that is designated criticism.

While I agree with Cheryl Turner that women's "sex had a profound influence upon their place within the patriarchal power structures,"[6] I do nevertheless want to discourage the creation of a separate canon of female literary critics. As Turner herself notes, even today "[t]hose interested in eighteenth-century women's fiction who turn to the secondary sources for the first time will probably be struck by the way in which (with conspicuous exceptions) these novelists have been squeezed into the margins and corners of our literary heritage."⁷ While more women novelists have made inroads into course syllabi, for the most part, critical studies of them and their work remain ghettoized in the world of scholarly publication. Turner's own introduction illustrates that the canonical secondary sources on the novel's origins, *The Rise of the Novel*, *The Origins of the English Novel*, and most recently *Before Novels*, continue to be those works which neglect and/or misinterpret the contribution of women writers to the rise of the novel.⁸

In my juxtaposition of male and female novelist-critics, then, I seek to dismantle the binary canon that twentieth-century critics continue to construct when we treat male and female authors separately. I consider the writing of Charlotte Lennox, Jane Collier, and Sarah Fielding to be part of the *same* enterprise in which Richardson and Fielding are said by twentieth-century critics to be engaged; their writing takes part in the same literary dialogue about literature, reading, authorship, and professionalism.⁹

I want as well to resist more traditional approaches to male- or female-authored texts, ones that, for example, encourage us to rewrite the gendered public/private split into our criticism. Richardsonian criticism has focused more on the private contexts of epistolary writing in its interest in Richardson's relationship to and representations of female sexuality. Conversely, Fielding criticism has focused more on the public contexts of Fielding's writing, the political and economic conditions of the mid-eighteenth century, with very little discussion of how circumstances in his private life might have influenced his literary output. Very few critics have considered women's novels as public responses to their male peers. Rather than focusing on either the private circumstances of a writer's life, or the public context's impact on writerly production, I will attempt to focus on both factors in my examinations of novelists and their work. I believe that focusing on both the socio-historical and the personal conditions influencing each author's participation in the literary critical debate leads to richer readings of these texts.

Constructing Readers and the Privileges of Literacy in Periodicals

Before we look at novelistic constructions of readers in the novels of the mid-eighteenth century, we need first to examine the evolution of print culture's obsession with reading and readers, and its development of an ideology of criticism based largely on gender and class distinctions. In this section, I wish to address the questions:

How do male-authored periodicals write men and women as readers? How do writers define various interpretive positions and roles for members of society in and through language? According to these periodicals, who occupies an authoritative critical position in the public space of print culture?

The critical discourse of early periodicals attempted not only to shape their audience's taste, but to control their access to literary cultural forms and the modes of their production. One way by which periodicals such as *The Gentleman's Journal*, *The Spectator*, and *The Female Spectator* sought to restrict access to literature and the literary field itself was to exploit the binary categories of public and private in their constructions of writers and readers. In particular, Addison and Steele's *The Spectator* and, later, Eliza Haywood's *The Female Spectator* papers reveal a literary cultural desire to separate more distinctly the public from the private sphere, to separate the public from the private functions of language, and to separate the private, refined cultural producer from the mass public consumer. Most important, the periodicals reveal a cultural ambivalence about reading in their compulsion to define the rules for making judgments about texts for each sphere, for each function, and for each role. They also begin to lay the groundwork for the distinction that later novelists will make between professional and amateur readers.

Terry Eagleton locates the roots of professional critical practice in Addison and Steele's *The Spectator* essays, and the prototype for the modern critic in their fictional character Mr. Spectator. Other scholars have concurred, noting that in terms of early eighteenth-century periodicals, "the influence of *The Spectator* on English manners and taste has been described as being only slightly less than that of the Bible."[10]

Modern criticism's roots go back further than that, however; some twenty years prior to the publication of Addison and Steele's periodical, writers such as Peter Motteux create a hierarchy of critical authority when they distinguish between literacies, link one kind of literacy to the development of a particular sort of private sensibility, and imply that class and gender either limit or enhance one's ability to develop the brand of literacy that entitles one to assert critical authority. Motteux's *The Gentleman's Journal* (1691–93) suggests that in society as a whole, educated upper-class men are responsible for the dissemination and interpretation of literary texts. Moreover, the discourse of this periodical's short stories, what it calls "novels," sets forth the male subject as the cultural norm in terms of authorship, whether that authorship be creative or critical. Finally, Motteux's *Journal* represents the power of fiction itself to shape interpretive practices, to define, that is, the work of criticism. Almost two decades later, Addison and Steele employ many of the same strategies and communicate many of the same biases when they create Mr. Spectator, a fictional spectator-critic whose private sensibility imbues him with the authority to make public his critical judgments.

Motteux began his journal in England in 1691 as a newly married and financially strapped Huguenot refugee from France. As a non-native speaker of English, Motteux seemed to sympathize with those people in society who could not yet read, but who might hear his journal read aloud in the coffeehouses and taverns: "Writing . . . being only by Institution, and different almost every-where, is understood but by few."[11] Like many people of the era, Motteux believed that language had enormous power to distort the "real," or "Truth." In his *Journal*, he implies that the outward, public behavior of individuals is a more accurate representation of their true natures than their language, oral or written. Perhaps for this reason his criticism of published drama indicates that he preferred the visual spectacle of a play: "And indeed the Wit which is diffus'd through it, makes it lose but few of those Charms in the Perusal, which yield such pleasure in the Representation."[12]

This sympathy for those who prefer the spectacle to print, however, is tempered by bias. Motteux suggests that class, gender, and, most important perhaps, education, have a great deal to do with an individual's ability to encode properly, and also to interpret or "read" public behavior so that he might achieve his goals in his relations with others. Those who cannot read or write, Motteux implies, have no ability to control how they are judged or interpreted by others. He demonstrates this ideology of literacy in his periodical's "novels," what his biographer refers to as "brief short stories, dealing with much the same matter as the drama of the day."[13]

These "novels" illustrate, among other things, that what will distinguish the professional critic from the amateur reader in many eighteenth-century writers' imaginative representations of life and literature is the degree and kind of literacy each type of reader develops. From the late seventeenth century onward, authors distinguish between print literacy, the degree to which individuals can read, decode, and encode the written word, and cultural literacy, or the degree to which people can decode and encode social processes and behaviors. As the century progresses, the literary market expands, and the number of literate people with literary ambitions swells, class, educational, professional, and especially gender traits increasingly become critical factors in authors' constructions of privatized readers of both sexes. In their early representations of literacy and critical authority, late seventeenth- and early eighteenth-century periodicals help to shape and influence later metaphoric representations of professional critical practice in the novel.

For example, in one of Motteux's "novels," "The Noble Statuary," an illiterate sculptor falls in love with a wealthy aristocratic woman. When his mistress will no longer see him because he is of an inferior class, a nobleman steps in for the sculptor and writes a passionate letter to her. The letter represents the sculptor's true nature as aristocratic; it appeals to his mistress, and persuades another nobleman who enjoys the fiction of the letter to dub him a knight. Having thus risen in status and class, the illiterate sculptor gains the title of Noble Statuary and becomes the husband of his wealthy mistress.

Certainly "The Noble Statuary" demonstrates language's enormous power to effect social, political, and economic change even as it distorts truth. The sculptor's inferior class status makes him subject to others' whims; he is a puppet rather than an individual with any visible agency. His transformation from illiterate sculptor to noble statuary reveals the control that the upper class has over language production and consumption. The illiterate sculptor does not have to embody the values of the aristocracy, he merely has to present a letter that says he does. Once the upper class has bestowed knighthood on him, once he has been named through the letter, he rises in the class structure and becomes worthy of the gentlewoman's hand in marriage.

Importantly, as an allegory of critical authority in late-seventeenth-century Britain, "The Noble Statuary" also suggests that not only the sculptor's class but his illiteracy, his inability to write himself properly in the world, prevents him initially from marrying the wealthy gentlewoman. In Motteux's story, the sculptor's illiteracy makes his behavior so natural and readily interpretable by others that even "the dullest could easily read thro it."[14] All of his thoughts are externalized and made public to the world because he does not know how to keep them private—a skill that only comes with literacy. Literacy endows a subject with self-consciousness; an individual becomes more cognizant of the ways and means by which he or she can transcribe, or not, private thoughts onto a text of public behavior. Moreover, literacy makes one aware of the *need* to control others' power to judge one's self as text, to inhibit their ability to so "easily read thro" one's behavior. That is, "The Noble Statuary" suggests that education produces interiority—or a private sensibility—in an individual.

Motteux's "novel" suggests that fiction can be a very powerful form of art in its ability to effect change in material culture—but it suggests too that whether or not material culture is transformed depends on fictions' readers, specifically in terms of their ability both to discern truth in those texts and, in response, to author new texts that will make those transformations come into being. In this process, gender, education, and class matter. The sculptor's lover *mis*interprets the sculptor's forged love letter because of the kind of interiority that she has developed as a woman. Her "naturally" sexual and emotional sensibility limits her ability to read well or authoritatively. Her passion causes her to distort the truth; she fails to recognize that her lover could not have written this text because he cannot read or write. Moreover, despite her belief that the sculptor is worthy of her love, she has not the power or authority to ignore the difference in class and marry him until a man "names" him, or writes him as a member of the nobility. Unlike the two noblemen, she has no power to effect change in the public realm.

In contrast, the first nobleman's literacy allows him to "read thro' " the sculptor's lovesick behavior, and rewrite it as a text that transforms the way that the sculptor's mistress "reads" him. And the second nobleman's superior literary critical judgment—as opposed to the gentlewoman's naiveté—ensures that he recognizes that the letter is fiction. In order to achieve fully a happy ending for the fiction created by the first nobleman, the second nobleman "reforms" the text it names into "the Noble Statuary" by knighting him. As a man of the upper class, the nobleman's reading and judgment of the letter also transform the way that society "reads thro' " the sculptor's public behavior and ensure that it bestows upon that reformed text, the Noble Statuary, its cultural esteem and recognition. As a work of fiction, then, "The Noble Statuary" ultimately reveals that critical authority derives from one's ability both to read and rewrite the world with authority, an ability bolstered by one's gender, class, and education.

In the context of eighteenth-century society's attempt to distinguish between the private and public functions of language, reading practices often depended upon a text's perceived function.[15] Moreover, print culture typically associated readers of a particular gender, class, educational background, or profession with one sort of text rather than another. Newspapers and broadsides, for instance, were believed to serve a public function—the dispersal of information—and were usually consumed in public spaces—

coffeehouses, pubs, or even the street. Furthermore, these journalistic vehicles of information were primarily consumed by merchants, businessmen, or other professionals who, besides being entertained by the contents of these media, relied on such dissemination of information to help them make progress in their business, social, and political lives.

Printed discourse which was understood to serve a private function—to effect an emotional or psychological or spiritual response—including such material as novels, plays, and poetry, was usually consumed, literary historians tell us, in an extremely private space, that is, by women in their closets.[16] As a group, upper- and middle-class women received a restricted education and were virtually excluded from the public spheres of politics and industry. As production of essentials like food and clothing moved from the domestic to the public, economic sphere, middle-class women in particular had more leisure time for diversions such as reading. Conduct manuals, devotional literature, and diaries whose primary function was to teach women how to structure their inner worlds or their behavior in their private lives as citizens, made up their recommended reading material. Much of it argued that women belonged in the domestic space and that their language should also be private, serving private purposes like the improvement of their morals.[17] Women seemed, however, in the private space of the boudoir, to prefer to read novels, plays, and poetry.

At least initially, society apparently saw this desire for the latter sort of texts as a moral problem—novels, plays, poetry and romances were considered to be literature that would excite the emotions, particularly those emotions associated with the content most often at the center of this kind of written discourse, i.e., love, or more reprehensibly, lust. In the same way that women of the period who masked their identities in the theater were considered to be behaving illicitly, those who read silently and in the closet were considered to be behaving potentially immorally. Both behaviors were seen as strategies to evade public surveillance, to transgress the proper rules of womanly conduct. For the moral safety of society as a whole, then, there was a need to monitor what kinds of texts were read in women's closets.[18] But, paradoxically, reading "novels" and romances in the closet was, as we will see below, the best preparation for "reading" in a fashion that Addison and Steele's Mr. Spectator or Eliza Haywood's Female Spectator would recommend.

Within print culture, another paradox to which the differing connotations of privacy gave rise was that depending on one's position and status in society, the literacy associated with a private sensibility might be viewed either as a privilege or a privation. To those who enjoyed the privileges of a private sensibility, literacy gave the power to exclude, to control, to "own" critical authority. For others, the literacy that shaped their private sensibilities limited and constrained their movements in the world. Like Mr. Spectator, for instance, eighteenth-century women were encouraged to cultivate private sensibilities; however, within the periodicals of the late-seventeenth and early eighteenth century, reading for them is linked to a retreat from the world. As noted before, conduct manuals were a primary source material for this aspect of their schooling. These texts were meant to teach women the necessity of reserve, the advantages of silence, and the need to become more private, more distant, and more enclosed in their relationships with society at large.

Men and women alike who were deprived of an education that provided a well-developed, cultured, genteel sense of interiority and literacy were not only denied power, authority and ownership in the public sphere, but were also encouraged to withdraw altogether from that realm. Society's desire to "privatize" the responses of the majority of its members can be easily understood in light of the actual power that individuals within society had in influencing literary culture. An entry from the diary of Samuel Pepys serves to illustrate this.

In this entry, avid reader Pepys makes reference to a performance of a play called *The Black Prince* (1667). Toward the end of the production's first performance, one of the actors reads aloud a letter which explains and ties up the loose ends of the plot. This letter takes upwards of fifteen minutes to read; the audience greets the introduction of the extremely literary and literate device with derision. They laugh and hiss. Pepys himself laughs all the way home as he is struck by what he calls the audacity of an author who does not take into account that his audience has not the desire nor the attention span necessary for them to be able to take in and interpret this document: "though the letter of itself at another time would be thought an excellent letter; and indeed an excellent Romance . . . at the end of the play, when everybody was weary of sitting . . . to trouble them with a letter of a quarter of an hour long was a most absurd thing."[19]

Interestingly, Pepys returns to the play on another night, at which time he notes that copies of the letter have been made for members of the audience to read—or not—at their own discretion, and that the actor now only makes passing reference to it and its contents.[20] This example demonstrates, first, that certain kinds of discourse were meant, in the minds of some seventeenth-century readers anyway, to be read in a particular space; romances, excellent or not, were meant to be read in the privacy of the home, not in a public space such as the theater. Second, it undoes a popular stereotype: not only women read romances during this period, nor were these romances only read illicitly. Samuel Pepys was a member of the Royal Society, who worked every day, who read books that helped him move freely in the political and economic world, but who, apparently, also liked to read "romances"—at his own discretion, but not always in the privacy of his closet. Sometimes he participated in group readings of fiction. And while sometimes he read to himself at night, he often had his wife read to him, particularly after his eyesight began to fail. But finally, and most importantly, the diary entry reveals the power of an audience, comprised of all classes, various professions, different levels of literacy, and both genders, to influence the production and then reproduction of a literary text. The anxiety this power provoked fueled literary culture's desire to regulate the ambitions of a growing population of readers and spectators.

The material conditions of Restoration theater had created an environment in which the roles and practices of spectatorship were, as a number of historians and critics will tell us, dynamic and changeable.[21] For one thing, patrons such as Pepys "spent many a night at the theater" not only watching the play but watching the behavior of those to whose rank they aspired. Deborah Payne has argued that in the desire to be like aristocrats, upwardly mobile patrons "often [filtered their] aesthetic response to a play through an aristocratic lens." Hence, "by the sheer ability to alter the viewer's reception of spectacle, the aristocrat [helped] to constitute the aesthetic status of the literary artifact."[22] Moreover, patrons—in particular, women—were often repeat viewers and readers of printed versions of the plays. The upwardly mobile and members of the leisured class—including some women—these types of readers would comprise a major portion of Addison and Steele's audience for the periodical called *The Spectator*.

Joseph Addison and Richard Steele, both of whom were active in the theater and political scene of the early eighteenth century, create Mr. Spectator in the attempt to condition both the social *and* the reading behaviors of the theater-going public.[23] Authors' attempts to solicit the type of spectator who frequents the theater after the Restoration—a citizen who spends a good deal of time "reading" plays, either as they are performed on stage or within the privacy of his or her closet—can be readily found in eighteenth-century periodicals. Their desire to convince audiences to demur from participating in literary critical practices can also be seen as readily. Mr. Spectator embodies and displays the characteristics of private interiority necessary both to the proper viewing of plays and to the proper interpretation of their printed versions. He is not the only model of spectator/reader that Addison and Steele develop in their periodical; as critics have pointed out, Addison and Steele constructed three types of spectator-as-reader in *The Spectator* papers: 1) those "mortals who have a certain Curiousity without Power of Reflection . . . whose judgments are provoked by their passions and therefore rendered moot";[24] 2) those who filter their response through an aristocratic lens, and finally 3) the aristocrat himself. But it is the aristocratic lens that best makes use of the privilege of privacy—a privilege that primarily develops from one's aesthetic and literary education.

Nearly twenty years after the publication of *The Gentleman's Journal*, Addison and Steele embody in Mr. Spectator—the viewer or reader who communicates his judgments only in writing—the critical authority that arises from one's ability to rewrite the world. As with the two noblemen who literally transform the life of Motteux's illiterate sculptor, Mr. Spectator's aesthetic judgment and private sensibility are privileges because he can express both publicly, with authority and in writing. As in "The Nobel Statuary," Mr. Spectator embodies the notion that the function of education is to produce interiority, what Daniel Cottom refers to as "a kind of higher literacy that excludes the common crowd from its discourse."[25] Mr. Spectator's literacy helps to separate him as a member of one class of spectator from other classes of spectators, and from other groups of spectators, most notably women. Unlike the noblemen of "The Noble Statuary," however, Mr. Spectator's cultural authority as an observer/reader derives first and foremost from his public identity as an author in print culture. So too will the cultural and critical authority of the novelists I examine in this book derive principally from their identities as authors.

Eagleton asserts that Mr. Spectator's self-ascribed role was to educate "a socially heterogeneous public into the universal norms of reason, taste and morality."[26] Daniel Cottom has more recently argued, however, that the critical stance adopted by Addison and Steele's Mr. Spectator, its discourse of taste, is "not only an aristocratic discourse but a discourse of aristocracy." To put it more bluntly:

> The law that governs criticism is that a perceptual event will not be judged to have occurred unless it can be proved to have been the result of both nature and education, which work together to form taste, which is a mechanism for discovering that the aristocracy is the universal class within the state and the state, in effect, an internal government to the body.[27]

In effect, the seemingly democratic discourse of Mr. Spectator also sought to control society's access and experience of culture. Addison and Steele were particularly concerned to restrict access to the growing business of reading and writing itself.

A periodical such as *The Spectator* was, argues Terry Eagleton, "a primary constituent of the emergent bourgeois public sphere,"[28] but Eagleton fails to take into account fully the ways and means by which Addison and Steele attempt to distinguish and then to naturalize the subjects of male and female discourse, as a means to restrict access to the literary marketplace. To that end, and under the guise of criticizing social biases against women's trustworthiness in matters of love, number 11 of *The Spectator* (Tuesday, 13 March 1711) exposes their bias against women's participation in the public world of letters. Kathryn Shevelow has argued that Addison and Steele represent women as subjects of their own private discourse, a paradoxically public one.[29] Nonetheless, it is crucial that we keep in mind that this female discourse is not the discourse of public life; women are deprived of participation in the economic and political spheres.[30] In its unfolding of the story of Arietta, number 11 begins to illustrate the ways in which *The Spectator* contributes to the critical neglect of women authors and critics two centuries later.

Essay number 11 suggests that women cannot express their aesthetic judgment publicly with authority. Literacy is a mixed blessing for them. In this issue, Arietta responds to a story that is critical of women's constancy in love with a fable about a lion and a man:

> The Man, walking with that noble Animal, showed him, in the Ostentation of Human Superiority, a Sign of a Man killing a Lion. Upon which the Lion said very justly, 'We Lions are none of us Painters, else we could show a hundred Men killed by Lions, for one Lion killed by a Man.' (Bond I: 48–49)

Arietta continues with the moral of her story: "you Men are Writers, and can represent us Women as unbecoming as you please in your Works, while we are unable to return the Injury." She protests that throughout history, women have been drawn as hypocrites by

"Authors who leave behind them Memorials of their Resentment against the Scorn of particular Women, in invectives against the whole Sex" (Bond I: 49).

Steele, in the guise of Mr. Spectator, appears at first to defend women when he allows Arietta to show us how the story of the Ephesian maid unjustly stereotypes all women as being inconstant. He shows that art is political, that artists' representations, such as those depicting men as superior, elevate a particular group or class of individuals. All artistic productions engage in a power struggle.

Yet Arietta's analogy between lions and women acknowledges society's belief in women's "natural" inferiority to men. Moreover, like lions, women are situated outside of culture. Arietta implies that women have no access to a particular kind of discourse. It is not simply a matter of their having no education; it is that, like the lion, they do not have the innate ability to access cultural representation of any kind. Granted, the lion of the story speaks, but the lion cannot represent his experience artistically. Nor, says Arietta, can women. They can be the objects of representation but not subjects who represent. Her story denies that the discourse of women writers has any authentic cultural power or authority. Thus, Steele ultimately undermines his original defense of women. What is particularly interesting about Arietta's assertion that women cannot write is that women *are* writing at this time, not only privately but professionally, and Steele indeed knows this.[31]

Earlier works of criticism suggest a reason why Steele depicts Arietta as one who mistakenly asserts that women cannot write, even as she objects to the stereotype that all women are inconstant. In *A comparison between the Two Stages* (1702)[32] three men, Sullen, Ramble and the Critick, discuss plays performed at Drury Lane and Lincoln's Inn Fields during the past season or so, their reception by the audience, and their own personal judgments of these plays' vices or virtues. Rather than refer to *The Royal Mischief*, a successful play written by Mary de la Rivière Manley during the period under question, Sullen draws readers' attention to her failed *The Lost Lover*.[33] At Sullen's mention of Manley's play (her name is never used), the Critick rails: "I wonder in my Heart we are so lost to all Sense and Reason: What a Pox have the Women to do with the Muses? I grant you the Poets call the Nine Muses by the Names of Women, but why so? not because the Sex had any thing to do with Poetry, but because in that Sex they're much fitter for prostitution."[34]

As Joan B. Landes argues and the Critick's dismissive comment seems to confirm, in the mind of the eighteenth century, a "public woman is a prostitute, a commoner, a common woman."³⁵ Much of society remained convinced that for women to write was immoral. For Arietta, then, who speaks of proper women and who is herself a proper woman, women cannot write, because to do so would be to prostitute themselves.

A comparison between the two Stages also hints at why Addison and Steele's audience might not quarrel with Arietta's assessment that women cannot or do not write. An audience that read such a review of plays performed in London's two theaters presumably did so because it wanted to know how well these plays were received and written. During this period, plays had very short runs on the stage even if successful (a play was considered a hit if it ran six nights). As a result, playwrights could usually make more money by having their plays printed than by having them produced, although successful runs certainly ensured better sales of printed copies.³⁶ In a sense, *A comparison between the two Stages* would have served the same purpose as an essay in the *Times Literary Supplement*. A reading audience who wished to know what play to buy for at-home reading pleasure might well have been leery of buying women's plays simply because this dialogue among the three male theatergoers forces the reader to focus on the raillery against women playwrights, rather than on how well their plays were either written or received. We assume, for example, when Sullen mentions Mary Pix's *Ibrahim* while discussing other failures of the season, that it too was "damn'd." In fact, during a particularly unpopular period for new plays in the theaters, *Ibrahim* was successful enough to have been revived several times after its first run.³⁷ Like Manley's *The Royal Mischief*, the women's texts disappear even in the criticism of them.

Of course, there were probably relatively few women who could have pursued a literary career during this period; most women were not literate enough to write even if they could read.³⁸ But given that women had been publishing and talking about their work as productions of women, that these women had acknowledged other women readers' responses to their work at least since the time of Aphra Behn, and that male critics were also talking about women authors' work, however derisively, Arietta's declaration still rings hollow. For Addison and Steele, it appears to be a matter of believing that there's writing and then there's Writing. Perhaps, like many male writers, they see female writing as less competition than perversion: "I hate these Petticoat-Authors; 'tis false grammar, there's no Feminine for the Latin word, 'tis entirely of the masculine Gender, and the Language won't bear such a thing as a She-Author."³⁹

Since women who publish their writing for money in the eighteenth century are considered "punks," or prostitutes, the writing of female authors can be seen as a kind of sexual misbehavior, not to be considered "writing." In the *Spectator* papers, Addison and Steele primarily represent women's writing as a diversion, as writing which serves a private function and which is meant to be consumed in a private space, invisible and non-existent because it rarely moves into the public domain, and invisible as well because, even if it does enter the public domain, it rarely receives written public commendation or sanction. Steele creates an Arietta who believes that women "can't write" because their writing is by definition not writing. More importantly, however, when Arietta bemoans that women cannot repay men the injury they do to women with their pens, she suggests that what women really cannot be is critics.

With this in mind, Arietta's fable can be read subversively. The essay implies that the need to represent women and lions as inferior to men comes from men's fear of both. When men find themselves in Nature without the tools of culture that give them power—like rifles—lions win every time. Think of what might happen if lions were inside culture. Likewise, if women were allowed to move more freely in culture, if they were given the power to use cultural systems of representation, and particularly the power of criticism, women might wrest economic and political power from men's hands.⁴⁰

This anecdote may signal the reason for the obsession with the role of women as readers that one can locate, interwoven with the dismissal of women writers, in the essays and criticism of the period. This obsession may have its origins in the underlying anxiety that the story of Arietta reveals, and in historical circumstances of the Restoration period when it became increasingly acceptable for women to attend the theater, where they became a powerful force. Restoration playwrights' appeals to women as spectators and readers in the prologues and epilogues of their drama illustrate their importance. In her preface to the published edition of a play which failed in performance, for example, Aphra Behn implies that it failed because the women in the audience were swayed by male critics who labeled it immoral.⁴¹ She suggests that critics appealed to women's fear of being thought immodest when they said her plays were, and discussed the sexual content of her plays in ways they did not when they dealt with plays authored by men. Besides pointing out the critical double standard which already existed in the Restoration period, Behn's appeal seems to suggest that women made up a large enough portion of the audience to make a significant difference. Her preface suggests that, at least in one writer's mind, if a play failed to win the support of women as consumers, and by implication as critics, it failed altogether.

Addison and Steele's *The Spectator* also suggests that this obsession with women as spectators and readers of cultural discourse arose, in part, from writers' ambivalent desire for women's patronage in the face of their fear of women's power as consumers and as critics—even if those judgments were not written publicly. Mr. Spectator asserts that one of the purposes of his essays is to "make an innocent if not improving Entertainment, and by that Means at least divert the Minds of my female Readers from greater Trifles" (Bond I: 47). He justifies his spending more time instructing the ladies because "Most Books [are] calculated for Male Readers, and generally written with an Eye to Men of Learning." Unfortunately, however, women, he argues, usually prefer to read "trifles," romances. In number 37, Mr. Spectator criticizes Leonora's library and bemoans her reading habits:

> When I think how odly this Lady is improved by learning, I look upon her with a Mixture of Admiration and Pity . . . What Improvements would a Woman have made, who is so susceptible of Impressions from what she reads, had she been guided to such Books as have a Tendency to enlighten the Understanding and rectify the Passions, as well as to those which are of little more use than to divert the Imagination? But the manner of a Lady's employing her self usefully in Reading shall be the Subject of another Paper, in which I design to recommend such particular Books as may be proper for the Improvement of the Sex. (Bond I: 158)

Mr. Spectator never does give his own recommendations for "improving" texts for women. In number 92, he catalogues for us the books recommended for women by three groups of people: the Booksellers, who recommend books that will procure them a profit; the husbands, who recommend conduct manuals and literature that encourage women to be obedient and stay at home, like *A Dissuasive from the Play-house* and *The Government of the Tongue*; and the Ladies themselves, says the Spectator, who recommend plays and romances: *All for Love, Pharamond, The Innocent Adultery*. He refuses, hoever, to name books recommended by a fourth group, Men of Learning. Instead, he offers the excuse, "I shall defer . . . till I am further acquainted with the Thoughts of my judicious contremporaries, and have time to examine the several Books they offer to me" (Bond I: 392). Given that Mr. Spectator in his first essay announced,

> during the Space of eight Years . . . I applied myself with so much Diligence to my Studies, that there are very few celebrated Books, either in the Learned or the Modern Tongues, which I am not acquainted with (Bond I: 2),

his lack of acquaintance with all or some of the books recommended by these men of learning seems odd—especially since the self-confessedly learned Spectator seems so well acquainted with all the books recommended by the other three groups. What books are these men of learning recommending if not the books which Mr. Spectator claims he read at the University?

One suspects that Mr. Spectator deliberately keeps private his knowledge as a means to exclude not only women, but men of an inferior class. In eighteenth-century periodicals such as *The Spectator*, aesthetic judgment, or taste, was rapidly becoming a class prerogative as well as one of gender, the privilege of an aristocratic sensibility, a matter of privacy.[42]

Expressing an aesthetic judgment in the public discourse of print culture excluded not only those individuals who could not read, but also those who could not afford this periodical. Mr. Spectator's literacy helps to separate him as a member of one class of spectator from other classes of spectators. His development of a private, reserved, and solitary sensibility increases his status and authority as both a writer and a reader. As Addison and Steele work to endorse the privilege and status as a reader which Mr. Spectator's privacy affords him to a readership comprised primarily by nobility and gentry, they endorse as well the need for certain members of the audience who do not share his status to keep their readings private and therefore marginal. When taste becomes the privilege of an aristocratic sensibility, a matter of privacy, it necessarily becomes a privilege of that individual who can best represent that private sensibility, that superior judgment, in writing or within some other public forum. Essay number 93 seems to corroborate this notion.

There, Mr. Spectator addresses the male readership, particularly the Man of Business, in order to instruct him on ways to fill the "Gaps and Chasms, which are neither filled with Pleasure or Business." He proposes several methods for filling these empty spaces, such as the exercise of virtue (doing good deeds), praying, and conversation. Last but not least, "of all the Diversions of Life, there is none so proper to fill up its empty Spaces as the reading of useful and entertaining Authors." He refuses to pursue this notion any further, however, because reading interferes with the third method of filling time, i.e., conversation. So while he argues that reading is a useful diversion, he worries that it will interfere with men's learning how to comport themselves in public. It is, after all, conversation that best "eases and unloads the Mind, clears and improves the Understanding, engenders Thoughts and Knowledge, animates Virtue and good Resolution, sooths and allays the Passions, and finds Employment for most of the Vacant Hours of Life" (Bond I: 395–397).

This interesting contradiction in Addison's argument, his definition of reading as both the most and least productive use of time, is followed by an essay in which Mr. Spectator promises to pursue the topic of instructing the Man of Business in the pursuit of knowledge so that he might "[fill] up those empty spaces of Life which are so tedious and burdensome to idle People." Again Mr. Spectator neglects to recommend any specific titles, saying instead, "I shall not here engage on those beaten Subjects of the Usefulness of Knowledge, nor of the Pleasures and Perfection it gives the Mind, nor on the Methods of attaining it, nor recommend any particular Branch of it, all which have been the Topicks of many other Writers" (Bond I: 398). Thus, Addison and Steele withhold the titles of books that would help many of their readers, male as well as female, to acquire power in the political, social, and economic world. They do so to restrict the privilege of a private sensibility to a certain class of men.

Mr. Spectator never enters "into the Commerce of Discourse with any but my particular Friends, and not even in publick with them." (Bond I: 21). In terms of reading-as-criticism, one of *The Spectator*'s purposes was to make clear that when it came to matters of interpretation, the mass public's view belonged backstage; the center stage was reserved for the private, objective observer of manners. As spectators, the lower classes were thought incapable of keeping their opinions to themselves or of expressing those opinions through written language, which thereby lowered the value of their judgments. To reiterate Voltaire, " 'Taste . . . belongs to a very small number of privileged spirits.' "[43] There are any number of men who Addison and Steele see as insufficiently 'privileged,' and would therefore wish to discourage from pursuing a literary career.[44]

Addison and Steele certainly withhold crucial information from their male as well as female readers when they refuse to name books that they consider important to read. Still, many men had access to a particular public space in which "a sort of communal reading" took place: the coffeehouses. Here they gathered to discuss politics, finances and literature: "It is a mark of the literary societies of the age that membership was entirely heterogeneous, including politicians, surgeons, actors, and so on, besides the poets and other writers."[45]

Within that particular space, the activity of reading does not interfere with the third method of filling up the "Gaps and Chasms" of leisure time that Steele describes in number 92, conversation among men, but encourages and propagates it. It is there, presumably, perhaps in Will's Coffeehouse, that Mr. Spectator will "further [acquaint himself] with the Thoughts of my judicious contremporaries" on the books which he refuses to name for his readership. So too might his Men of Business learn there which books might serve their needs in their pursuit of cultural power.

The point remains that the majority, if not all, of the coffeehouses and literary societies of which Eagleton speaks were not so heterogeneous as to include women; women were not allowed to participate in the "egalitarian public discourse" of the coffeehouses. Addison and Steele's need to withhold book titles seems specifically tied, then, to a need to restrict women's access to the public realm.

Women Readers and the Privileges of Private Literacies

Kathryn Shevelow has already traced a number of the outcomes of print culture's obsession with women as readers in terms of its development of the gender-specialized periodical. One theme of particular relevance here is how women exploit (or fail to exploit) in their own writing the various positions and roles in and through language that print culture has assigned to them. Specifically, I wish now to address the question of how women write themselves and other women as readers by examining the ways in which a woman's periodical, a journal specifically written by a woman for women, envisions an authoritative critical position and role for them in the public sphere.

Eliza Haywood's *The Female Spectator* reveals her to be a resistant reader of Addison and Steele.[46] While she learns from *The Spectator* to parrot what it designates as women's values, such as their place in the private sphere and their proper roles as wives and mothers, Haywood also recognizes that culture will accept women as subjects of their own discourse if they produce the discourse of private life. Moreover, she recognizes that it is through the appropriation of Addison and Steele's trope of the private, solitary spectator/reader as the producer of this discourse that women can gain access to the public sphere and a public power and authority as professional participants in the literary field of criticism.

As a novelist whose choice of writing material sullied her reputation in the early years of the century, Eliza Haywood may have created the periodical *The Female Spectator* as a means of both reauthorizing herself as writer, and increasing her ability to compete in the world of fiction writing.[47] At the very least, by 1744, Haywood seems to have recognized that a writer must construct herself as one who has developed superior moral judgment if she is to achieve any status at all in the critical establishment. This means that, just as Addison and Steele did through the character of Mr. Spectator, she must exhibit the capacity to perform the labor of criticism. Hence, during a period when the function of criticism continues to be the moral reformation of society, Eliza Haywood creates in the guise of a Female Spectator a woman who has already achieved her own moral reformation: "I shall acknowledge, that I have run through as many scenes of vanity and folly as the greatest coquet of them all."[48]

But Haywood's appropriation of Addison and Steele's trope of spectator-as-social critic involves a permutation of that trope. Establishing her authority to write as a woman in the genre of the periodical essay necessitates the construction of a woman who is a public spokesperson for her gender, a problem in a period when to be a "public" woman is to be an immoral one. As an author who wishes to present herself as a (now) proper woman, she circumvents that problem by asserting that the Female Spectator is an amalgamation of female voices: her own, that of Mira, the wife of a gentleman of wit, along with "a widow of quality . . . [and] confidante of secrets," and "the daughter of a wealthy merchant . . . [whom she calls] Euphrosine, since she has all the cheerfulness and sweetness ascribed to that goddess" (I: i, 4).

Most critics have heretofore analyzed *The Female Spectator* only under the general aegis of women's journalism—as a "manner and morals" conduct book written exclusively for a female audience. *The Female Spectator* extends, argues Kathryn Shevelow, "the tendencies contained in the periodical from the beginning, but, on the other [hand, recasts] the way in which the essay periodical persona represented her authority to address her audience."[49] That is, from a twentieth-century critical perspective, Haywood's periodical apparently continues to make distinctions between the public and private realms of experience and women's relation to each. It helps to perpetuate, in other words, the beliefs that women's place is in the home, that women are to nature as men are to culture, and that their primary interests are and should be courtship, marriage, and the family.[50] Shevelow argues further that Haywood's authority to address her female audience is predicated upon her methodical reinforcement of the notion of women's essential difference from men in both their natures and their social roles. I believe, however, that what Haywood does *not* reinforce is the notion that women are essentially different from men intellectually. Rather, Haywood suggests, women's intelligence suits them as well as does men's for participation in the aesthetic realm—and in the public space of that literary and cultural world.

Thus, under the subterfuge of training women to become better daughters, wives, and mothers, Haywood-as-female-spectator attempts to train women to participate in the public world of the culture industry. *The Female Spectator* will help them as women to develop private sensibilities, but not simply in terms of their acceptance of the domestic sphere (as Mr. Spectator recommends) as the space within which to cultivate this interiority. Rather, *The Female Spectator* also claims for women what *The Spectator* implied was true only for men—that their cultivation of a private sensibility will give them power to effect change in the public realm.

As Shevelow indicates, the Female Spectator becomes a figure of the reader contained within the text, a model for the reader outside of it. The Female Spectator's recommendation to read is couched within an argument for her audience to continue to see the reading of her periodical as a useful activity. According to the periodical's rhetoric, it follows that they should also hold Haywood, as its author, in their highest esteem: "books are the channel through which all useful arts and sciences are conveyed. . . . Authors, therefore, can never be too much cherished and encouraged, when what they write is calculated for public utility, whether it be for instruction or innocent amusement" (II: vi 38). Haywood-as-author also becomes the model of an ideal reader because she understands that the development of aesthetic taste is one of the best means by which women can achieve what society considers to be an important goal, "to know [themselves]." Finally, women's "naturally" cloistered domestic life gives them ample opportunity to develop a version of aesthetic judgment that presages William Wordsworth's: "reflection and recollection are as necessary for the mind as food is for the body" (I: iv, 187). The development of the kind of aesthetic judgment that Haywood endorses will aid women in their participation in "the construction of civil society"[51]: "a proper love of solitude at some times, [enables] us to relish with more pleasure, as well as to be esentially the better for conversation at others, and also to select such for our companions as may be likely to answer both these ends" (I: iv, 164).

The Female Spectator reminds her readers that the development of their private sensibilities can serve to help them achieve goals beyond those related to the family, particularly when, as a collective group of spectators speaking in one voice, they influence what gets produced for themselves and other consumers of cultural discourse. The theater, the Female Spectator exhorts, is a proper amusement for women because of its capacity to teach them further how to become good spectators ("a good play is an elegant entertainment for those of the brightest and most elevated capacities, and cannot but afford some improvement to the dullest and least informed" [I: v, 261]). Haywood then calls her female readers' attention to the ways in which their critical capacities, as spectators, have already given them access to a public power in society: "Some ladies indeed have shewn a truly public spirit in rescuing the admirable, yet almost forgotten Shakspear, from being totally sunk in oblivion . . . in preserving the fame of the dead bard, they add a brightness to their own which will shine to late posterity" (I: v, 263).

Thus while Haywood often seems to be encouraging women to become even more private and self-enclosed, she actually encourages them to develop the kinds of critical skills that can potentially make them equal participants in culture: "What is the true taste but a fine fancy blended with a strong judgment—what indeed, but that just manner of thinking I have been all this time recommending. . . . It is therefore the business of *everyone* (italics mine)" (I: iv, 212).

Upon closer examination, however, one finds an even more subversively political edge to Haywood's argument. When she suggests that life can be otherwise for women if they learn how to read both texts and Nature well, she implies further that women's aesthetic achievement may give them better access to power and authority in the political theater as well. Having established women's critical skills as spectators within the public space of the theater world, she counsels them to make use of these skills in the world of texts that surrounds them. She encourages women to use their opera glasses as microscopes, tools with which to penetrate more clearly into the meaning of life in Nature. These opera glasses allow women to read their own potential for power and authority in the world of culture, particularly when they examine life in the bee hive: "a glass hive . . . will tell you such wonders of their oeconomy, order, and policy, as might render them patterns for the best regulated government" (III: xv, 131). Women may of course take note that it is the female bee who reigns in the hive. Haywood makes clear how she would like her female "spectators" to interpret what they see: "We could not, indeed, do better than to become their imitators, since what we call instinct in them is, in fact, the immediate direction of Divine Providence." (III, xv, 131). God intended the female to reign; in many species of animals, it is the norm. To lessen the subversive sting of her message, she offers up a disclaimer—of course she does not mean that women should rule the world—but one senses that she does so merely to appease, and not because she believes that women should really ignore the lesson of apiary government.

On the surface, Haywood creates an image of a female "spectator" of the world of texts whose morals and manners are improved by her reading of the world of Nature, or what she refers to as natural philosophy. This female spectator seems to know her place to be firmly in the home, but she is nevertheless a woman whose literacy, whose ability to read the world of the domestic and to instruct the denizens of that space morally and aesthetically, gives her access to a public power that society is reluctant to afford to women of the period.

The Female Spectator is a call-to-arms, an appeal for women to come together to form a collective much like the fictional amalgamation of women whose joint venture results in this publication. The women whose voices make up the journal meet regularly, after all, to converse in the manner of Mr. Spectator and his friends. While Mr. Spectator's authority to speak for the group is self-generated, the Female Spectator relies on the consensus her group generates. The point is, however, that when women form communities, things can and often do happen to make their lives better. Certainly we can see that Haywood herself succeeds here in forming a collective of women readers who will in turn support her next writing venture, a novel.

Ros Ballaster argues that from mid-century on, "women writers of the novel were forced to go to sometimes extraordinary lengths to avoid any identification between themselves and the disreputable . . . Haywood."[52] Ballaster refers here to Haywood's disreputable amatory fiction, written prior to *The Female Spectator*. As suggested above, however, Haywood recuperates her reputation when she authors this periodical and creates a new critical and moral persona with which she again identifies herself when she writes her novel, *Betsy Thoughtless*. In subsequent chapters, I argue that from mid-century on, women novelists will go to great lengths to identify with this new, reputable Haywood, and with the critical persona of the Female Spectator that Haywood develops in the eponymous journal. Because she defends fiction as a more successful instrument of reform than direct assertion, Haywood also helps to pave the way for women to use novel writing as a means to write criticism. The critical authority that Haywood constructs for herself in *The Female Spectator*, her image of women's power as reader, is one that novelists Charlotte Lennox, Fielding-Collier and Austen later embrace.

Charlotte Lennox authors a book on Shakespeare, the first full-length critical study of Shakespeare in the eighteenth century. Sarah Fielding and Jane Collier seem particularly open to the power of Haywood's call to arms when they literally collaborate on *The Cry*, arguing similarly for authors to create collectives rather than hierarchies.

And some years later in *Mansfield Park*, Austen embraces the privilege associated with the private sensibility that Mr. Spectator endorsed in the Spectator papers, while also giving her character Fanny Price access to the more subversive aspects of the reader-as-spectator trope that Eliza Haywood develops in *The Female Spectator*. Fanny learns to use her education—an education meant to teach her to be merely a passive spectator—to achieve instead critical authority, and therefore a public power and status within the society of Mansfield Park. As the final chapter in this study, then, the example of Jane Austen serves two purposes: it traces the trajectory of the novel-as-criticism, and it serves as well to illustrate that the novel did allow some women authors to develop a critically authoritative voice.

All of these authors' novelistic constructions of readers were to some degree shaped by the audience who awaited their novels. The awareness that women of the period were avid readers, for example, greatly influenced the construction of a female subject who reads for both the eighteenth-century periodicalist and subsequently, even consequently, the novelist. Writers desired female readers not only as consumers, but as instruments to promote one group of authors over another. Nancy Armstrong asserts, for example, that Samuel Richardson, who deplored much of the period's "dramatick writing," used fiction as a means to protest what he perceived as the immorality of the drama, and as a tool "for redefining the desirable woman."[53] All readers were potential raw material in an ongoing power struggle—a struggle certainly, as Janice

Haney-Peritz suggests, of male rivalry, but sometimes of female rivalry as well.[54] Writers' desire for power and control over their audience's reactions colored their depictions of reading and readers. Many of these depictions continue to play a role in "producing cultural subjects" today.[55]

Eighteenth-century novelists create a hierarchy of readerly desires and behaviors.[56] Michel Foucault has observed of the discourse of sexuality that in the eighteenth century it had as much to do with power as it did with sex itself.[57] Constructing reading subjects in terms of their sexuality is one strategy by which the novelists I discuss here contest the qualifications of the professional who will be authorized to judge their fiction. For example, in *The Spectator* as well as in *Clarissa* and *Tom Jones*, female characters are denied access to certain texts because these narratives define women as both less rational or intellectual and more sexual and emotional than their male counterparts.

Authors Samuel Richardson and Henry Fielding exploit the legal system as well as gender stereotypes to empower their male inheritors of Mr. Spectator's legacy. Literature's relation to law in the mid-eighteenth century was rapidly changing. Court cases such as *Pope v. Curll* increased authorial rights while decreasing those of printers and booksellers. Changes in eighteenth-century copyright law gave rise to the concept of intellectual property, while also creating a professional crisis of sorts for Samuel Richardson. In *Clarissa*, Richardson argues for his own right to continue to share in the ownership rights of any text he edits as a printer, and argues as well for an increase in his power as the author of the novel itself. To achieve this goal, Richardson claims that women are vulnerable as readers, that they need a benevolent and paternal man working to protect them from those texts which might potentially seduce them, as Clarissa is seduced by Lovelace's fictions, into making "an error *against* judgement." Hence, he constructs an editor who often parrots Mr. Spectator, a man whose superior interpretive skills and paternal instincts give him the power and authority to "reform" and to make public Clarissa's story.

A crisis of a more personal nature shapes Henry Fielding's representations of critics and criticism. His scandalous marriage to a servant affected not only his public reputation but his ability to compete with "moral" authors (such as Richardson and his sister Sarah). In his periodicals, Fielding frequently attacked partisan reviews by critics; he was the subject of such virulent attacks during the gestation of *Tom Jones*. He did not want the new professionals, hack reviewers, to wrest from him the power to define himself as an author or to harm him in his position of Magistrate. For both professional and personal reasons, therefore, Fielding attempts to limit the power of these reviewers and others to damage his career. In *Tom Jones*, the world of criticism is highly politicized and polarized. As a justice of the peace, Allworthy has the socially sanctioned voice of judgment; as a woman who knows that she properly belongs in the private world of the home, Sophia represents the ideal privatized reader who chooses not to articulate publicly her judgments of texts. But it is Fielding-as-narrator who best represents and articulates the critical authority and biases promulgated by Mr. Spectator.

The women writers I examine rely more heavily on the kinds of strategies developed by novelist Eliza Haywood to give her female spectator an authoritative critical persona, in constructing for themselves and their characters authoritative voices as reader/critics. Charlotte Lennox treats satirically women's exclusion from the public sphere of literary criticism, arguing by way of Arabella and the countess that women can be literary critics, but that the education they receive, the education that society sanctions, teaches them that they must be silent, merely spectators rather than participants in the world of texts.

Lennox picks up on a theme developed by both Richardson and Fielding; most *men* should not practice criticism either. She reveals more fully than they, however, why literary culture is just as biased toward many males-as-professional-readers as it is towards women. The male characters in *The Female Quixote* struggle to eradicate the discourse of romance because of its power to seduce them, to engage their passions rather than allowing them to develop the dispassionate persona of a critic such as Mr. Spectator. Reading, for most men, involves the danger that it will inhibit their ability to perform in the world of economic and political relations. The new moral discourse is reserved for the privatized sensibilities of those educated to negotiate between the private and public spheres: the clergy and the authors of periodicals such as *The Rambler*. Only professionals such as the learned divine can practice the business designated as criticism in the eighteenth century—the reformation of social (and readerly) behavior.

Richardson, Fielding and Lennox create in their novels a private domain of culture for women that is independent of the political and economic world of relations. They suggest that the language which women use within that world has no public power; their language deals only with matters of courtship and marriage.

In *The Cry: A New Dramatic Fable*, however, Sarah Fielding, with Jane Collier, creates a narrative which subversively uses the education designed to silence women to empower them to re-enter the public realm. They create in Portia a character who makes use of what she observes and "reads" to empower herself as not merely a censorious spectator like The Cry, but as a player on the stage of life, a stage much like the one on which she presents her story. Fielding and Collier interpret the Bible as lessons of moral instruction in the negotiation of the network of human relationships. As Bible readers, women become moral voices of authority by re-inscribing into their own texts the Christian values their society propounds to uphold. Portia becomes the ultimate social critic, a female savior of her text's society wherein hack critics like the Cry use language to gain economic and political control, either through sexual or financial exploitation.

Jane Austen represents a singular case of a woman author accorded critical authority by twentieth-century scholars. To address why this is so, I explore the ways that the protagonist of *Mansfield Park*, Fanny Price, mirrors behaviors that Addison and Steele's Mr. Spectator and Haywood's Female Spectator reveal in their respective fictionalized worlds. In this novel, Austen calls into question society's propensity to invest individuals, whether they be real, or imagined, like Mr. Spectator, with moral and critical authority purely on the basis of their institutional and/or professional affiliations. In particular, she treats as suspect the tendency of the field of letters to represent men (especially men of property or men of the cloth) as the moral guardians of the public domain, and its subsequent tendency to represent men-educated-at-Oxford as best suited to the profession of literary criticism. I suggest as well that *Mansfield Park*, with its Oxonian image of the ideal critic, foreshadows the displacement of the battle over literary criticism from the world of the novel to the academy.

2
A Will to Read: Intellectual Property and Critical Practice in *Clarissa*

IN THE REALM OF CRITICAL PRACTICE, MR. SPECTATOR'S REFINED AESthetic sensibility had entitled him to articulate in writing his judgments of texts and to assume that the more genteel members of his audience would follow his rules of judgment. In turn, by identifying with the sentiments and behaviors of Mr. Spectator, a certain percentage of this audience might have come to believe that this sort of aesthetic critical authority "belonged" to them as a class. By the time Samuel Richardson published *Clarissa* in 1748, however, the stakes of critical authority were considerably higher. With the development of the concept of intellectual property in the mid-eighteenth century, critical authority became a technique by which to declare legal and material ownership of a text.

While the fictional author Mr. Spectator enjoyed critical authority in the literary cultural imagination, Samuel Richardson as a professional editor and printer enjoyed a critical power and authority of a much more material nature. Before he ever turned his hand, at age fifty, to writing fiction, Richardson's profession as editor, printer, and sometime publisher had brought him economic and political status. Elected to the ruling body of the Stationer's Company, the Court of Assistants, in 1741, Richardson was among those most interested in protecting the position and rights of his fellow members of the publishing industry. As an editor, Richardson deployed his critical authority to read texts and then to reform them; that is, he not only effected changes in the printed version of the text but often added explanatory notes as well. Prior to the mid-eighteenth century, these changes automatically entitled Richardson to share in the copyright of the text.

Legal rights of ownership, questions of authorship, and matters of critical judgment, however, were matters increasingly brought to the fore in both the field of letters and the courtrooms of mid-eighteenth century England. Between the publication of *Pamela* and that of *Clarissa*, for example, one such legal decision limited the powers and rights of those in Richardson's profession while increasing those of authors. Alexander Pope's suit to prevent the bookseller Edward Curll from publishing Pope's letters in a collection of Jonathan Swift's correspondence, *Pope v. Curll* (1741) "established the rule that copyright in a letter belongs to the writer."[1] This foundational case in copyright law led Lord Chancellor Hardwicke, in his decision, to draw a distinction between "the receiver's property in the paper and the writer's property in the words." That is, an author could now claim ownership of the words used in a manuscript or text, even though the bookseller or printer might still own the physical property of the book itself. "In this moment," argues Mark Rose, "the concept of literary property as a wholly immaterial property [i.e. the concept of intellectual property] might be said to have been born."[2] One outcome of this new concept of "intellectual property" was that "invention" and "originality" became important criteria by which to establish an author's rightful ownership of his or her text.[3] Interestingly, a number of scholars have noted that the publication of "novel" fiction, original narratives, fell off significantly between 1740 and 1752. Catherine Gallagher speculates that "either the trade had not yet caught on to the advantages of [these ephemeral productions] or the assumed demand had not yet been created by the 1750s,"[4] but perhaps actually Pope's victory in 1741 increased booksellers' and printers' reluctance to publish "novel" discourse. They might have worried that those who could claim legal rights to the text itself would now be more likely to sue for proprietary control of the printed book as well. Certainly Pope's legal action warned of authors' ambitions for more power and authority in the industry, and it is in part to these ambitions that printer and editor Richardson responds in *Clarissa*. If he is to print fiction, especially if it is not his own, he wishes to maintain property rights.

In Richardson's capacity as editor and printer, he had profited greatly from a number of books he had helped bring to market, such as Robert James's *Medicinal Dictionary*.[5] He was particularly concerned that literary professionals like himself would continue to reap the rewards of printing and publishing books, since he owned, among other kinds of patents and copyrights, many of the copyrights to texts published during the period.[6] He must have been equally interested in controlling the ambitions of any author with whom he might do business. Richardson's best hope of maintaining copyright privileges in texts authored by others was to represent the literary critical writing of an editor as an original contribution to the text, as justifiably the editor's intellectual property.

By 1741, the date of the *Pope v. Curll* decision, Richardson had already established himself as the author of England's most popular novel, *Pamela*. Thus, while drafting *Clarissa*, Richardson was in a unique and paradoxical position. He was at once an editor who desired to maintain ownership and control of those printed manuscripts he had helped to shape, and an author who desired to maintain control and ownership of his own text.

According to Glen M. Johnson, "Richardson considered his editorial voice, especially in the footnotes and interpolations within the text, an integral part of his strategy of presentation in *Clarissa*."[7] His strategy has a clear goal; in *Clarissa*, Richardson appropriates, manipulates and exploits the century's new concept of literary property as a means of increasing his own control over the text and limiting his audience's appropriation of Clarissa's story.[8] Readers might sympathize with her character but they cannot presume to "reform" her story, or to elevate their own interpretation of the story's goals and purposes above Richardson's as the narrative's author and editor.

In *Clarissa*, Richardson responds to such changes in copyright law by creating a book and text that legally and intellectually belong to their editor. The editor's professional skills reform a manuscript into a printed book; his superior interpretive skills help him to reform that manuscript into a morally instructive text. Because the writer(s) of the manuscript authorize his selection and emendation of letters, and approve his creation of a critical apparatus, he can reform the two sets of correspondence into a printed document that serves the public's interest. His literal and figurative reformations of this collection of letters sanction him as legal owner of the book, and make the text his intellectual property as well.

Technical skills alone do not authorize this editor to transform a text and usher it into print. He must first demonstrate a refined aesthetic taste, a superior morality, and a head for business. In order to establish his editor's aesthetic and, particularly, his moral credentials, and to enlist the predominantly female audience as supporters of fiction, Richardson exploits the social view of women as the moral guardians of the domestic sphere. As Haywood's *The Female Spectator* illustrated, the proper female spectator/reader knows her place to be firmly in the home. With her moral judgment properly shaped by her education in conduct books and the Bible, this woman guides the moral education of those who live with her in the private sphere.

Elizabeth Heckendorn Cook notes that the epistolary genre insistently underlines "the contradictions between private document and public book."[9] Clarissa demonstrates her superior moral judgment in what are considered to be private documents—the letters that she writes to other characters in the novel.[10] Cannily, Richardson creates a male spectator/reader who acquires the legal right not only to "own" these feminine qualities of moral judgment, but the legal right to usher them into the public world of print culture via their publication.

He also implies that such a male presence is a necessary safeguard. In matters of literary judgment, in matters where the primary purpose of discourse is to transform, reform, and to interpret, Clarissa's story demonstrates that for women, a desire to leave the private space of the home, either literally or literarily, places women in danger. As readers, their "naturally" emotional and sexual sensibilities make them more susceptible to the machinations of seductive authors such as Lovelace and to the plots of such "public" women as Mrs. Sinclair. Thus, proper women writers need the guidance of an objective, dispassionate man—an editor who can make clear their intentions and protect their privacy as he teaches the audience how properly to consume and interpret their texts. They need a spectator-critic not unlike Mr. Spectator, an editor, argues Richardson in *Clarissa*, whose private, moral sensibility gives him the right not only to make public his critical judgments in the body of the text, but to consider the articulation of his judgment, and indeed the text itself, to be his intellectual and literal property. The editor's participation in all aspects of the transformation of a manuscript into a printed book blurs the distinction between the writers of the letters and himself as reader, and then interpreter of them. The editor of *Clarissa*, in the character of Belford, becomes Addison and Steele's literate spectator turned professional.

Echoing Eliza Haywood in his assumption that fiction can be used as an instrument of moral reform, Richardson creates Belford, a character who learns how to effect moral reformation in and through texts. Belford's appropriation and exploitation of traits normally associated with the feminine play a significant role in this character's rise to power as a reader.

Gender and profession figure significantly in Richardson's portrayal of critical practice. Perhaps no one knew better than professional printer and editor Samuel Richardson the crucial role that women played in the field of letters as both producers and consumers—in both roles, they helped him to make a very nice living.

Surely many of the letters Richardson received "from unknown and often anonymous correspondents about *Pamela*" were written by women; social mores encouraged women writers in any genre to keep their identities secret. It is no secret, however, that Samuel Richardson has traditionally been viewed as a writer interested in and supportive of women. His relationship with a female coterie of readers is almost legendary and has been used as evidence of his feminist tendencies, especially in contrast with his rival, Henry Fielding, who is considered chauvinistic by most feminist critics.[11] As Richardson himself famously noted, "My acquaintance lies chiefly among the ladies." Eighteenth-century women themselves viewed Samuel Richardson as more interested in and supportive of women writers than most other men in the publishing business save, perhaps, Samuel Johnson.[12]

In private, Richardson often shared his writing with his women friends, asked for their opinions, and incorporated their suggestions, apparently respecting their ability to make sense of what they read. Men, he once wrote in a letter, are more concerned with trivial details than women are: "The men are hastening apace, dwindling into index, into common-place, into dictionary learning. The ladies, in time, will tell them, what is in the works themselves—only taking care, as I hope, not to neglect their domestic duties."[13]

As this last quotation implies, however, women's ability to read well, to "tell them what is in the works themselves," also makes them potential usurpers of men in the area of critical judgment. The latter half of the sentence suggests that this might have caused Richardson some anxiety, since such a skill might well lead women to abandon the domestic space for the more public space of the critical and publishing world. What he might have hoped, at least on an unconscious level, was that they would *not* aspire to do this kind of literary work instead of housework.[14] In a period when women writers, such as Eliza Haywood, are constructing themselves as morally superior writers on the basis of their literary-critical skills, Richardson creates Clarissa as an attempt to limit women readers'—and women authors' and critics'—power and authority in the literary marketplace.

While Richardson solicited female response to his work, as Eagleton notes, he "certainly [remained] the smugly ensconced patriarch . . . ; there is little doubt that wittingly or not, he [exploited] his literary powers to tighten his hold over women."[15] Richardson's behavior toward women authors was supportive, but paternalistic. In his fiction, he showed little faith in their abilities to desire moral texts, or to make the proper judgments about those texts without authoritative help from him or some other paternal figure.¹⁶ His patriarchal attitudes toward women as critics are figured in *Clarissa*: becoming critics such as the one he defines in this novel would give women a political and economic power he does not believe they ought to have.¹⁷ Richardson firmly believes that the brand of literary criticism he performs as editor is properly, and should be, the labor and property of a particular class of men. Especially in the formal apparatus of his novel *Clarissa*, in the preface, postscript and footnotes, Richardson represents the moral, middle-class, male editor as the best judge and interpreter of what transpires in the narrative.

In both the preface and postscript to the novel, which discuss, respectively, male and female reader response, Richardson first implies that the ability to read well depends on gender. The preface details the editor's submission of the letters contained in these volumes to the perusal of several "judicious friends."¹⁸ Angus Ross suggests that the "gentlemen" Richardson refers to here are the "professional men of letters" with whom he associated (introduction to *Clarissa*, 15)—all of whom would have been aware Hardwicke's assessment of familiar letters as aesthetically and morally valuable literary property, and the way it served as precedent for Richardson's argument defending the moral superiority of epistolary fiction.¹⁹

On an aesthetic level, these gentlemen's comments take into account traditional literary opinion "that in all works of this, and of the *dramatic* kind, *story* or amusement should be considered as little more than the vehicle to the more necessary instruction" (emphasis Richardson's preface, 35–36). Most of their suggestions relate to how the deletion or inclusion of material will affect not only the entertainment quality, but particularly the instructional value of this work. While the editor opts to hear from these men, he retains ultimate authority, and makes clear that he has the final say with regard to what he publishes of the collection. Ownership of the manuscript rests squarely in his hands. Still, his solicitation of male readers' opinions makes the preface a radically different treatment of the audience from that in the postscript.

In the latter, Richardson no longer pretends that an editor of these volumes of letters exists. Instead, he takes the full responsibility of ownership, and rejects his female readership's criticism: "This error they have been led into by a ridiculous doctrine in modern criticism that they are obliged to an equal distribution of rewards and punishment and an impartial execution of poetical justice" (postscript, 1495). The preface and postscript imply an important distinction: man is to professional reader as woman is to amateur reader. While the editor remains the dominant critical voice in the preface, he allows other professional men to voice their opinions, and he treats those opinions respectfully.

In contrast, Richardson-as-editor lays down the law to women readers, correcting them for their errors in literary judgment. In discussing letters "directed to him by the gentler sex," he focuses on these women readers' desire for a happy ending: "as the notion of poetical justice seems to have generally obtained among the fair sex, and must be confessed to have the appearance of good nature and humanity, it may not be amiss to give it a brief consideration" (postscript, 1495). His voice resonates with critical authority; he establishes himself as literary inheritor of Mr. Spectator's critical legacy as he exploits the authority that culture has invested in such critics as Aristotle and Joseph Addison.

Richardson's female readers have apparently confused "poetical justice," the necessity of a plot to trace the pattern of God's just, providential design in history, with "happy ending." He quotes directly from *The Spectator* papers in order to liken his own aims in this novel with Addison and Steele's. While a "learned," read male, reader would certainly have read in the original Aristotle's rules regarding plot, the author implies that unlearned women might find Addison's translation more accessible. Here in the postscript, Richardson's public attitude toward women as readers is condescending—it differs little from that of Mr. Spectator toward Leonora and her library in that respect.

The response that Richardson claims in his Postscript he has received from some of "the gentler sex" implies that women readers are seduced by the fictions they read, and have more trouble "penetrating" the less noble and moral characters than educated, professional, "judicious" men do. Because they are less skillful readers, it argues, women want Clarissa to marry Lovelace. Yet in reality, at least one woman, Sarah Fielding (see *Remarks on "Clarissa"*), did not wish the novel to end with the marriage of Lovelace and Clarissa, while at least two men did: Colley Cibber and Sarah's brother Henry.[20] Richardson's unfair stereotyping of professional male readers as judicious and his female readers as misinformed may derive from his anxiety at knowing that his novel provokes writing from women as well as from men. Fictional women such as Clarissa or historical ones such as Sarah Fielding wish to enter a public critical debate about writing, and desire more critical power and authority than Richardson wants to give them.[21]

Thus Richardson goes on to advise his "fair readers" to "attend to what a celebrated critic of a neighboring nation says on the nature and design of tragedy" (postscript, 1497). While the preface asks male readers for advice, the postscript assumes female readers deficient in critical skills, and attempts to instruct them. Moreover, the preface *foregrounds* men's interpretive skills; the postscript suggests that Richardson believes, as did Addison and Steele, that when it comes to matters of literary interpretation, women's judgments belong in the background. Finally, Richardson's Postscript carries all the more weight because within the novel proper, he has demonstrated that with regard to fiction in particular, women such as Anna and Clarissa are prone to make such "errors against judgment." As such, he portrays them as incapable of properly carrying out the kind of professional reading practices that he executes in his capacity as an editor.

Anna Howe opens the correspondence between the women of *Clarissa* with an apologetic request: "I know how it must hurt you to become the subject of the public talk . . . I long to have the particulars from yourself . . . write to me therefore, my dear, the whole of your story—with the expectation of an example" (L1: 39–40). Richardson's writing reflects the same prevalent views of women writers as Addison and Steele's; society has very little anxiety about women's writing as long as they do not themselves feel it of much consequence. Such are the sentiments, in any case, that Anna expresses to Clarissa:

> That you and I, my dear, should love to write is no wonder. We have always from the time each could hold a pen delighted in epistolary correspondencies. Our employments are domestic and sedentary, and we scribble upon twenty innocent subjects and take delight in them because they *are* innocent; though were they to be seen, they might not profit or please others. (L12: 74–75).

Anna's and, by implication, Clarissa's attitudes toward writing reflect a private sensibility encouraged to withdraw from the world. Their literacy itself encourages this withdrawal; Anna and Clarissa do not escape the inactivity of their domestic lives by going out into the world or by looking for ways to become more active. Instead they retreat further into their private space by spending large portions of time "scribbling" in their closets. Anna's self-deprecatory attitude toward her own and Clarissa's writing is very much like

Arietta's attitude toward women's writing in *Spectator* essay 11: Women's writing is for their amusement only, to divert a narrow audience within the private space, and not to instruct a larger public.

Nonetheless, as Eliza Haywood pointed out in *The Female Spectator*, the type of writing and reading Clarissa and Anna most often practice with each other provides them with the opportunity for introspection, contemplation, and the development of a more reserved and private sensibility. Paradoxically, of course, Anna's and Clarissa's belief, at least initially, that their correspondence is a private one ensures that their letters will carry more moral weight when finally made public.

As a reader of Clarissa and Lovelace, Anna is very like those members of "the gentler sex" to whom the editor refers in his Postscript. Like them, she is "enamoured . . . with the principal character," and so is, also like them, "warmly solicitous to have her happy." Unfortunately, Anna's taste has been shaped by her consumption of heroic dramas. Anna delights "in subjects of heroism"; her choice of reading material includes such plots as those that turn "upon difficulties encountered, battles fought, and enemies overcome, 4 or 500 by the prowess of one single hero" (L46: 209). She would prefer, therefore, a man who "would show the ardour of [his] passion." Her dissatisfaction with her suitor, Mr. Hickman, stems from his meekness, and his lack of "a decent spriteliness, a modest assurance." He is not much of a hero for one who desires a knight in shining armor to sweep her off her feet. Anna turns to fiction and Clarissa's letters in the hopes of finding, or constructing, such a hero. As a result, even before Clarissa herself becomes susceptible to Lovelace's fictions, Anna begins to read Clarissa's letters as an heroic romance.[22] As a spectator of this drama of her own construction, she begins to reform her correspondence with Clarissa into a tale that recounts the difficulties that Clarissa encounters in her dealings with Lovelace. The trials that Clarissa faces in her interactions with Lovelace are romantic battles, contests that will end when Lovelace proves himself worthy of Clarissa's hand.

> But is not his inducing you to receive his letters, and to answer them, a point gained?—By your insisting that he should keep this correspondence private, it appears that there is one secret that you do not wish the world should know; . . . He is indeed *himself*, as I may say, that secret!—What an intimacy does this beget for the lover! . . . a close examination into the true springs and grounds of this your generosity . . . [i]t is my humble opinion . . . will come out to be LOVE. (L10, 71)

At several points in the narrative, she will advise Clarissa to think of her reputation, or to think of how much more attractive and interesting a man is Lovelace than most men. Marry Lovelace, she advises, completely unaware that in this new moral age, a reformed rake does not make a good husband. While on the whole Richardson draws Anna very sympathetically, we are meant to learn from her mistakes as a reader: "Upon the whole, we may say, That if Clarissa was not fit to be her own Judge in this Case . . . , Miss Howe was much less fit."[23] In the same way that Clarissa suffers for believing she could survive in the world without a father figure, Anna must learn via her friend's death her own proper place in a relationship with a man: Richardson wrote that Miss Howe was "to be corrected for her Flippancies with regard to [Mr. Hickman]."[24]

If Anna is a fallible judge, she nonetheless has a good enough share of critical acumen to represent some danger to Lovelace: "Miss Howe is a charming creature; but confoundedly smart, and spiritful. I am a good deal afraid of her" (L104: 416). His fear results in his most famous deployment of his editorial skills; he intercepts one of her letters and makes numerous "additions and connexions" (L239.1: 811). Here, Richardson demonstrates that all men are not suitable for the office of editor, because there are those who would, like Lovelace, alter the text for immoral purposes. While an aristocrat, Lovelace has not the refined aristocratic sensibility that will become the hallmark of the middle-class critic. Only Belford, through his self-discipline and self-control, demonstrates an aptitude for the job of professional editor.

Richardson takes up the issue of critical authority very early in the novel when Clarissa explains to Anna how she has become the subject of so much "public talk." What has made Clarissa a topic of discussion is a correspondence begun because she has accepted Lovelace's request to participate in the writing of a manuscript. Her uncle has commissioned Lovelace, who has a reputation as "a great plotter and a great writer" (L4: 50), to compose this narrative:

> My uncle has a young gentleman entrusted to his care, whom he has thoughts of sending abroad a year of two hence, to make the Grand Tour, as it is called; and finding Mr. Lovelace could give a good account of everything necessary for a young traveller to observe on such an occasion, he desired him to write down a description of the courts and countries he had visited, and what was most worthy of curiousity in them. (L3: 47)

Attracted to Clarissa while still paying suit to her sister Arabella, Lovelace decides to use her uncle's request as an opportunity to get closer to Clarissa. He "[consents], on condition that [Clarissa will] direct his subjects." In other words, he asks that Clarissa be assigned to be his editor.[25] Clarissa's qualifications as an amateur reader will be shown not to be readily transferable into the public world of print; she has not the dispassionate, objective sensibility required of one who would be a professional editor. Her participation in this correspondence will reveal, on the contrary, that the professional world of literary culture is no place for a single, improperly chaperoned young woman writer.

The morality, as well as the politics, of literature continued to be the source of cultural and legal debate well into the eighteenth century. Richardson himself supported, for instance, moral, if not political, censorship of the stage; he was not among those who believed that society could properly reform its manners by "reading" Drama, whether in performance or in print: "A good Dramatick Writer, is a Character that this Age knows nothing of." Part of his rationale was founded in class prejudices; "plays make the young person discontent by giving 'a Taste for a station *beyond his own* [emphasis his]'" (*SR*, 54). Like many in the literary world, Richardson worried that reading fiction or viewing dramatic performances would quicken the ambitions of the mass public.

In *Clarissa*, he attempts to squelch those ambitions by portraying writers of dramatic fictions as irresolute and rakishly immoral reprobates, and the naive or willing consumers of them as doomed. In Richardson's world of letters, there are potentially two kinds of problematic female readers of any sort of fiction. First, there are those amateur readers who would, like certain members of Richardson's audience, be willing to overlook a Lothario's immorality in the name of romance and happy endings. This audience might also be presumptuous enough to attempt to persuade the author to change the story, to write a happy ending. Reading fiction might even inspire a second group of women to attempt to reform the genre of fiction writing itself, either as professional authors or as critics. In *Clarissa*, gullible or ambitious readers of such fictions are encouraged to reform their reading practices, to learn to prefer moral discourse, to develop more private sensibilities, and to keep private their interpretations. In *Clarissa*, Richardson attempts to teach literate spectators, and especially female literate spectators, to prefer what he considered to be a more moral discourse form: the familiar letter. Familiar letters announce their status as private discourse and encourage a more privatized consumption of their contents as well.[26]

Belford's and Lovelace's letters comprise a correspondence "between two gentleman of free lives; one of them glorying in his talents for stratagem and invention, and communicating to the other in confidence all the secret purposes of an intriguing head, and resolute heart" (preface, 35). These lines identify Lovelace as an author, a flawed character who nevertheless "preserves a decency, as well in his images as in his language, which is not always to be found in the works of some of the most celebrated modern writers, whose subjects and characters have less warranted the liberties they have taken" (preface, 35). In describing Lovelace thus, the editor compares Lovelace to those contemporary "Dramatick" writers whom he despises and would wish to censor. This comparison is borne out in the novel, where correspondents refer to Lovelace's skill at writing, and particularly his skill at creating fictions.

Lovelace "delights in writing. Whether at his uncle's or at Lady Betty's, or Lady Sarah's, he has always, when he retires, a pen in his fingers." Miss Howe suggests that Lovelace writes "dramatick" fiction and considers himself a dramatic performer of sorts: "He had once the vanity upon being complimented on these talents (and on his surprising diligence for a man of pleasure) to compare himself to Julius Caesar, who performed great actions by day and wrote them down at night" (L 12: 74). That Lovelace is, by comparison, more moral than the playwrights reveals both the depths of Richardson's antipathy for them, and implicitly, the pressing need for society to monitor more closely the reading habits of young women such as Anna and Clarissa.

As critics have noted, Lovelace becomes the symbol of "Art," a literary figure whose primary audiences are Clarissa and Belford. Anna Howe interprets Lovelace's desire to write at all as morally suspect. Eighteenth-century society as a whole believed that there must be something wrong with a man who wants to spend all of his time writing. (See my discussion of Sir George in Chapter 4.) In comparing Lovelace's love for writing to her own and Clarissa's, Anna exclaims, "But that such a gay, lively young fellow as this, who rides, hunts, travels, frequents the public entertainments, and has *means* to pursue his pleasures, should be able to set himself down to write for hours together, as you and I have heard him say he frequently does, this is a strange thing." *Clarissa*'s depiction of Lovelace echoes, then, Addison and Steele's bias that the majority of men should be active, out and about in the public world, pursuing public goals, rather than closeted with pen or book in hand. Such privatized behavior as that associated with the writing and reading of fiction seems transgressive for men.

Clarissa agrees to edit Lovelace's texts because she assumes that editing his text will not result in a public display of herself. Her direction of his travel narrative requires her only to construct in writing a literate persona who travels, an observer not unlike the personae created by Addison and Steele and Eliza Haywood. Clarissa's education as a woman has helped her to develop a proper interiority, or private sensibility, for a woman of her class. In her writing she can control which of her thoughts will be made public to her audience because she knows how to keep them private, a skill (see Chapter 1) that comes with literacy. She makes "the less scruple" to write because she thinks "he could have no opportunity to address me in them, since they were to be read in full assembly before they were to be given to the young gentleman" (L3: 47).[27] She assumes, that is, that her correspondence with him will serve a public function. Her voice will be that of a dispassionate, objective editor. The correspondence will not cross the lines of propriety by probing her private thoughts and emotions.

The problem is that Lovelace has no intention of writing travel narratives. He does mean to construct a romance. But no sooner has Clarissa begun the correspondence than her parents try to marry her off to Mr. Solmes. While Solmes appears to be a physically unattractive man, what makes him most repulsive to Clarissa is his "narrow mind . . . , [his] coarse and indelicate aspect." If she is to be compelled to marry, she implores her uncle Anthony, "let it be in favour of a man that can read and write—that can teach me something" (L32: 151). The belief that she might be trapped and isolated in a world of illiteracy provokes Clarissa's breach of filial duty.

Literacy, whether in the hands of men or women, is power. Lovelace's very different attitudes toward Clarissa and Rosebud suggests that like Clarissa, his opinion of members of the opposite sex depends on their level of education. He intends to shelter Rosebud from his own and others crass machinations and plots because she is illiterate: "no *self*-dependent, *thee*-doubting watchfulness (indirectly challenging their inventive machinations to do their worst) will she assume" (L34: 162). Unlike Clarissa, Rosebud has not developed interiority and hence she can not criticize Lovelace, challenge his plots, attempt to reform him. Lovelace's protective attitude toward Rosebud suggests that his desire to ensnare and to seduce Clarissa arises in part from the resentment that he has for any literate woman who would, as a proper and moral spectator/reader, reject him and his plots.

In a letter to Sarah Chapone some three years after the publication of the novel, Richardson wrote, "Well, Dear madam, do you observe, that 'I designedly drew Clarissa with some Defects in Judgement, and that even in palpable Cases, in order to give an Air of Probability to the Character.' And I have made her ever ready to point out, and accuse herself of those Faults. . . ."[28] That is to say (as critics before me have also noted), that Richardson always intended for Clarissa to misread Lovelace, even though he hoped his readership would not make the same error. As a spectator/reader of Lovelace, Clarissa speaks to Richardson's fear that "plays make the young person discontent by giving 'a Taste for a station beyond his own.'" Lovelace's dramatic fictions give Clarissa a taste for a station beyond her own—that of a literary critic, an editor who reforms as well as directs the writer's subjects. In the letter to her uncle in which she rejects Solmes as potential husband, Clarissa admits that she "may be vain of my little reading"; in turn, Lovelace's request for her to act in the capacity of editor of his texts indicates that he recognizes Clarissa's healthy respect for her own private sensibility. He exploits her pride in her own judgment; it plays a key role in his future plots to undo her.

As Clarissa's story unfolds, Richardson makes clear that her so-called "error *against* judgment," her loss in status as literary interpreter, arises in part from her initial breach of filial duty. She disobeys her parents' order to discontinue corresponding with Lovelace, and her continued correspondence leads to her being tricked by Lovelace into leaving her parents' home. Once outside that home, bereft of parental authority, guidance and protection, and guided by her desire for public authority as a reader and "reformer" of Lovelace's fictions, she becomes more apt to be seduced by these texts.

Clarissa begins to trust Lovelace when he promises her, that "it was now his part, *in earnest*, to set about recommending himself to my favor, by the *only* way he knew it could be done . . . It is high time to be weary of it, and to reform; since, like Solomon, I can say, There is nothing new under the sun." What persuades her to continue their relationship more than this promise to reform, however, is his request that she "will have the goodness to undertake" the editorial task of directing this process. Clarissa's uncle had only asked her, as an editor, to direct Lovelace's writing; Lovelace himself offers Clarissa the opportunity to reform him and his texts. As his spiritual "editor," she will be the author of his new morality. Lovelace tempts her with an offer to intellectually and morally "own" him. He tells her he would prefer reading her example to reading conduct books: "I have read in some of our *perfectionists* enough to make a *better* man than myself either run into madness or despair about the grace you mention; yet I cannot enter into the meaning of the word, nor into the modus of its operation" (L116: 444).

He shows her that he desires *her* critical language, "instead of using such words, till I can better understand them." Such rhetoric on Lovelace's part convinces Clarissa to continue in her role as Lovelace's reader. In response, Clarissa immediately directs her writing to the task of making Lovelace into a moral man: "And twenty things of this sort I even preached to him . . ." When he tells her that he once wrote verses despising his former courses, she looks forward to reading and offering a critique of them: "He has promised me a copy of the lines; and then I shall judge better of their merit" (L116: 444). In turn she reads to him cautionary lines from Homer's *Odyssey*. By asking that Clarissa help to reform him, Lovelace succeeds in engaging Clarissa's interest in himself as "rakish" text. He flatters her, praises her judgment, and correctly judges her desire for her own critical language, a desire evidenced by Clarissa's eager "preaching." However, her desire to be a critic, to edit Lovelace himself, blinds Clarissa to the fact that his desire to reform is itself a fiction and a plot to seduce her.[29]

Dramatic fictions, particularly those which are performed publicly, have the power to evoke powerful emotional responses from their spectator/readers. Because Lovelace constructs himself as subject to Clarissa's authority as a reader, he unsettles her assumptions about the way his narratives function and how she ought to interpret them.[30] Hence, the line between the kind of private discourse that inflames the passions and the sort of private discourse that disciplines them blurs for her.

At one point in the novel, Clarissa attends a play with Mr. Lovelace and Miss Horton. She writes to Anna: "It is, you know, a deep and most affecting tragedy in the reading. You have my remarks upon it, in the little book you made me write upon the principal acting plays. You will not wonder that Miss Horton, as well as I was greatly moved at the representation" (L200: 640). Obviously, Clarissa has herself acted the part of literate spectator, has previously interpreted literary evidence. She has read such moral dramas as the tragedy she views here with Lovelace in the privacy of her home and then articulated in writing her judgment of them (though that writing remained private).

Nonetheless, this scene exemplifies the danger that dramatic writer's fictions, such as Lovelace's, present to women like Clarissa and Anna. These seductive texts often contain images that charm and unsettle their female spectator/readers, who are by nature more sexual and emotional than male spectator/readers. Lovelace embodies these texts' seductive qualities. He has the ability to disguise his immoral nature and responds "properly" to the play they witness with a performance of his own. Lovelace skillfully displays how he has "been sensibly touched" and gives reason for Clarissa to "praise . . . the author's performance" (L200: 640).

Lovelace, then, brings to a crisis Clarissa's relationship with language. He has seemingly given her the authority to pass judgment on him, to voice her moral judgments in a way denied her by her family. In asking Clarissa to assume the role of editor, he unsettles Clarissa's assumptions about her role as a woman within this literate and literary relationship. He tricks her into believing she has more power than she in fact has. Such power gives Clarissa pleasure, a pleasure that arises from her desire to reclaim Lovelace—to save him with her own moral discourse (L40: 183). Essentially, what gives her pleasure is a desire for her own critical language. Such pleasure provokes her to read more of Lovelace's texts, to read more of Lovelace himself—and to "write" about it, to attempt to discourse upon him as a moral critic would.

Having forgotten Lovelace's earlier warning that it often serves his purposes to make a woman angry with him, Clarissa easily falls into Lovelace's emotional snares while living with him at Mrs. Sinclair's. There, Lovelace continuously teases her and she blushes, weeps, and shows all the signs of a body overwhelmed by its readings. More than once Clarissa is overcome by emotion when in Lovelace's presence: "My heart struggled violently between resentment and shame to be thus teased by one who seemed to have all *his* passions at command, at a time when I had very little over *mine*" (L137: 489). Such passion reveals a growing physical attraction ("I was not displeased to see Mr. Lovelace in his riding habit."). As Clarissa becomes gradually more caught up in her desire for Lovelace as text, she loses control.[31] She begins to read in Lovelace's words and actions a moral sincerity where there is in fact none. As a spectator of his public performances, Clarissa's "[judgment is] provoked by [her] passions and therefore rendered moot."[32] Lovelace's fictions force Clarissa to recognize her own unfitness as an editor, to acknowledge that while she is herself moral, and capable of distinguishing between morality and immorality, she cannot herself reform an immoral text into a moral one.

In *Clarissa*, Richardson implies that, as in a traditional romance, there are moments when a rake may present himself attractively. Romances themselves can seduce readers with their narrative forms. From the moment that she admits her confusion concerning Lovelace, Clarissa gradually loses her role as the primary interpreter of the events of the novel. Lovelace's and then Belford's letters become the reader's primary source of information.[33] It is also only at this point that her narrative loses some of its unity and coherence, and prior to the rape, opens itself up to misinterpretation by Anna.

If however, as recent critics suggest, we can read Clarissa's letters about Lovelace as texts that give us her interpretation of Lovelace,[34] then we can treat Richardson's caution "that a reformed rake does [not] make the best husband" (preface, 36) as a metaphoric caution to women that an immoral text is equally dangerous. Women readers' attempts to interpret, to re-write, or to "reform" an immoral, rakish text may lead to their being seduced into believing that a text holds a moral truth that it does not hold. Therefore, women should not be allowed to judge those texts which could potentially seduce them into making, as Clarissa does, "an error *against* judgement."

The distinction between an error *in* judgment and an error *against* judgment is an important one. Clarissa makes this distinction while discussing the probable danger of getting involved with Lovelace: "that such an husband might unsettle me in all my own principles, and hazard my future hopes . . . that I knowing these things, and the importance of them, should be more inexcusable than one who knows them not; since an error against judgement is worse, infinitely worse, than an error in judgement" (L40: 186). In other words, Clarissa acknowledges that her error does not arise from her failure to recognize Lovelace as an immoral text, but from her failure to stop "reading" him once she has recognized him as such. Her continued involvement with him via the correspondence and her consequent departure with him from her father's house prove to be her undoing. Clarissa's distinction between the two types of errors suggests that while Richardson believed women capable of recognizing a text's immorality, he believed them incapable of eluding, without male guidance, its negative power.

He believed their bodies to play a key role in their inability to elude immoral fiction's seductive powers. Mr. Spectator's development of a private, reserved and solitary sensibility, his refusal to enter "into the Commerce of Discourse with any but my particular Friends, and not even in publick with them," (Bond I: 21) increased his powers of judgment, his objective and rational reflections upon that which he read or viewed. In order to construct himself as a dispassionate, critical observer, Mr. Spectator became a disembodied self, a self he exhibited only in writing. When Lovelace tricks Clarissa into exhibiting her "self" to him in person, she as a spectator/reader also must confront Lovelace's physical self as text. Clarissa's body stands in the way of her becoming a critic; she cannot reform Lovelace until she represses it as Mr. Spectator repressed his.[35]

In the end, only one correspondent reads properly the history of this narrative; only one can make use of what he learns to reform both texts and his peers: Lovelace's friend, Belford. In order to emphasize Belford's superiority as a professional reader of all the correspondence contained in this novel, Richardson draws each of the four main correspondents as a potential editor of the manuscripts that come into his or her hands. Our job as extratextual readers is not simply to examine the dynamics of the relationship between Lovelace and Clarissa, or Lovelace and Belford, or Anna and Clarissa, or even between Clarissa and Belford. Our job is to judge who, in his or her description of the events that transpire, constructs the most moral narrative, who the least; who reads morally and accurately, and who does not. Our job is to read how Clarissa writes her story to Anna, and how well Anna interprets it. We are to compare this type of literary transaction to the way that Lovelace writes his narrative, and how well Belford interprets that narrative.

Belford's letter to Lovelace two days before the rape prepares us for the narrative shift that occurs when Clarissa must give up all authority as interpreter of her own story;[36] it deals explicitly with judgment and the danger that Lovelace, as fiction maker, poses to women. In this letter, Belford recalls his first meeting with her, and his admiration for her wit, discernment, and fine mind. Belford's discussion of Clarissa's noble nature and her superior "judgement" is tempered by his critique of Lovelace:

> Such is the woman, such is the angel whom thou hast betrayed into thy power, and wouldst deceive and ruin—Sweet creature! did she but know . . . what is *intended* . . . —And how effectually would her story, were it generally known, warn all the sex against throwing themselves into the power of ours . . . (L222: 713)

Here, Belford's words imply that Clarissa's story may eventually serve as a warning to other women—thus repeating, almost verbatim, what the fictional editor says in the preface. As the letter to his friend continues, Belford alludes to the passion, or desire, which draws a woman to Lovelace: "are there not hundreds of women, who . . . would be taken with thee for mere *personal* regards . . . With regard to the passion itself, . . . [s]ee what fools this passion makes the wisest men! What snivellers, what dotards, when they suffer themselves to be run away with it . . ." (L222: 713). Belford's critique of Lovelace, his attempt to portray Clarissa's skills in discerning true wit from false, true modesty from vanity and true politeness from false design in a most favorable light, ultimately succeeds in indicting Clarissa for being unable to see through Lovelace's "frothy jest[s]." Clarissa is identified as a "sweet deluded excellence"—she is blinded by her own desire for Lovelace as text, and deluded in her belief that her critical language has any real power to reform a rake like Lovelace. Her critical judgments as a result carry less authority.

Belford's role as critical reader begins shortly after Clarissa leaves her father's house with Lovelace. In a letter dated April 21, not quite two weeks after Clarissa's and Lovelace's flight from the Harlowes', Belford shifts from desiring Lovelace's fictions to desiring his own critical language when he writes:

> Thou, Lovelace, hast been long the *entertainer*; I the *entertained*. Nor have I been solicitous to animadvert, as thou wentest along, upon thy inventions and their tendency . . . But now that I find thou hast so far succeeded as to induce [Clarissa] to come to town, and to choose her lodgings in a house, the people of which will too probably damp and suppress any honourable notions which may arise in thy mind in her favour, I cannot help writing . . . (L143: 500)

For his friend's sake, Belford writes to persuade Lovelace against dishonoring Clarissa. However, from here on, Clarissa-as-morality-tale will attract Belford more than the fictions of his friend. Furthermore, Belford will become "this fatherless lady's father," in numerous ways—not just, as he initially requests, as symbolic stand-in for her father at her wedding to Lovelace.[37] He will assume patriarchal authority for her letters, and for the entire text, when Clarissa recognizes his morality and names him the executor of her will.

To assume critical authority in the novel, Belford must first exorcise his own desire for the types of intrigues and plots Lovelace creates: "I am far from hating intrigue upon principle. But to have awkward fellows plot, and commit their plots to paper, destitute of the seasonings, of the *acumen*, which is thy talent, how extremely shocking must their letters be!" (L190.1: 608). Paradoxically, Belford must first learn how to read more like Clarissa, in order to read better than she. He begins to act in the capacity of editor during Clarissa's long illness after the rape, when she asks that he read her correspondence: "I undertook to read some part of [Lovelace's letter], resolving to omit the most exceptionable." It is in this capacity that he begins to see the error he made aiding and abetting Lovelace: "For my own part, I am more and more sensible that I ought not to have contented myself with *representing against*, and *expostulating with thee upon*, thy base intentions . . . [emphasis his]" (L340: 1080). As Richardson sets the stage for Belford's legal and moral acquisition of the literary property that he will ultimately publish, Belford becomes increasingly censorious of Lovelace's immorality and more complimentary of Clarissa's virtue. He begins to write himself more and more in the image of Mr. Spectator.

A literate spectator represses bodily passions; thus Belford's desire for Clarissa as text is not the passionate, sexual desire that motivates Lovelace's reading of her. Clarissa's subsequent denial of her body after the rape, her refusal to eat, makes it all the more possible for Belford to idealize her; "she is, in [his] eye, all mind": "Were she mine, I should hardly wish to see her a mother unless there were a kind of moral certainty that minds like hers could be propagated. For why, in short, should not the work of bodies be left to *mere* bodies?"(L169: 555).[38] Unlike Clarissa's or Lovelace's earlier readings, Belford suppresses the bodily response that often propels an audience's consumption of a text, whether or not that text is moral. Belford's idealization of Clarissa as both "angel" and "mind" seeks to establish a relationship between writer and reader based on spiritual and moral esteem.

Thus, partly from Clarissa's example after the rape, Belford educates himself to be the type of objective, dispassionate spectator/editor that Richardson aspires to elevate. In fact, as an apprentice editor Belford behaves very much in the manner recommended by Richardson in his pamphlet, *The Apprentice's Vade Mecum*.[39] He begins to read the texts upon which Clarissa has always relied most heavily for strategies of interpreting the world: the Bible and other spiritual-conduct books. For instance, Belford obtains a copy of a meditation that Clarissa has extracted from the Scriptures. He writes to explain to Lovelace what Clarissa's text teaches him:

> You and I always admired the noble simplicity, and natural ease and dignity of style, which are the distinguishing characteristics of these books, whenever any passages from them by way of quotation in the works of other authors, popped upon us . . . indulge me, Lovelace, a few reflections on these sacred books.
> We are taught to read the Bible when children, and as a rudiment only; and, as far as I know, this may be the reason why we think ourselves above it when at a maturer age. . . . Odd enough, with all our

> pride of learning, that we choose to derive the little we know from the undercurrents, perhaps muddy ones too, when the clear, the pellucid fountain-head is much nearer at hand, and easier to come at . . . (L364: 1125)[40]

In reading the fictions of his friend Lovelace, and then subsequently Clarissa and her letters, Belford comes to understand that the conduct books and Bible that shape Clarissa's writing are far better sources of knowledge, particularly moral knowledge, than Lovelace's fictions, however entertaining they might be. From Clarissa's example, he reforms and refines his role of spectator/reader of texts, a reformation that qualifies him, by the end of the novel, to wield the power and authority to interpret and make public narratives such as *Clarissa*. Clarissa herself merely reflects the Bible's morality; she becomes a sign of morality, not an agent of it. And because she merely represents, at this stage of the novel, a properly moral and utterly private sensibility, Belford can take possession of that quality. Her symbolic morality will literally become his property.

Belford's apprenticeship under the tutelage of this dying woman earns him her request that he take charge of publishing her story for those who ought to know it.[41] Clarissa's faith in him as the custodian of her literary and material properties convinces her cousin Morden to make him, likewise, the executor of his will. He becomes financial adviser for his friends Mowbray and Tourville, both of whom, after seeing the error of Lovelace's ways, "[take] their friend Belford's advice: [convert] the remainder of their fortunes into annuities for life . . . their friend Belford managing their concerns for them" (conclusion, 1490). Belford also inherits from Lovelace's uncle, Lord M, "his Hertfordshire estate" (conclusion, 1493), which should have passed to Lovelace himself. "Happy is the man who in time and strength sees and reforms the errors of his ways!"—he gets all the power, economic and social.[42]

In the Preface to *Clarissa*, the editor hastens to reassure us that the novel is "not only the history of the excellent person whose name it bears, but includes the lives, characters, and catastrophes of several others, either principally or incidentally concerned in the story." He then spends a good deal of time defending his primary male characters, Lovelace and Belford. Having only briefly mentioned Clarissa's and Anna's correspondence in one line of this preface, the editor devotes three paragraphs to his discussion of the correspondence between Lovelace and Belford. Such an effort to focus his audience's attention on the novel's male characters rather than its eponymous heroine suggests that in actuality, the correspondence between the men may be the more important exchange for its audience to scrutinize.

Within those three paragraphs, Richardson refers specifically to Belford's role as one who reforms and provides an antidote for "the poison which some might otherwise apprehend would be spread by the gayer pen and lighter heart of the other." Richardson's analogy between critic and doctor is an interesting one in light of a scene that comes late in the novel, after Clarissa has already died, a scene that depicts the effects of both moral and physical poisons on the body. It is also the moment when Belford fully inherits the role of the ideal spectator/editor in the text.

Having fallen down a flight of stairs and broken her leg, Clarissa's nemesis, the prostitute Mrs. Sinclair, calls Belford to her bedside. When he arrives, she lies howling with pain, surrounded by some eight of her fellow prostitutes. Belford later writes to Lovelace, describing the "spectacle" of those hovering around her bedside:

> There were no less than eight of her cursed daughters surrounding her bed when I entered. . . . seven seemed to have been but just up, risen perhaps from their customers . . . and their nocturnal orgies, with faces, three or four of them, that had run, the paint lying in streaky seams not half blowzed up . . . (L499: 1387).

Belford's description of the scene is footnoted. The footnote reads, "Whoever has seen Dean Swift's "Lady's Dressing Room" will think [it] not only more natural but more decent painting, as well as better justified by the design, and by the use that may be made of it."[43] A reader might indeed ask, What is Belford's design and what use can the reader make of it?

Robert Erickson highlights the aesthetics of Belford's editorship when he argues that Richardson drew Belford as "a kind of ideal editor, the artistic role Richardson finds most congenial for himself."[44] For Richardson, the act of "reading" an immoral scene and then rendering it into an instructive and moral text demands an aesthetically gifted editor-cum-author/critic. Hence, when he renders the scene wherein Mrs. Sinclair seems to have been struck down by divine justice, and then comments on it again in a note, Belford "designs" to call attention to the aesthetic skill he demonstrates in painting this picture of debauched morality. As an author, Belford must be judged to be an even better author than Swift because his morality has helped to produce a more decent and moral depiction of the depravity he witnesses. He is a more refined spectator of the city's underbelly than Swift. In this, Belford has profited greatly from his active cultivation of friendship with the dying Clarissa, from having momentarily become her pupil. Clarissa shows Belford how to develop a properly moral, private sensibility—a sensibility that colors his perceptions of the world and that helps him to paint a scene of depravity in such a manner as will encourage others, in turn, to reform morally and spiritually.

Like the editor in the Preface to *Clarissa*, Belford here links the discourse of medicine to the discourse of criticism when his discussion of the women's physical bodies quickly shifts to a consideration of the discourse of Mrs. Sinclair's doctors. Though horrified by the gruesome spectacle before him, Belford is as dismayed, if not more so, by Mrs. Sinclair's attendant doctors' professional conduct and language. He despises them for puffing themselves even as they show themselves incapable of restoring Mrs. Sinclair to health:

> I cannot but say I have a mean opinion of both these gentlemen who, though they make a figure it seems in their way of living, and boast not only a French extraction but a Paris education, never will make any in their practice. How unlike my honest English friend Tomkins, a plain, serious, intelligent man whose art lies deeper than in words; who always avoids parade and jargon: and endeavors to make every one as much a judge of what he is about as himself. (L499: 1391).

The proper professional's practice mirrors his discourse and teaches those making use of that discourse to heal themselves, physically in the case of patients and morally in the case of readers. Unlike Mrs. Sinclair's physicians, who speak only to elevate themselves, Belford writes this letter to Lovelace not simply to impress him, or to convince him of his superior critical skills (though, arguably, the footnote suggests otherwise). He writes in the hope that Lovelace will attend to the letter's lesson and mend his ways. The footnote implies that Belford's tasteful and moral discourse provides a better antidote to, as well as a better picture of, the poison of the scene before him than the discourse of such a writer as Swift. As a proper professional critic, Belford's art lies in his ability to read the lesson of this scene and to find a remedy for the immorality of "the lives [that] rakes and libertines lead," to reform and cure many "worthy women betrayed by that false and inconsiderate notion, raised and propogated by author[s such as Lovelace] of all delusion, *that a reformed rake makes the best husband*." (L499: 1393). His echo of the preface's announced moral of Clarissa's story confirms that in Richardson's mind, Belford's morality and his critical writing skills as an editor and printer confer upon him the right to share in the ownership of any and all texts that he helps usher into print. Having established the power and authority of editors like himself in the novel proper, Richardson constructs a powerful authorial subjectivity who can now, more authoritatively than in the preface, defend his authorial choices in the postscript.

To his credit, Richardson never represents women (even in the postscript) as totally incapable of critical judgment. Clarissa does have superior powers of judgment, but they are of a particular kind. Richardson represents her as having superior powers to recognize the morality of a certain kind of literature, spiritual texts, and conduct manuals. The morality of these texts is, however, self-evident; Clarissa copies meditations from Scripture, rather than reforming, or rewriting, them to produce new texts that she could claim as her intellectual property. As I have suggested earlier, conduct manuals and the Bible also define women as subject to male authority, as the caretakers of the private sphere. They represent women who pursue spiritual rather than worldly goals, who prefer spiritual rather than material or bodily enrichment. Clarissa herself best represents a moral judge after Lovelace brutally uses her body as a means by which to succeed in his plot against her. One can speculate that after the rape, Clarissa recognizes fully that he has figuratively used her body-as-reader to undo her; hence her refusal to see him or to read any more of his letters, her repression of her own body through literal starvation, and her self-immersion into Scripture. In *Clarissa*, Richardson implies that women's bodies prevent them from making proper moral judgments because their sexual natures make them prone to fiction's power to arouse them sensually. Capable of recognizing the morality of conduct books, Clarissa cannot properly judge immoral fictions because she remains incapable of effecting their reform.

In the figure of Clarissa, Richardson confirms that women are not adequately qualified for the profession of editor or critic and that as authors, therefore, they remain subject to the authority of the professional man who would properly usher their stories into the public realm. When she wills her story to Belford, Clarissa negates the distinction between "the receiver's property in the paper and the writer's property in the words,"[45] that would make this story hers. Moreover, in admonishing Belford to edit the text in what ever way he deems appropriate, Clarissa further empowers him to claim ownership of both text and the book itself: his interpretive notes, emendations and additions or deletions to the story proper are original contributions, even "inventions." As noted at the beginning of this chapter, these qualities had become important criteria by which to establish an author's rightful ownership of copyright.

While Belford learns to read accurately during Clarissa's prolonged illness, Clarissa herself becomes increasingly removed from the real world of reading. Lovelace begins to lose his power as writer, and both Belford and Clarissa learn powerful lessons regarding the ability of desire to interfere with critical judgment. Both reform, but while Clarissa's reformation means that she must renounce her desire to read and write in the social world,[46] Belford's reformation means he can become a more powerful force in that world.

The novel ends, therefore, by reaffirming male authority in all realms of literary production. A critic always gets to write his or her judgments; because of her "tragic" mistake, because she has been temporarily seduced by the fictions of Lovelace, Clarissa must give up her right not only to read but to write. Upon her death, Clarissa becomes for Belford and the readers of these volumes of letters only an image of a moral exemplar—the subject of our reading, the conductor of our desire as critics to write. As current critical discourse about *Clarissa* illustrates, the majority of critics discuss Clarissa as the subject of others' readings, rather than as an actively reading subject whose readings have any authority. She has become our intellectual property just as she, her story and her moral judgment, become the intellectual property of Belford in the novel itself. As an ideological construct, *Clarissa* successfully reproduces an ideology that seeks to exclude women from critical practice.

Richardson's attempts to exclude women from the literary critical enterprise are subtle; only recently have scholars begun to uncover his more patriarchal attitudes.[47] His major competitor in the field of letters, Henry Fielding, whose desire to exclude women from the professional field of criticism was much more overt, has been treated more harshly, dismissed or scorned by most critics interested in gender issues. The ways in which Fielding treats the issue of gender and interpretation warrant some examination, however; as we shall see, his attitudes are much more complex than previously acknowledged, particularly when one takes into account the nature of his relationship to his sister Sarah, and perhaps to Samuel Richardson as well.

3

No Jury of his Peers: Reading *Tom Jones*

WHILE RICHARDSON WAS WRITING *CLARISSA*, HIS ARCH-RIVAL IN THE field of letters, Henry Fielding, was also hard at work on what most consider to be his greatest novel, *Tom Jones*. All during the 1740s, the world of print was busily constructing a "battle of the authors" between the two. In fact, in London's eighteenth-century literary circle, Fielding's and Richardson's rivalry was as closely followed as the rivalry between Blifil and Tom is followed in the novel; "the private correspondence of the period awaited the publication of *Tom Jones* and *Clarissa*, sensing what would in fact prove the case: that Fielding and Richardson, for the better part of the decade acknowledged rivals in the art of fiction, were about to produce their masterpieces" (*HF*, 412). I argue here that we might in fact read the rivalry between Tom and Blifil in the novel as Fielding's fictional representation of this rivalry, his struggle for power within the field of letters with authors and critics such as Richardson.[1] It was a rivalry that had begun with the publication of *Pamela* and Fielding's satiric responses, *Shamela* and *Joseph Andrews*—responses Richardson had resented.[2] At the very least, Tom and Blifil's rivalry can be read to represent Fielding's rivalry with other writers, particularly his critics, who attempt—as Blifil does with Tom—to lower Fielding's status in the literary world.

By 1747, Fielding was well known to his novel's potential reading public and to the political and literary worlds at large. *Tom Jones* was written during a period of personal crisis. After his first wife died in 1744, Henry, in his grief, sought comfort in the arms of her servant, Mary Daniel. He married the woman, then six months pregnant, in November of 1747 (*HF*, 422), an action that left many in the literary world, including Samuel Richardson, morally outraged. The marriage was bad publicity for a man trying to pass himself off as a moral author.

Given his participation in the literary and political warfare of the 1730s, and having in the past suffered economic and political sanctions for his writing, Fielding had good reason to worry about the public's reaction to news of his marriage.[3] To try to avoid any embarrassment, therefore, he moved himself and his bride from Bath to Twickenham. But his enemies "[gloated] over his huddled match with [her]" (*HF*, 423), mocking both Fielding and his wife in print and in private. This response to his hasty wedding must have fueled his anxieties about how the world would receive him and his writing thereafter. He may have seen writing *Tom Jones* as a means to apologize, both to defend and show remorse for his actions.

The month of his marital union, November, 1747, in fact, "affords the earliest documentary evidence that it [*Tom Jones*] was on the way" (*HF*, 423). One year after the birth of his son William, Henry Fielding published what he referred to as "The Author's Offspring, and indeed the Child of his Brain."[4] As its author, Fielding had already endured intense public scrutiny and criticism. *Tom Jones* seems a purposeful attempt to persuade his audience to focus on one "child" and not the other, to educate readers to judge his writing based on its aesthetic beauty and inherent morality rather than by the "politically" (im)moral criteria by which his enemies would like him to be judged, and to persuade them to be wary of how or whether they articulate those judgments.

Twentieth-century critics have generally downplayed the relationship between Fielding's private life and his fiction; he was a man who left behind very little evidence of his innermost thoughts, feelings and personal habits.[5] Still, such contemporaries as Samuel Richardson believed that Tom Jones's ribald adventures mirrored Fielding's life, that Sophia was modeled on Fielding's first wife, Charlotte, and that his previous fiction was also autobiographical, particularly in terms of its apparent revelation of the most intimate (read sexual) details of his private life as a man.[6] In the face of scandal and public criticism, Fielding's worries about his reception as man and author within print culture inform his fictional attempts to define the laws by which one can participate in the developing profession of criticism. He mines both his private and public lives, relying on his career as a public representative of the law, his life as a writer, and his amorous and familial experiences to help him draw distinctions between and among writers and readers.

Through his characterization of Tom, Fielding admits and minimizes the charges of immoral conduct being levelled against him in print and in private, and proves himself to be the superior writer.[7] Through his characterization of the immoral Blifil, Fielding condemns the socially powerful critic and attempts to limit the amount of cultural authority that society invests in other male authors such as Samuel Richardson. Tom's errors prove to be lapses of youthful judgment, or sins of excess, which can be corrected because of his inherent humaneness; Blifil's flaws arise from his lack of "heart," because his narratives and readings of other characters develop from callous manipulation. Thus, Fielding uses the trial(s) of Tom Jones to exonerate his own private life and to justify his own superiority as an author/critic. He shows that, like Tom, he is capable of moral reform and is himself a worthy inheritor of the literary world's critical legacy.

Recent scholarship has examined commentary on writing and reading in Fielding's novels as his attempt to restrict access to fiction writing. As critics like Linda Zionkowski, John Richetti and Katharine Rogers have argued, he assiduously tried to uphold and to sustain the class and gender hierarchies that existed within the literary field.[8] Like Richardson, Fielding also wrote fiction in the attempt to achieve the kind of cultural authority that would raise him as an author economically, politically, and socially above his competition. Scholars' emphasis on Fielding's desire to "create a canon of accepted legitimate writers that would limit the dangerously open traffic in letters"[9] has nevertheless deflected attention away from his corresponding attempt to restrict access to the profession of criticism. Even the most recent book on the century's "new species of criticism" examines the "explicit commentary . . . by the earliest novelists and critics" only as it relates to the practices of authorship[10]; "criticism" in the eighteenth-century novel is assumed to be about the writing of novels, rather than about the nature of critical practice itself. Hence, despite occasional references to *Tom Jones*'s "overriding [interest] in the problems of assessing evidence and passing judgments," i.e., the activities of criticism as well as "the activities of the courtroom,"[11] no one has read *Tom Jones* as a novel that deals explicitly with the developing profession of criticism.

Certainly the historical and social circumstances of literary production during the 1740s played a significant role in Fielding's representations of literary critical practice. The literary marketplace that would usher Fielding's *Tom Jones* into the world was in the process of destroying "the canon of courtly letters centered on the classics, and in a revolutionary, democratic manner [leveling] all books in a continuous surge of new, ever-accumulating print products."[12] Simultaneously, the reading public was itself becoming increasingly democratized, with authors more and more dependent upon this audience's "patronage." Many members of this reading public continued to turn to sources like periodicals for advice on which of the new books, fiction or otherwise, to purchase. By providing such advice, the new literary professional, the hack reviewer, acted as the middleman between the author and the general public.

This new profession threatened to democratize the practice of criticism. No longer was criticism only the business of an elite group of authors, of classically educated men who, through the authorship of "courtly letters," had earned the culture's esteem and authority to judge other writers. Now it was potentially the business of any literate citizen, of any man or woman who could read a novel and express an opinion in and through writing. Henry Fielding's *The History of Tom Jones, A Foundling* also reflects the anxiety and ambivalence he feels as a would-be member of this elite group of authors in an era in which the authority—and ambition—of the general reader seems to be increasing exponentially.

Whereas in *Clarissa* Richardson exploited the law's relationship to the literary world in general through his response to changes in copyright law, in *Tom Jones* Fielding exploits his professional experience as a lawyer and Magistrate to obtain for himself the cultural authority to make judgments about literature. He compares certain legal practices with certain literary practices, specifically the practices of bearing witness, hearing testimony, weighing evidence, and arriving at a judgment, implying that in its similarity to the practice of law, the practice of criticism in the public sphere of print culture necessitates that certain citizens' authority to pass sentence on an author or his work be restricted or denied altogether. In *Tom Jones* Fielding metaphorically juxtaposes literary and juridical interpretation as a means to limit the access of various members of society, particularly women, to the professional practice of literary criticism.[13]

As a number of feminists before me have argued, Fielding believed women's place in culture to be in the private space of the home as wives and mothers;[14] he wished to encourage them to keep their literary judgments private as well. Women with economic or political ambitions are drawn harshly in *Tom Jones*; women with literary ambitions are drawn perhaps the most harshly of all. Still, while he did not wish for women in print culture to gain any more power than they already had, Fielding knew as well as Richardson the central role that they had as readers in the literary marketplace. He had no desire to alienate them as potential buyers of his novels. Thus Fielding, like Richardson, exploits society's stereotype of women as the moral guardians of the private sphere, and privileges their judgments within that space, even as he denies them the right to articulate them publicly.

As I have shown, in *Clarissa* Richardson's characterization of his four correspondents blurs the lines between the activities of writing and reading. While he tries to make clear that most individuals have no authority to "reform" an author's work, Richardson did not successfully convince many of his readers, who clamored in and through letters to persuade him to change his novel's ending. Fielding appears to circumvent that difficulty by teaching his audience to view writing and reading as separate activities, performed differently in separate realms. For instance, he attempts to distinguish between public acts and private acts of reading, and to distinguish between reading as production and reading as consumption, in order to create clearer boundaries between author and reader.

Changes in the material conditions of authorship had already helped to initiate such a separation of writerly and readerly practices in literary culture. To return briefly to the 1740 *Pope v. Curll* decision discussed in the previous chapter: Mark Rose argues that Lord Chancellor Hardwicke's decision in this case affected culture's representation of authorship in the following way:

> in severing the immaterial from the material aspect of literary property . . . he severed the act of writing a letter from that of receiving it. In this way Hardwicke separated writing from social exchange, constructing it as a solitary and self-sufficient act of creation . . . Hardwicke's decision also implied an author who created in privacy a work he might either bring to market or not as he chose. And this representation of writing implied a reciprocal representation of reading as a private act of consumption.[15]

But of course whether or not it was a private act of consumption, reading was not for that reason, as both Richardson and Fielding well knew, a necessarily passive activity. A private act of consumption could well result in a public act of literary production—as it did, for example, when Sarah Fielding read *Clarissa* and then published her critical pamphlet, *Remarks*.

To discourage such readerly ambitions in women and in men of the lower classes, Fielding tries in *Tom Jones* to emphasize novel writing as emanating from the private sphere, the product of an author's private sensibility and intended to be consumed, as well, privately within that sphere. More specifically, he attempts to encourage the general population of readers to be more passive in their private acts of reading through his deployment of gender. *Tom*

Jones ends with the marriage of Tom to Sophia; it ends metaphorically, that is, with an ideal reader forging an alliance with the best writer. Fielding suggests in *Tom Jones* that the proper relationship between the writer of literature and his readers is like that of husband and wife, because by his definition, both relationships depend on love motivated by esteem and gratitude, rather than a desire for political or economic gain. The relationship is also like that of husband and wife because by Fielding's definition, both relationships guarantee one party more power and authority than the other; the Reader/Wife is meant to complement the Writer/Husband's role as producer with hers as tasteful consumer. Proper readers view themselves as subject to the writer's laws, in much the same way that women remain subject to their husbands' authority.[16]

Having made all readers "naturally" inferior by representing them as potential "wives" of writers, Fielding further undermines the authority of the new professional critic. To do so, he defines "Critic" as "Every Reader in the World" (VIII: i, 396), and thus "radically democratizes the term, erasing the conventional discrimination between critic and common reader, denying the special skill and training by which his audience would recognize a critic as a privileged judge of letters."[17] By democratizing the term, he equates common criticism with mere opinion and opens up a space within which to argue that only an individual properly educated and (s)elected by his peers may truly pass judgment in the public sphere of letters.

In *Tom Jones*, Fielding therefore distinguishes between public and private readers as a means by which to make the privatized reader appear morally superior to the public critic, even as he actually locates the cultural authority for the public articulation of the rules, practices, and qualifications for the evaluation of literature in a particular kind of judge. This ideal professional reader of fiction mediates between the socioeconomic and political arena and the private sphere, and is a man whose education has trained him to be both a fair-minded legislator and an objective interpreter of evidence: an ideal Spectator in judicial robes, Fielding himself.

There is already a legal precedent for Fielding-as-Narrator's representation of himself as superior author and literary Judge. During the period in which Fielding wrote, some of the Lord Chancellor's juridical practices paralleled those of the new professional literary writer, the critic. As Mark Rose contends, "[W]hat we should observe [from the *Pope v. Curll* verdict] is that the issue in the case led to a circumstance in which a legal question—were letters on familiar subjects protected?—required [Lord Chancellor Hardwicke] to make a literary critical proclamation from the bench."[18] As Fielding well knew, the Lord Chancellor's duties included reading and judging whether a new play ought to be licensed and staged. The Lord Chancellor was a literate spectator; like Mr. Spectator or the Female Spectator, his spectatorship was a function of his ability to read scripts and to make judgments about those texts in and through writing. In other words, the job of Lord Chancellor necessitated that he be a skilled reader both of texts that serve a public function and of those that serve a private function, a skillful reader of the law and of texts on human nature. Of course, an important difference between literary-cultural spokespersons and a spokesperson of the Law is what motivates their spectatorship. While Mr. Spectator and the Female Spectator drew themselves as cultural commentators, the Lord Chancellor's role was that of a legally and professionally authorized official of the State, appointed by the King, a status which conferred upon him as a reader much more authoritity and power. As one whose literary behavior is modelled upon the Lord Chancellor's, and as one who also draws himself as the King of his text, Fielding-as-Narrator explicitly determines the legal and professional qualifications that bestow upon him the rank and status he assumes for himself. Fielding-as-Narrator draws his audience's attention to the ways in which his social and legal education as a barrister, his professional experiences as an author, and his ability to negotiate between public and private texts better suit him to the office of Critic than do the professional experiences of other men.

In effect, he creates in *Tom Jones* a five-tiered hierarchy of readers: within the public sphere, he designates a state-appointed official as print culture's highest authority, the Author/Critic. The next level of judges in this realm consists of those elected by other members of their communities, the professional critics who ostensibly serve the interests of society as a whole. On a third level, he places those readers who behave as jurors or lawyers do—those whose judgments about texts or testimony influence others, but who nevertheless remain subject to judges whose legal or professional status gives them more authority.

Within the private realm of the novel, he distinguishes between two kinds of readers, those who judge properly but whose class, gender, education or morality legislates against their judgments having any public authority, and those whose class, gender, education, or morality clearly demonstrates why their judgments should have no public power or authority. As did Mr. Spectator and the

Female Spectator, Fielding creates these categories to help him to authorize a particular kind of private sensibility.

In "the world of Law, justice is not guaranteed."[19] In the material world of letters, as in the world of the courtroom, power relations define the interpretation of evidence. In contrast, acting as a beneficent, omniscient Lord Chancellor, Fielding-as-Narrator creates in his novel a world in which justice for well-meaning characters and texts is guaranteed, where the intentions and meanings become clear and fixed: the world of the professional male Author/Critic.

Jurors, Judges and the Interpretation of Evidence

An author of fiction earns the esteem and gratitude of his readers by prudently representing his own and others' human nature. Authors are ultimately responsible for ensuring that readers recognize their moral superiority, genius, benevolence, and good heart, but readers' judgments of such texts should be based on their knowledge of human nature, rather than their desire for economic or political gain. A good reader/critic of human nature will be able to distinguish between hypocrites, those who behave affectedly, and those who behave truthfully, just as a judge and jury should be able to distinguish false testimony from true. Throughout *Tom Jones*, Tom and/or Blifil commit "crimes" for which they are called upon to defend themselves; witnesses are heard, "jurors" deliberate and a justice of the peace announces a verdict, and metes out—if necessary—punishment. *Tom Jones* the novel defends its author, testifies and presents evidence as to his superior writing skills and powers of judgment, and calls upon the extratextual readers to render a positive verdict. Its narrator, nevertheless, instructs his jury as to what rules should guide them, and so in the end only he, as the metaphoric Lord Chancellor of the novel, can deliver the final verdict.

In chapters 3 and 4 of book 4 of *Tom Jones*, Fielding first metaphorically "tries" himself and his rival(s) as authors. It is here, moreover, that he invites his readers to evaluate his characters' critical acumen as metaphoric spectators, jurors, and readers. In the first of these two chapters, young Blifil sets free the bird that young Tom had given Sophia as a present, and Tom attempts to rescue it. In the second, Thwackum, Square, Allworthy, Western, and the lawyer evaluate the evidence presented to them by the children. Notably, while also a witness to Blifil's thievery, Sophia refuses to utter her judgment publicly. She remains an objective female spectator of the sort Addison and Steele encouraged.

In order to critique as critics men who have achieved education and status similar to his own in the public sphere (thus limiting their authority and access to the profession of criticism), Fielding represents them as metaphoric jurors. Thwackum's and Square's weighing or interpretation of facts influence whether Tom or Blifil is either damned or praised, in turn, by justices of the peace Allworthy and Western.

Using the bird incident, Fielding attempts to make clear distinctions between "political" and "literary" criticism. In this novel, both the desire to condemn others and one's own physical appetites, such as hunger, lust, or the impulse to strike others violently, give rise to "political" criticism—typically overly legalistic or cunningly self-serving. A properly "literary," or heartfelt and moral, criticism issues from benevolent and sincere feelings of respect and gratitude, from an internal, privatized recognition of an author's or text's moral worth. The bird incident in particular makes clear that few individuals in society have the ability and authority to make public these latter kinds of judgments.

Because none of the men, not Thwackum, Square, the lawyer, Western or Allworthy, is physically present when Blifil sets the bird free and sets the subsequent events in motion, all of the men privilege testimony provided by the culprit Blifil himself, an unreliable source. They base their judgments on the testimony of Blifil, rather than the facts of the case, the events that actually transpire.

Moreover, all of them, like Fielding's Bad Critic, adhere to "the lifeless letter of" laws set down in the learned texts they read, and mistake mere form for substance (V: i, 159). All fail to judge accurately a situation that reveals something about the nature of human behavior because of their immersion in texts that neglect the element of emotion, and that create and promote political hierarchies dependent on class, social status, and property. None of these gentlemen is particularly interested in the facts themselves; for each one of them, it is the way that Blifil presents himself that matters. Because Blifil gives the appearance of a sober, virtuous boy, they apparently mistake the appearance of virtue for virtue itself. Since Blifil can also skillfully articulate proper motivations, which he has derived from his learning, his actions may be excused, no matter what the consequences of those actions. A conflict only develops when what he articulates does not correspond to laws valorized by a particular individual. In interpreting the evidence by the laws of their respective professions, Thwackum and Square lack compassion. Having no natural goodness of heart themselves, they do not consider the consequences of Blifil's actions, nor do they consider that Blifil's actions may have been motivated by less-than-virtuous emotions. Any notion of "heart"-felt behavior is beyond their vision.

Fielding indicts them most adamantly, however, because their judgments are politically rather than morally motivated. Their favorable interpretations of Blifil's actions are an attempt on their part to elevate themselves in Allworthy's eyes. Indeed, "[Tom and Blifil] are not always received in the World with the different Regard which seems severally due to either; and which one would imagine Mankind, from Self-interest, should shew towards them. But perhaps there may be a political Reason for it" (IV: v, 165). Blifil's mother, Bridget Allworthy, is an eligible commodity available to join in an alliance that would be favorable to either man. To establish an alliance with Blifil would, they think, make it easier for one of them to ally himself with her. Hence they are improper readers not only because they read the actions of the children based on laws they have derived from texts, but because they misread what the proper relationship between jurors (themselves) and witness (Blifil, as constructor of the narrative they "read" here) should be. Thwackum and Square judge Blifil favorably because, unlike the bastard Tom, he has the legitimacy, social position, and power to have his actions merit their esteem. To judge Blifil unfavorably in public would be politically imprudent for both these individuals. Their desire to elevate Blifil's story over Tom's is motivated by simple greed.

Importantly, Allworthy also judges Blifil's testimony in a favorable light. Allworthy, who has a benevolent disposition and a good heart, often has trouble distinguishing motive from appearance. At times he is capable of discerning the truth—for instance, that Tom's motivations are usually good though his actions may appear bad—but he is inconsistent. As a Justice of the Peace used to hearing evidence after an incident occurs, this is usually what he judges—the testimony of others. Allworthy oftentimes censures actions, or rather works, he has not himself read, as in the case when he harshly, indeed illegally, judges Partridge on the basis of his wife's testimony. Much later in the novel, Allworthy vociferously resists Mrs. Miller's assertion that Tom, who has "the most humane tender Heart that ever Man was blest with" (XVII: ii, 878), has been wronged by Blifil. Though Mrs. Miller reveals incriminating details of Blifil's plot against Tom, for Allworthy her testimony is hearsay, and carries very little weight in the world of courtroom testimony

(XVIII: v, 932–33). Thus, although Allworthy has a benevolent nature, he is at several points in the narrative guilty of abusing his power to judge.

In Fielding's definition of this kind of abuse of power, Allworthy is guilty of slander when he censures the actions of others without having witnessed them himself, particularly when he throws Tom out of Paradise Hall on the basis of Blifil and Thwackum's report of Tom's behavior during Allworthy's illness: "Such Censurers as these, whether they speak from their own Guess or Suspicion, or from the Report and Opinion of others, may properly be said to slander the Reputation of the Book they Condemn" (XI: i, 570).

The man who comes closest to the truth among those discussing what happened among the children, Squire Western—who is, like Allworthy, a Justice of the Peace—ultimately fails to render a fair and humane judgment as well. He bases his judgment of Blifil's actions on what he has learned from reading inferior journals and political newspapers. These texts have taught him that money and property confer power and authority. Not even the lawyer's interpretation of the events (which is that the bird was nobody's property and hence no blame can be attached to Blifil's actions) can convince Western that Blifil did not violate his daughter's rights as owner of the bird.

None of these men discerns Blifil's ulterior motives, his perjury, because they do not read human nature; they read words spoken or written by authoritative and authoritarian figures on abstract concepts or points of law. Without the wisdom that results from the study of human behavior, they have trouble interpreting properly the written texts they read. Allworthy breaks the law of his learned texts when he accepts the testimony of a wife against her husband; Western interprets from texts that the law regarding the use of money is to "lay it up" (VI: ii, 278); Thwackum interprets the law of Authority as one recommending violence. Fielding suggests that one should be properly educated in Nature, or the world, before being allowed to pursue knowledge from certain kinds of books. Nature, honest society and books about human nature are better able to instill proper morality in individuals, while learned texts seem to develop only an individual's political side. For this reason, these male "jurors" are also what Fielding labels "bad critics." Their partisan judgments are often motivated by their "appetites," or their desire for power.

Fielding protests against the sort of partisan critical practices which these men indulge in *Tom Jones*. Nevertheless, the boundaries between "political" and "literary" criticism often blurred elsewhere in Fielding's own writing because he himself always had a propensity to use discourse, such as his journalistic essays or plays, for political or partisan ends. As a dramatist and journalist, Fielding specialized in political satire. During the 1730s, for instance, Fielding often wrote plays that criticized then-Prime Minister Robert Walpole. In 1737, the Licensing Act—instigated and legislated by his worst political enemies, legislators supporting Walpole—effectively and legally silenced him. Ironically, he experienced the impact of "criticism" on his material circumstances much more strongly and tangibly than did those he criticized or than had the powerful and comfortably well-off printer Samuel Richardson. No longer able to stage his plays, Fielding was called to the bar in 1740, but throughout this period he remained an active journalist and hack writer.

As such, he often wrote positive reviews as a means of supporting fellow authors, but also as a way to express gratitude for past patronage or as an investment against future financial reward: for example, "Fielding's laudatory review of [James] Thomson's *Castle of Indolence* suggests the puffing of a friend rather than the cool judgment of a critic" (*HF*, 326). James Thomson was apparently the man responsible for introducing Fielding and his work to Andrew Millar, the publisher who eventually would give Fielding, with Thomson acting as intermediary, a £200 advance for *Joseph Andrews*. And more importantly, perhaps, Fielding indulged in those censorious practices of political criticism that he condemned when, in several of his literary reviews, he set up fictional Courts of Censorial Enquiry (see for example *The Covent Garden* Journal, no. 5; *The Champion*, no. 80; and *The Jacobite's Journal*, nos. 6 and 7), "trying" such figures as Poet Laureate Colly Cibber.

Like Thwackum's and Square's, Fielding's judgment was often politically motivated. As Jill Campbell notes, "the same man who came to the attention of the London public in the 1730s as an inspired Opposition satirist—who in fact was credited with precipitating the passage of the Stage Licensing Act in 1737 by so effectively attacking Walpole's administration on the stage—was to serve in the final years of his life 'as the government's most dutiful and effective apologist.' "[20] *Tom Jones* in fact implicitly acknowledges the contemporary literary world as a political arena in which writers vie for position, status, and power. And for Fielding, it was an arena in which he and most of his critics would continue to use "political" rather than merely "literary" criteria to judge an author's work.

In *Tom Jones*, Fielding metaphorically highlights the politics of the world of literary criticism and suggests that the work of those authors with more power and status will usually receive more praise than those who have little or no power or status, even as he calls for the reformation of criticism. His strategy to undercut the cultural authority of his rivals by elevating writers like himself on the basis of genius or a "humane tender [heart]," rather than attacking the rivals themselves through character assassination, remains a political one nonetheless.

For instance, it is Blifil himself who seems best to mirror Fielding-as-Narrator. Both Blifil and the narrator manipulate and "plot" in every sense of the word. Moreover, like the narrator, Blifil performs the work of author-as-critic when he constructs the fictions about Tom that he presents in turn to others. Blifil reflects, however, the temperament of those authors whose appearance of morality hides a corrupt private sensibility.

As far as Blifil's testimony is concerned, his narrative is one built on carefully managed circumstantial evidence. He attributes his own behavior in taking Sophia's bird to his desire to set free a creature which (he implies) Tom has unjustly entrapped for Sophia's amusement. Appealing to the sensibilities of two of his jurors, Thwackum and Square, he couches his explanation for his behavior in rhetoric that will satisfy both of them. Blifil asserts that to domesticate an animal is against the Laws of Nature and Religion. In effect, Blifil justifies his actions, placing them in an advantageous light, while casting indirect aspersions on Tom—a behavior that he will continue to cultivate throughout the novel.

In the character of Blifil, Fielding suggests that the privilege of a private sensibility associated with class, status, and education may be a double-edged sword. Those motivated by greed and ambition can often exploit their education in order to mask their baser side. Particularly in relation to Tom, Blifil looks for means to discover his faults, reading Tom's actions with a malevolent slant. As a critic of Tom throughout the novel, Blifil exhibits those characteristics which Fielding ascribes to slanderers. Like the Slanderous Critic's readings, Blifil's readings of Tom's behavior are a means of revenge. Blifil usually does his readings at times when Tom seems to have more power than him; for example, in the bird incident he perceives that Tom's present to Sophia makes Tom superior to Blifil in Sophia's eyes. Moreover, the account of Tom's behavior that precipitates Tom's expulsion from Paradise Hall comes very soon after Blifil discovers that Tom is Bridget Allworthy's son, his own half-brother and potential heir to the Allworthy fortune.

Blifil's ability to "write" his judgments of Tom, to construct narratives which give his readings substance, and which allow him to manipulate those asked to act as his jurors or judges, distinguishes him from other characters. Some of Blifil's success as a constructor of narratives is based on his ability to "read" skillfully how the elder men wish him to articulate that interpretation publicly. Yet this is also a reflection of his dominant social, economic, and political position. As is true for Blifil, some authors' literacy skills will always achieve for them more cultural authority than they deserve.

Blifil is the first one asked for his judgment about the actions and behaviors of himself and others because throughout most of the novel, he is perceived by others to be Allworthy's rightful and legitimate heir. He therefore has the most powerful voice. Throughout most of *Tom Jones*, Blifil owns the discourse of political and moral power. While Blifil may be a Bad Critic, he is also an apparently successful one. His reading of Tom's behavior during Allworthy's illness and recovery results in Tom's dismissal from Paradise Hall.

When he offers his testimony about what has happened among the children, Blifil seems quite adept at interpreting what his jurors wish to hear. Fielding later makes it quite clear, though, that Blifil is not, in terms of morality, a good reader at all, and therefore not a very good writer, either. Blifil's desire to interpret does not arise from the esteem or gratitude he feels upon reading a text: "he [was] altogether well furnished with some other passions that promised themselves very full Gratification . . . Such were Avarice and Ambition, which divided the Dominion of his Mind between them" (VI: iv, 284). Notwithstanding his ability to discern the political wishes of others, for example, his own baser appetites prevent him from judging accurately Sophia's enmity for him. He merely considers her "a most delicious Morsel, indeed [regards] her with the same Desires which an Ortolan inspires into the Soul of an Epicure" (VII: vi, 262).

Fielding ultimately banishes Blifil from the world of the novel. It is important to note, however, that he does not, metaphorically speaking, banish him from the public realm of discourse, nor does he condemn Blifil to a life of poverty and infamy. Allworthy settles £200 a year on him,

> to which Jones hath privately added a third. Upon this income [Blifil] lives in one of the northern Counties, about 200 miles distant from London, and lays up £200 a Year out of it, in order to purchase a Seat in the next Parliament from a neighbouring Borough, which he hath bargained for with an Attorney there. He is also lately turned Methodist, in hopes of marrying a very rich widow of that Sect, whose Estate lies in that Part of the Kingdom. (XVIII: xiii, 979)

Fielding seems, like Tom, to maintain a certain amount of affection for Blifil, not wholly unlike the affection Fielding is said to have felt for his rival Richardson.[21] Of course, Fielding cynically suggests that Blifil's brand of narrative skills, particularly in terms of his political savvy and prudence, will serve him well in explicitly political arenas. Even when Blifil is proven to lack Tom's better qualities, his capacity to "re-write" his actions so that they appear good continues to stand him in good stead. Despite the fact that Tom Jones is shown to be morally superior at the end of the novel, Fielding does not preclude the possibility that Blifil will regain a measure of economic and political power. In the world of authorship, writers who can cloak their immorality can still wield power; Blifil can eventually buy a seat in Parliament and help to enact legislation. What Fielding may hope to do through his characterization of this culprit is to limit the ability of authors such as Blifil to achieve economic and political status within those branches of literary production in which he himself is most anxious to compete—fiction and criticism—by undermining their cultural authority to speak about moral and literary matters.

The Erotics of Reading

To achieve his readers' esteem and gratitude as a Spectator/Judge of literature, Fielding must prove he can perform the labor of critic. That is, he must prove that he can reform immoral discourse and the manners of society in and through his own writing. Given his marital circumstances at the time of writing, Fielding must also convince his audience that he can or has reformed his own "immoral" ways as well. He does so through the character of Tom.

Given the time other characters spend judging Tom's actions, a reader of Fielding's text might be justified in saying that Tom inscribes himself, and is in turn written and re-written by others: "[Thwackum] produced the Record upon his Breast, where the Handwriting of Mr. Jones remained very legible in Black and Blue" (VI: x, 235). Fielding-as-narrator makes a more explicit comparison between Tom and the novel proper when he says: "For as no one can call another Bastard, without calling the Mother a whore; so neither can any one give the Names of sad Stuff, horrid Nonsence, etc. to a book, without calling the Author a Blockhead" (XI: i, 433). Tom Jones is the primary text to both Fielding's readers and to other characters in the novel. As such, we can see Tom as the "book" which Allworthy judges, for instance, without first having read it himself.

Nevertheless, as the example of Blifil illustrates, the writer or text that will be judged most moral has at least to appear moral in his (its) public behavior or character and through his (its) use of language. As was true for Motteux's Noble Statuary, Tom Jones must become more cognizant of the necessity to transcribe properly his private thoughts and emotions onto a text of public behavior. As the novel progresses, Tom becomes aware of the *need* to control an audience's power to judge him as text, to inhibit their ability to interpret (usually negativively) his behavior. Tom must reform his physical, erotic body into a prudent and moral text. That is, Tom's journey after his initial expulsion from Paradise Hall produces in him an interiority—or a private sensibility—which will later give him access to the Paradise Hall of the literary world, as the proper inheritor of Mr. Spectator's legacy.

In many ways, in the early stages of the novel, Tom is pre-linguistic—at least his "readings" are—perhaps because "he was not at this time perfect master of that wonderful power of reason" (V: x, 257). Unlike the sober and articulate Blifil, Tom imparts his judgments of others' behavior in primarily non-verbal ways:

> He was indeed a thoughtless, giddy Youth, with little Sobriety in his Manners, and less in his Countenance; and would often very impudently and indecently laugh at his Companion for his serious Behaviour. (III: v, 100)

Without thought there is no language, and Tom's "violent animal Spirits" (V: ix, 191) often cause him to act unthinkingly—Tom's interpretations of events are usually "written" in gesture, rather than in speech. It is in discussing Tom's wantonness, wildness, and want of caution that Fielding-as-Narrator intrudes within the text of Tom's story to caution:

> It is not enough that your Designs, nay that your Actions, are intrinsically good, you must take Care they shall appear so. If your Inside be never so beautiful, you must preserve a fair Outside also. This must be constantly looked to, or Malice and Envy will take Care to blacken it so, that the Sagacity and Goodness of an Allworthy will not be able to see thro' it, and to discern the Beauties within. (III: vii, 106)

Although his actions are not intrinsically good, Blifil has the ability to make them appear so because of his serious appearance; more importantly, he has the skill to make his actions appear moral *through language*. As Allworthy later tells Tom:

> you have much Goodness, Generosity, and Honour in your Temper; if you will add Prudence and Religion to these, you must be happy: For the three former Qualities, I admit, make you worthy of Happiness, but they are the latter only which will put you in Possession of it. (V: vii, 244)

What Tom lacks before his "journey to Wisdom" is the prudence (the capacity for judging in advance the probable results of his actions) and the religion (morality) to inscribe himself properly through his actions. Tom does not possess Blifil's capacity to "rewrite" his actions so that they appear good, though, as we have seen, this is partially a result of his inferior political position in the novel. Tom's journey will teach him how better to "write" himself in the world.

As a metaphoric text, Tom has a good heart and learning, because he has been instructed by Square and Thwackum. But he lacks experience and Judgment: "A blameable Want of Caution and Diffidence in the Veracity of Others, in which he was highly worthy of Censure." Fielding-as-Narrator goes so far as to say what Tom lacks is "Genius": "As *Jones* had not this Gift from Nature, he was too young to have gained it by Experience" (VIII: vii, 428). After his eviction from Allworthy's estate, Tom's odyssey leads him to the discovery of knowledge and conversation with all ranks and degrees of human nature, including members of the "fair sex."[22]

Unfortunately, as Peter J. Carlton so blithely argues, women always appear to be "the aggressor[s] in Tom's affairs.... 'Poor' Tom comes off as a relatively innocent bystander, a kindly and generous stallion beset by mares in heat."[23] For example, Jenny Waters's esteem and gratitude to Tom for saving her life, and for his superior "Good nature," somehow get waylaid into sexual appetite. Mrs. Waters does not make proper use of her knowledge—she is chastised twice by Allworthy for not making better use of it. Her immoral alliances with other men are even more grievous because Jenny has "Learning," and should know better the laws of moral behavior.

A moral text reveals its author to be in possession of that power of mind that is "capable of penetrating into all things within [his] Reach and Knowledge" (IX: i, 490–91). Despite the fact that women appear to be the aggressors in the novel, Tom Jones-as-text penetrates, bodily, all women within his reach. Notably, his sexual exploits are not motivated, like Square's, for instance, by acquisitive lust. He has affairs when the opportunities present themselves, but he does not manipulate his partners in order to control or dominate them. His sexual exploits are good-natured; he genuinely wishes to please his female suitors. In his inability to repress his body throughout much of the novel, however, Tom, like Lovelace and Clarissa, fails to show his capacity for moral interpretation. When Tom allows Sophia's image (an image that represents wisdom) to slip his mind, he is unable to discern the difference between the essence of women like Molly, Jenny Waters, Lady Bellaston, and that of Sophia. It is only when Nightingale makes clear the contrast between Lady Bellaston and Sophia through his stories of the former's promiscuity that Jones is ready to acquire the judgment that the possession of Sophia represents:

> From his Disgust, his Mind, by a Natural Transition turned towards Sophia: Her Virtue, her Purity, her Love to him, her Sufferings on his Account, filled his Thoughts, and made his Commerce with Lady Bellaston appear still more odious. (XV: ix, 819)

Tom's sexual liaisons raise an interesting problem; for the most part, he becomes involved in these immoral escapades because of the ways women read him (see, for example, XVI: x, 871). Fielding thereby also implies that Tom's inability to elude the erotic is the woman's fault rather than the man's; women desire erotic titillation.[24] Metaphorically speaking, this also serves to suggest that authors have difficulty producing wholly moral fictions in a literary marketplace wherein the majority of consumers, women, themselves prefer erotic romance. This strategy is a means by which Fielding also competes with women authors of the period, as many are the authors of those works which he denigrates as "romances."

For instance, while in the public sphere of print culture the only perceived literary rivalry was that between Richardson and Fielding, Fielding's biographer Martin Battestin points to another important rival, Sarah Fielding. According to Battestin, the relationship between Richardson, Henry, and his sister was "a fascinating, intensely personal triangular [one] in which all three authors, jealously interacting, spurred each other on to their best work, as well as to less appealing displays of pettiness and spite" (*HF*, 379). Some of *Tom Jones*'s less appealing female characters may display some of Henry Fielding's anxiety about competition from women authors like his sister.[25]

Reading "romance" tends to create in the women who read *Pamela*'s and *Clarissa*'s stories, if his sister Sarah is any evidence, a desire to write fiction, and a desire to write their judgments of others' fictions. Reading "romance" creates a desire to compete within the field of letters—and Fielding knows that this can potentially lead to a desire for power in the public realm. Writer today, barrister tomorrow. Like Richardson, Fielding attempts to counteract this power by constructing an ideal female reader, an exemplary daughter who like Sophia, to quote Janice Haney-Previtz, needs "someone to speak about, as, and for" her.[26]

Certainly *Tom Jones* expresses some hostility and ambivalence toward women who are either seductive, scholarly, or both. Equating a desire for learning with sexual deviance in women provides Fielding with a reason to exclude women from the profession of literary criticism: readers like Jenny Waters, Lady Bellaston, and even Tom's own mother, the novel implies, are often incapable of controlling their sexual desire for Tom Jones.

For women, erotic reading is the male version of a desire for control over texts. Sexual as these readings of Tom by women characters may appear, like the readings of male characters, they also seem to arise from an improper desire for control or power—according to Fielding, a masculine desire.[27] For example, Molly's "[b]eauty was not of the most Amiable Kind. It had indeed very little of Feminine in it, and would have become a Man at least as well as a Woman. . . . Nor was her Mind more effeminate than her Person" (IV: vi, 174–75). Molly reads in Tom a "Backwardness" that leads to her aggressive "[m]eans of throwing herself in his Way". She also correctly reads that in order to win Tom she must make it appear that he seduced her:

> Molly so well played her Part, that Jones attributed the Conquest entirely to himself, and considered the young Woman as one who had yielded to the violent Attacks of his Passion. He likewise imputed her yielding to the ungovernable Force of her Love towards him . . . (IV: vi, 175)

Fielding demonstrates a male fear of women using their sexuality to control men, implicitly alluding to the biblical tale of Eve's seducing Adam into eating the forbidden fruit. Lady Bellaston is another example of a woman reader of Tom whose pleasure in reading him is played out sexually. But the narrator slyly implies that even Tom's real mother exhibits signs of sexual desire for him.[28]

> When Tom grew up, and gave Tokens of that Gallantry of Temper which greatly recommends Men to Women . . . [s]he was so desirous of often

seeing him, and discovered such Satisfaction and Delight in his Company, that before he was eighteen Years old, he was become a rival to both Square and Thwackum; and what is worse, the whole Country began to talk as loudly of her Inclination to Tom, as they had before done of that which she had shewn to Square. (III: vi, 139)

An improper desire for political power is a primary reason that Fielding advances for women's exclusion from the public office of criticism, and those women who desire the right to air their judgments publicly and authoritatively suffer harsh treatment in his hands. Fielding writes a chapter whose title ironically calls our attention to Sophia's aunt's interpretive skills: "The Character of Mrs. Western. Her Great Learning and Knowledge of the World, and an Instance of the deep Penetration which she derived from those Advantages." This "Great Learning and Knowledge" derives from "all the modern plays, Operas, Oratorios, Poems and Romances; in all of which she was a Critic" (VI: ii, 272–73). In other words, Mrs. Western not only reads stereotypically bad literature, but she also has the audacity to think her opinions on fiction are worth hearing. Mrs. Western reads other women's behavior for the arts of affectation they use to encourage men to court them, for their hypocrisy. She cannot read properly "the plain simple Workings of honest Nature" (VI: ii, 208).

More importantly, Fielding satirizes Mrs. Western because, unlike others of her gender, she has no interest in performing woman's proper role as either wife, mother or daughter, and indeed, is unrecognizable as female: a "masculine person, [of] near six Foot high, added to her Manner and Learning, possibly prevented the other Sex from regarding her, notwithstanding her petticoats, in the light of a woman," Mrs. Western prefers having the upper hand in her relationship with her brother. She steps out of her proper place by assuming that Squire Western should serve her out of gratitude for the way she has raised his daughter. She speaks with an inflated sense of her own authority; her judgments of others, like those of many of the male readers, are spawned by her desire for political power, a particularly inappropriate desire for a woman. And again, Mrs. Western cannot interpret human nature well. The only woman whom Fielding identifies explicitly as a critic must perforce be judged a very poor interpreter of the texts she reads.

Men can be bad jurors, but, Fielding implicitly argues, women should never be jurors, primarily because, like Mrs. Western, they are trained to affect airs in the pursuit of their goals. The majority of women in *Tom Jones*—in fact all save Sophia and Mrs. Miller—

are drawn as hypocrites and scandalmongers by nature. Unlike the men who discuss foreign and domestic affairs of importance at the Coffee-houses, women congregate in the Chandler's shop, "the known Seat of all the News, or as it is vulgarly called, Gossipping" (II: iv, 88). Those who deal with exaggerations of the truth, or those who disguise the Truth of Nature regularly every evening when they put on their make-up, cannot be expected to be able to distinguish truth from fiction in the stories they hear or read. Hence, when a soldier tells a ghost story, while only a few men believe him, all of the women present "believed it firmly, and prayed Heaven to defend them from Murther" (VII: xiv, 389).

It is important to recognize that Fielding's characterization of women as readers is not so much misogynist as ambivalent—and not altogether unconventional in any case. Women as readers had been very early on characterized as easily seduced by the fictions they read. The third Earl of Shaftesbury postulated in 1710, for instance, that Shakespeare created the character Desdemona, denoting superstition, to foretell the kind of woman reader of the romance thatwould spring up some 100 years later: "It is certain there is a very great affinity between the passion of superstition and that of [romance] tales. The love of strange narrations and the ardent appetite towards unnatural objects has a near alliance with the like appetite towards the supernatural kind . . . The tender virgins, losing their natural softness, assume this tragic passion, of which they are highly susceptible."[29]

Because he does seek the admiration and respect of such women readers as his sister Sarah, and in order to woo women as readers, Fielding suggests in *Tom Jones* that the majority of the reading public ought to judge texts more like a woman such as Sophia. Sophia, while looking askance at the sexual misbehavior of Tom, ultimately recognizes his moral superiority as a text, his genius, his benevolence, and his good heart, forgives him, marries him, and never utters a word against him in public.

In *Tom Jones*, the good women keep silent. Indeed, Sophia refuses at every opportunity the chance either to take sides in an argument or to utter her judgments about any texts with authority. She obeys all the laws that Fielding-as-Narrator sets down for those who wish to interpret a text. As metaphoric reader, she unites with Tom Jones out of the esteem and gratitude she feels when reading him as text. Fielding uses the character of Sophia to flatter his female audience and to create for women a limited role as readers. The refined upper-class female audience he seeks can identify with

Sophia, a woman whose reading is so superior that she need not say so.

When Blifil steals her bird, for instance, his actions speak louder than words for Sophia alone. Sophia, the narrator tells us, imputes the poverty and meanness of Blifil's actions to Anger, and judges his character solely on the basis of the way he behaves. Ostensibly, Sophia has gained some of her knowledge from the books she reads, books in which "[appear] a great deal of human Nature . . . and in many parts, so much true tenderness and Delicacy that [they cost her] many a Tear" (VI: v, 286). Sophia possesses, along with an ability to read human nature, a good heart, capable of sincere feeling. She reads none of those books recommended by Mrs. Western that teach hypocrisy. Fielding tells us "that whatever mental accomplishments she had derived from Nature, they were somewhat improved and cultivated by Art: For she had been educated under the Care of an Aunt, who was a Lady of Great discretion, and was thoroughly acquainted with the World, having lived in her Youth about the Court . . . By her conversation and Instructions, Sophia was perfectly well-bred" (IV: ii, 158). Sophia's education, then, has been almost purely experiential, her natural skills complemented and augmented by her intercourse with society rather than with books of learning, or books which would teach her to "act a part," to behave unnaturally.

In the episode described in chapter 3, only Sophia can be judged an adequate reader, because she alone bases her interpretation of Blifil's actions on what she knows about human nature, i.e., that one's actions reveal one's character. Nevertheless, she has no voice. The narrator gives us Sophia's interpretation.[30] He seems to be the only one privy to it; Sophia's response is not solicited within the chapter itself. Throughout the novel, Sophia resists publicly voicing her judgments. For instance, when Sophia hears the story of Tom and the partridge "she [says] nothing; nor indeed could her Aunt get many words from her" (IV: v, 166). However, when alone with her maid Honour, Sophia does communicate her feelings, and quite passionately: " 'I hate the Name of Master Blifil, as I do whatever is base and Treacherous" (IV: v, 166). This passage demonstrates Sophia's propensity to speak only in situations where her authority to do so is unquestionable. As a woman and a servant, Sophia's maid is even more powerless than Sophia herself. Sophia sees herself as not having the authority to judge outside the privacy of her own mind or her own closet. Although she is the best critic of the texts she reads, unlike Clarissa, Sophia never publicly desires her own critical language. She remains an objective female spectator of the sort approved by Addison and Steele. Her critical sensibility remains utterly and wholly private.

One might argue that Sophia discovers on her journey to London the liberty to choose not only for herself, but to speak freely for herself. Yet, in the scene in which she tells Tom of her judgment of him, Fielding undermines that authority. Immediately after Sophia gives Tom her assessment, he places her in front of a mirror and tells her that the image of her remains always in his mind. This is doubly significant; first, Tom puts Sophia on a pedestal. She remains an ideal, not really human. Tom reads Sophia as a paragon: "She is all over, both in Mind and Body, consummate Perfection. She is the most Beautiful Creature in the Universe."

Second, Sophia is not a human figure, but an artifact, something he can possess: "For what Happiness this world affords equal to the possession of such a Woman as Sophia, I sincerely own I have never yet discovered" (XV: ix 818). Fielding confirms this view of Sophia as an idealized character when he describes her at her bridal table: "neither [Tom nor Nightingale] could long keep his Eyes from Sophia, who sat at the Table like a Queen receiving Homage, or rather like a Superior Being receiving Adoration from all around her" (XVIII: xiii, 977). Sophia's marriage to Tom is also a decision to become Tom's subject. She plays the role of a woman who will remain the exemplary daughter, even in marriage: rather than asserting that she marries Tom for Love, she still "prudently" claims she marries him to obey her father. In essence, she verbally strips herself of authority.[31]

For Fielding, Sophia must also be judged the best reader because she does not, like other women readers, act out her desire for Tom sexually—at least not until she accepts subordinate status by marrying him. Christine Van Boheemen writes, "Sophia figures in the fiction only as a symbolic stand-in for Allworthy; access to her marks access to Paradise Hall."[32] In terms of how Sophia works as symbol of the relationship between Writer and Reader in the world, Fielding's access to the ideal woman reader, his possession of her as a purchaser and consumer of his texts, will give him access to the Paradise Hall of the Bookseller. She will be an "inestimable Treasure to a Good Husband," in Allworthy's words, because he

> never heard any thing of Pertness, or what is called Repartee out of her Mouth; no Pretence to Wit much less that kind of Wisdom which is the Result only of great Learning and Experience; the Affectation of which, in a young Woman, is as absurd as any of the Affectations of an Ape. No dictatorial Sentiments, no juridical Opinions, no profound Criticism.

> Whenever I have seen her in the Company of Men, she hath been all Attention, with the Modesty of a Learner, not the Forwardness of a Teacher. (XVII: iii, 882)

Allworthy's praise of Sophia alludes to the qualities of bad critics described by Fielding-as-Narrator: their assumptions of "Dictatorial powers" (V: i, 159), and their propensity to "act as a Judge would." In this manner, Allworthy makes it clear that what Sophia refuses to do is to be a critic, particularly when he goes on to praise her for refusing to judge an argument between Thwackum and Square. Sophia's response ("I will affront neither so much, as to give my Judgment on his Side" [XVII: iii, 883]) demonstrates to Allworthy that "she has always shewed the highest Deference to the Understandings of Men; A quality absolutely essential to the making of a good Wife" (XVIII: iii, 883).[33]

April London has contended that Sophia is the best reader in *Tom Jones*, and that Fielding actually validates Sophia's authority as an interpreter:

> female power, although most richly evoked in negative terms as an expression of carnality, also has its positive embodiment in the person of Sophia . . . Additional weight is given to Sophia's critical acumen by the narrative implications of her role as interpreter and arbiter of Tom's history. In this role she uses sources both oral (the maid Susan at Upton) and written (Tom's letter proposing marriage to Lady Bellaston), sifts the evidence, and finally delivers a sentence of banishment on her erring lover. Her magisterial act echoes Allworthy's earlier pronouncement, but while the latter's judgment is undercut by subsequent events, Sophia's is not . . . such interpretive abilities suggest a place in the narrative as surrogate reader . . .[34]

I would argue, however, that while Sophia's judgment itself may not be undercut, her authority to make public that judgment most certainly is. Without that public authority, her judgment has no power to effect change.

From the novel, then, we learn that women should not make public their own critical language. Fielding makes clear that women readers like Sophia are the best readers precisely because they never choose to execute their power to judge publicly. Sophia only reads in order to learn her proper role as a potential wife and mother. Her reading has helped her to see that men rightfully control the public sphere; they have jurisdiction in the economic and political world. Sophia's books on human nature teach her that women belong in the home, as wives and mothers, and that because they are so skilled at reading human emotion, they should execute their judgment only within that sphere. Since criticism is based on political and economic hierarchies, as Fielding shows in this text, women have no business within that realm of literary production. Female readers like Sophia, who understand the necessity of economically separating male and female roles in society, help to maintain the forms of patriarchal political authority within literary culture.

In denying women the right to speak authoritatively, Fielding denies them the right to "write" with authority their judgments of the actions they interpret. Certainly, when Fielding elevates Sophia as the best reader, as metaphorically the best mate for the superior writer, he also implies that those men who would learn to read as well as Sophia does should also refuse to make public their judgments.[35] In this way, he hopes to discourage a number of men from entering the literary marketplace as well. By not allowing women the authority for their judgments, however, he denies that those judgments are in fact superior to those of the male characters, whose gender ensures that they will always be believed before the women, whether they read well or not. The best reader becomes not Sophia, but Fielding-as-Narrator, because of all the characters in the text, he alone has the ability to read human nature properly, and the ability to apply what he has learned in texts to what he sees.

Sophia's judgment of Tom doesn't automatically make Tom a better person: "Whatever in the Nature of Jones had a Tendency to Vice, has been corrected by continual Conversation with this good Man [Allworthy], and by his Union with the lovely and virtuous Sophia" (XVIII: xiii, 981). Rather, Tom's "union" with (or possession of) her is what makes him virtuous—not *her* conversation. It is *Allworthy* who instructs Tom through language, and helps him to properly inscribe himself, despite his own questionable judgment throughout this text. As the socially sanctioned critic within the novel proper, Allworthy becomes the father-in-law of Sophia-as-reader, as well. With this image of the amateur reader as "daughter" to the professional critic, Fielding attempts to control readerly response to his novel, promotes the interests of male authors over those of female authors, and in addition promotes his own interests (as the metaphoric Lord Chancellor of the novel) over those of his male rivals in the field of letters.

In terms of readerly practices, Fielding attempts in *Tom Jones* to sever the censorious language of politics from that of literary criticism, and to divide the world of printed texts into two separate spheres: the world of fiction, a private, domestic world of courtship and marriage, and the world of non-fiction, a public world of socio-economic and political relations. Within these two spheres, there also exist, respectively, amateur writers and readers and professional authors and critics.[36] The only reader who both discerns truth from human nature and successfully presents his judgments or knowledge is the professional author/critic. Like Mr. Spectator, as Lord Chancellor of the Kingdom of his text, Fielding-as-narrator not only objectively sifts through the evidence presented in a text, but can "with the greater Sagacity consider [defendant's and prosecutor's] Talents, Manners, Feelings and Merits." As an author, Fielding becomes the best critic because he understands and interprets human nature well. Even the most benevolent of judges, Allworthy, is fallible when he allows his passions to interfere in his consideration of evidence or when he allows a man's relative status in society to influence his final decision. Fielding-as-narrator exhibits both intuitive knowledge and a dispassionate penetration into the motives and intentions of characters and authors and the circumstances of their respective plots. As a culturally sanctioned authority, he can express that superior interpretive skill in writing, within a public forum. As such the best knowledge can be learnt from the author of this novel, who alone most successfully demonstrates and transmits "a very extraordinary Degree of Judgment, and a most exact Knowledge of human Nature" (VIII: i, 405).

4
Writing Men Reading in *The Female Quixote*

LIKE RICHARDSON'S *CLARISSA* AND HENRY FIELDING'S *TOM JONES*, CHARlotte Lennox's *The Female Quixote* was a great success with its audience. First published in March of 1752, it went into a second edition in June, was immediately translated into French, Spanish and German, and, thereafter, was "often reprinted until 1820." Based on Cervantes' *Don Quixote, The Female Quixote* recounts the ways in which the reading habits of the quixotic protagonist Arabella interfere with her courtship with her cousin Mr. Glanville, who desires to reform her reading habits because of their problematic influence on her behavior. Like its precursor, Lennox's novel spawned "numerous imitations and allusions," one of them American Tabitha Gilman Tenney's *Female Quixotism* (1801).[1]

One might expect that since *The Female Quixote* was as popular as *Clarissa* and *Tom Jones*, it would have a fairly well-established place in the twentieth-century canon of eighteenth-century novels. Such is not the case. The critical backlash initiated by the nineteenth-century male-dominated literary institutions of production, described by Gaye Tuchman in *Edging Women Out*, certainly contributed to Lennox's disappearance from the canon after 1820.[2] Nonetheless, given Lennox's popularity and status in the eighteenth century as one of the best novelists, it seems odd that even now there have been relatively few attempts by feminist readers of eighteenth-century literature to retrieve Lennox's texts, in comparison to their attempts to resurrect, say, Anne Radcliffe or Aphra Behn. One reason could be that early criticism of Lennox was said to have been divided: "the men for Mrs. Lennox, the women against her."[3] Having accepted this hypothesis in their evaluations and interpretations of her work, subsequent critics' attempts to explain the reasons for this split have resulted in both Lennox and women in general getting short shrift as writers and critics.

More importantly, perhaps, *The Female Quixote* has remained a fairly marginal text in twentieth-century histories of the novel because any number of critics have explicated it as primarily revealing Charlotte Lennox's and women's vexed relationship to the romance.[4] These readings neglect, however, Lennox's more complex argument about the way in which the term "romance" functions in her novel. In *The Female Quixote*, Lennox points to eighteenth-century literary culture's use of romance as a tool with which to exclude readers and writers from participation in the new profession of literary reviewership, on the basis of class and gender.

Like Fielding, Lennox was an author who through much of her literary life suffered from money troubles. Apparently the daughter of a soldier and his wife (of whom little is known), as a woman, she had no access to an education like that received by Fielding. According to Miriam Small, she was sent to England in 1735 from North America to be educated, but when she arrived, found there had been no provision made for her. Left to fend for herself, she was reportedly taken in by a Lady Rockingham and then the Duchess of Newcastle. We have no evidence of what kind of education she received, if any, under the patronage of either of these two women; whatever her education, though, it was not the formal education with which many men of the upper classes were provided. Of course, Richardson did not have a formal, classical education either, and Fielding's academic credentials prepared him for little else but professional writing. It was only after his career as a playwright was ended by the Licensing Act of 1737 that he became a barrister—and only then because his records were doctored, and because a well-placed relative politicked for him (see Battestin). Like Henry Fielding's, then, Lennox's education prepared her for little else but writing;[5] like Samuel Richardson's, her education restricted her subject matter and style. She first wrote poetry, and perhaps because writing was an unstable and often unprofitable profession then (as it is now), she tried her hand at acting. She apparently showed no talent for the latter; Horace Walpole, for one, apparently considered her to be a terrible actress.

As Catherine Gallagher points out, the 1750s were not a "propitious" time to be an author of novels; booksellers were more interested in publishing old material. So, "although Lennox was among the twenty best-selling novelists between 1750 and 1770, constant economic distress was her lot, and she seems to have always been hatching schemes to end the drudgery of her 'independence' " as an author, though most of these projects, Gallagher tells us, failed.[6]

Furthermore, she married a man who did little to contribute to her financial stability: "Charlotte's husband probably never was able to fend for himself."[7] Unhappy in her marriage and always dependent upon the support of such patrons as the women mentioned above and men such as Johnson and Richardson, Lennox probably wished for more power and control over her own life and writing. Like Richardson, she probably resented those who dismissed her on the basis of her lack of classical education. Given the position of women in society and her own financial circumstances, she, like Richardson and Fielding, learned the necessity of playing within the rules of the writing game of that time. Like all writers, that is, Lennox was constrained by her material conditions to speak what the society considered to be "moral discourse" if she wanted a decent reputation and audience for her books.

What distinguished Lennox from Fielding or Richardson in her ability to eke out a living was that she did in fact have fewer occupational options open to her as a woman. She could not have learned a trade like Richardson's nor could she have become a magistrate like Fielding—even if she *had* had his familial connections. Nonetheless, it is important for us to remember that Fielding was a writer who was forced to stop writing plays by the Licensing Act of 1737; Lennox never actually lost her power and authority to write in this way. As Margaret Doody suggests, there is no reason to believe that Charlotte Lennox saw herself as abdicating anything.[8] Nor did she necessarily envision herself as a victim of the system to which she aspired to belong. Gender, in other words, is not the only interesting or determining factor in Lennox's writing. Lennox was a writer whose class and professional and personal circumstances, as well as her gender, influenced what she produced. Like Samuel Richardson and Henry Fielding, Lennox recognized that, in the age that saw the birth of the professional critic, a critic was no longer necessarily the best writer. Like them, she attempts to wrest the authority for literary judgment from both aristocratic dilettantes and upstart Grub Street hacks by presenting herself as performing the labor of criticism in *The Female Quixote*.

As literary criticism, Lennox's novel is not simply about the need to control and contain women's desire for the romance; it also represents culture's desire and need to control *men's* reading. Few have noticed that while the pivotal women characters of *The Female Quixote*, all women of leisure, are described as avid readers, virtually the only male character who reads is a man who also writes: Sir George. Lennox makes explicit that divisions of labor exist along class and professional, as well as gender, lines in the eighteenth-century field of letters. She metaphorically represents in her novel the struggle for economic and political power in the literary profession, and points to eighteenth-century literary culture's desire to ensure that within the profession of letters, only *certain* middle-class men have the authority to write or to judge others' writing.

In her own struggle for power, authority, and economic security as a writer and critic, Lennox undermines the critical double standard which governs the professional activities of writing and reading in the eighteenth century by exposing the economic, class and gender biases that are its foundation. But she also shares some of those biases—particularly those which involve class. I want here, then, to focus specifically on what Lennox contributes to the discussion of who does or does not belong in the literary profession designated "criticism," by reading the way Lennox writes the relationship between men and romance in *The Female Quixote*.

As I have implied in previous chapters, romance is the scapegoated discourse of the period; it is that discourse which, the dominant voices of the period argue, needs to be morally reformed into "novel" discourse. Lennox implies that there is another motivation beyond the moral one impelling writers and critics of the period to argue for the suppression of "romance" for all readers: reading romance produces the desire to write. All the major writers of the period use romances as source material for their own writing. For those who work within eighteenth-century England's rapidly developing industry of literary production, those who call themselves writers are also by definition critics—and thereby exert a certain amount of control over the modes of literary production. Those in control wish to maintain that control. They therefore have to limit who is allowed to read romances if they are to limit the reproduction of them, even if they are reproduced under the guise of their having been "reformed." And that means they have to convince most men that reading romances is bad for them too.

A crucial scene of reading occurs about midway through *The Female Quixote*. Sir George literally constructs a romance story in the attempt to woo the heroine, Arabella. As the only male character who actually reads, Sir George is also a nefarious and deceitful upper-class gentleman of leisure. Like Arabella, he has read romances and is aware of all the ways other novelists have used them in their work. Hence, he considers himself both a writer and a "very accurate critic," and consequently criticizes Dryden "for want of Invention, as it appeared by his having Recourse to [romance] for the most shining Characters and Incidents in his Plays."[9] Given Sir George's glaring lack of integrity throughout the rest of the novel, no reader trusts his negative appraisals of Dryden's borrowings from and re-writings of romance plots. Importantly, though, Lennox here shows that both the rakish and immoral Sir George *and* well-respected middle-class writers like Dryden feed off the romance, even while those same writers argue that the world in general, but particularly women, should not take romances at all seriously.

After Sir George relates his romance to an audience which includes Arabella, Mr. Glanville, Miss Glanville and Arabella's uncle, Sir Charles, there follows a scene in which this audience interprets and passes judgment on it. Sir Charles does not "penetrate into the Meaning of Sir George's story" (253). Rather than addressing the plot of Sir George's "romance," he exclaims, "it is a pity you are not poor enough to be an Author; you would occupy a Garret in Grubstreet, with great Fame to yourself and Diversion to the Public" (252). Because Sir Charles believes writing is economically motivated, in his mind there is no reason to publish one's writing unless one needs the financial recompense that such scribblings will bring. He holds this view because fiction serves no useful purpose for him—his previous occupation had not required that sort of literacy. He was a soldier in his youth, "and Soldiers, you know, never trouble themselves much with reading" (63). But while he does not see any useful purpose for Sir George's story, neither does he really see the dangers it poses for Arabella or his son. Having never read romances, he does not recognize them as tools of seduction, whether that seduction be political or erotic.

His son (Arabella's would-be beau, Mr. Glanville) recognizes that Sir George's romances pose a threat—but Mr. Glanville does not see that threat as being directed toward himself or Arabella. When Sir George tells Sir Charles that he has in fact produced a number of stories that he would consider publishing, Glanville angrily protests that Sir George's attempts at fiction are an attack on middle-class professional writers and critics:

> Nay, then, interrupted Mr Glanville, you are qualified for a Critic at the Belford Coffee-house; where, with the rest of your brothers, Demy-wits, you may sit in Judgment upon the Productions of a Young, a Richardson, or a Johnson; rail with premeditated malice at the *Rambler*; and, for the want of Faults, turn even its inimitable Beauties into Ridicule. (252–53)

Like Arietta's story of the lion, Glanville's response calls attention to the fact that writing is power in this culture. His criticism also reinforces the notion that during this period of history for the professional writer, writing and reading are not separate activities. The ability to write is perceived by other members of society as giving one the legitimate right to read authoritatively, to make public that judgment and to influence other readers' choices and practices. In the same way that Sir George implies that for many writers romances are a popular reading material, Glanville implies that many readers and writers of the romance are also "critics," to the degree that writing the romance gives them the power to judge others' writing in the public and male space of coffee-houses and periodicals. Lennox fully implicates a certain group of men in the production and reproduction of romances in eighteenth-century culture. At the same time, she shows that the form which dominant male voices decry as immoral reading material for women is an important part of those male writers' libraries because the romance is the very source of *male* writing, novelistic and critical. That is, Lennox yokes the terms "romance" and "men" in the same way that much of eighteenth-century popular discourse yokes the term "romance" with "women."[10]

Furthermore, she reveals a clear motivation for the derogatory stereotype of women readers of the romance. From a gendered perspective, if the romance is the source of male writing, it might also be the source of female writing. If women read romances productively, like Sir George and the Grub Street hacks, they may develop the urge to write—in fact they may attempt, like Sir George and the hacks, to "sit in Judgment upon the Productions of a Young, a Richardson, or a Johnson."[11] They may begin to write professionally as critics, thereby influencing those who would buy writers' books. Glanville's speech, on one level, valorizes a bourgeois ideology of morality, but on another uncovers a different sort of ideology. The suppression of romance rests on the capitalist economic desire to polarize the roles of women and men in language usage. It arises from culture's sense that romance discourse engages in a political power struggle. Moreover, those who write wish to create "consumers" for their products, rather than "producers." That is, the desire to suppress romance may arise from an anxiety felt by *all* writers who are fighting for a piece of the pie: if men like Glanville were actually to pick up a book and read it, they might give up their day jobs and become writers, or—even worse for women like Lennox who have no other means of economic support available to them—do both, like Henry Fielding, magistrate, and Samuel Richardson, printer.

While Glanville protests that Sir George mistakenly believes he is qualified to be a critic because he has read and written romances, the romance has actually taught Arabella superior critical judgment. Both Lennox and Arabella interpret the discourse of romance to be a critical language; like Mr. Spectator or the Female Spectator, Arabella expects her discourse to reform the behavior of those around her.[12] She reads the romance for its values, for the ways in which it teaches her to read the moral behavior of those around her; and her male relatives' responses show that she has the potential to use it influentially within the public sphere.

At Bath, for example, she "reads" the discourse of society when she has Mr. Tinsel relate the histories of other ballgoers. Arabella's and Mr. Tinsel's interaction literalizes the process of literary criticism; he holds up the partygoers' lives for ridicule. Arabella objects, arguing "there are very few proper Objects for Raillery; and still fewer, who can railly well . . . There ought also to be a great Distance between Raillery and Satire, so that one may never be mistaken for the other" (268). These and other comments reveal Arabella's semblance to Mr. Spectator and the Female Spectator, as well as to such contemporary critical voices as Fielding's Narrator.[13] To this demonstration of Arabella's superior judgment, Sir Charles exclaims: "I protest, Lady Bella . . . you speak like an Orator." Her cousin Mr. Glanville likewise expresses his admiration of her critical acumen. "One would not imagine . . . that my Cousin could speak so accurately of a Quality she never practises: And 'tis easy to judge, by what she has said, that no body can railly finer than herself, if she pleases" (269). Had Arabella been a male reader of romances who used the skills learned from these books to construct speeches, she might have "made a great figure in Parliament." In fact, Sir Charles is so impressed with Arabella's wit that he exclaims: "if she had been a man, . . . her speeches might have come, perhaps, to be printed, in time" (311)—i.e., she would have become a writer of some power and repute. Sir Charles's comment indicates that for all of these characters, language is power; all of them believe that the discourse of orators and writers works to elevate the perspective of a particular group or class of individuals. As a writer who competes for some of this power, Lennox wants to discourage men from reading romances for professional as well as for so-called moral reasons. Despite the fact that she convincingly shows the romance's power to produce superior judgment, none of her male characters takes advantage of this, not even Mr. Glanville, who will supposedly make the best mate for Arabella.

Certainly Mr. Glanville fails to recognize the romance's educational potential and, as certain events in the story reveal, his judgment suffers as a result. When early in the novel Arabella asks him to read one of her romances, he refuses because of the labor it involves. Counting the pages, he decides that to read these romances requires too much work; he only pretends to read, and provokes Arabella's anger when she discovers his deception (50–51). Because neither Glanville's nor his uncle's vocation requires that they read, neither feels the same desire to read that Arabella feels. Of course, neither man has been raised in isolation, or has ever had as much leisure time as Arabella. The important thing to note, though, is that Glanville seems to have neither the ability nor the desire to judge Sir George's story. His lack of reading practice leads him to assume the wrong motivation for its production—that is, he completely misses the point as a reader when he assumes that the story is a means of demonstrating Sir George's own superiority as a writer. Mr. Glanville does not realize that the story is actually an attempt to woo Arabella away from him. Because Glanville does not interpret properly he could never be the author of Arabella's reform from a literal reader of romance to a woman who rejects romances as unsuitable reading material. Because of Lennox's own professional and class loyalties, Lennox herself wishes to persuade her readers that there are very few men who can dispel romance; very few men demonstrate superior critical judgment, and thus very few men are suited to the new professional office of critic.

For Arabella to publish her critical discourse in the public realm would be to take on the labor of the literary critic, a role many designate as inappropriate for a woman. But it is as crucial for Lennox that Arabella is not simply a woman, but also a member of the aristocracy. The battle within the literary world among authors is also part of a larger class struggle, the struggle of the rising middle class to usurp the aristocracy's power even as it embraces a good deal of its perspective. On the one hand, to publish Arabella's speeches, which reflect the values she has learned from romance discourse, would be to validate the same aristocratic value system espoused by Mr. Spectator. On the other hand, because they emanate, literally, from an aristocratic body, were her speeches to be published, the aristocracy itself might again usurp the middle class's hegemony in the literary world. Lennox can more easily exclude Arabella from participation in the literary world than Richardson can exclude Lovelace, or Fielding can exclude Blifil, because of Arabella's gender. Sir George is a potentially more dangerous force than Arabella because as a man he already has access to the political sphere, even if Glanville is unable fully to recognize that danger. He appears less dangerous to Glanville initially because Glanville assumes that Sir George's fiction is a plot for public and political power—but only in the field of letters. Glanville fails to see it as a plot to gain economic and political power in the larger social world via a marriage to Arabella—via, that is, a private discourse that will transform Arabella from autonomous heiress to his wife, and property. Too, Glanville assumes that he cannot be morally or emotionally seduced by Sir George's rhetoric—or by Arabella's. Seduced by Arabella's person—a body that, for him, literalizes the eroticism of romance—Mr. Glanville ultimately find himself seduced and deceived by the rhetoric of romance, as well.

The problem with Arabella's rhetoric for characters like Mr. Glanville is, of course, that it is the rhetoric of the romance. Rather than apprehending the discourse of romance as only a figurative one, Arabella reads it as the discourse of her mother, which closely aligns it with a literal language of the body.[14] Those who wish to reform Arabella's use of language from the erotic discourse of romance into a moral, pious, and modest novelistic discourse valorize a discourse which not only excludes women from authoritative participation in the public sphere, but one which attempts to obliterate the body from the text.[15]

In her depiction of male characters as readers, Lennox also directs our attention to the role of desire in men's reading and its potential to inhibit their literary judgment. Eighteenth-century culture believes that passion makes one lose one's head and that romance supposedly leads to the buildup of erotic passions. These related beliefs in turn produce the male anxiety that the discourse most associated with women is more than capable of seducing men away from the "real" world of work, or inhibiting their performance within that world.[16] Mr. Glanville is consistently divided between his desire to accommodate his behavior to Arabella's, his desire to give in to the power that her "form" has over him sexually, and his desire to reform her. Mr. Glanville knows that "since [Arabella] was to be his Wife, it was his Business to produce a Reformation in her" (64). While Glanville continually expresses his discomfort at Arabella's odd behavior, he seems incapable of reforming her himself. Since Glanville does not himself read, there is already good enough reason for Lennox, an aspiring member of the club of middle-class writers who want to monopolize the business of social reform, to imply that in fact he has no business making it his business to produce a reformation in her. But even if Glanville could be the agent of her reform, it is important to note that, in fact, he often resists reforming her. What attracts him to her are the qualities of a romance heroine.

Arabella's folly in reading romances arises from her interpreting romance as a form which affirms a powerful role for women in the public sphere. As one who "writes" herself as a romance heroine, Arabella symbolizes on some level the romance itself. Arabella reads the world in terms of the romances she finds in her father's library, "supposing Romances were real Pictures of Life, from them she drew all her Notions and Expectations. By them she was taught to believe, that Love was the ruling Principle of the World; that every other Passion was subordinate to this; and that it caused all the Happiness and Miseries of Life" (7).[17]

These books were left behind by Arabella's mother, who died when Arabella was only three days old, and they prove valuable to a child "who had no other Diversion . . . and who had no other Conversation but that of a grave and melancholy Father, or her own Attendants" (7). They symbolically represent to Arabella her dead mother, the absent referent whose companionship and language she seeks. Her mother's death makes possible and necessary Arabella's attraction to the romance, thereby explicitly linking the romance, a highly abstract and ideational discourse, with both the literal and the figurative.[18] Unlike the son who would generate and privilege figurative substitutions to represent and control his mother's absence, Arabella longs for the literal, for a woman who speaks the language of the mother-daughter to be present ("she wished for nothing more passionately than an agreeable Companion of her own Sex and Rank" [67]). This desire to retrieve the language of the mother encourages Arabella to literalize her experience, to ignore the difference between sign and signifier: "Her Glass, which she often consulted, always shewed her a Form so extremely lovely, that, not finding herself engaged in such Adventures as were common to the Heroines in the Romances she read, she often complained of the insensibility of Mankind, upon whom her Charms seemed to have so little influence"(7).

Arabella's perception of her own image in the mirror is analogous to her relationship with romance novels; her economy of pleasure "consists in nursing her dual relation with the book (i.e. with the Image), by shutting [herself] up alone with it, fastened to it like the child fastened to the mother."[19] Arabella's reflection in the mirror represents "the paradisiac coalescence of subject and Image of the book."[20] Assuming the position of both the subject who desires and the object of male desire, Arabella negotiates back and forth between the literal and the figurative systems of language, valorizing the literal system, unaware that properly, in her identification with the literal, she ought only to be the silent object of representation (see Homans).

Instead, she wishes to ground the figurative language of romance in the literal system, to transpose the image of the heroine she sees within the books she reads onto her own reality. Arabella does not merely consume the discourse of romance; she attempts to reproduce it within the world of her experience. In her attempt to reproduce romance, she literally uses body language: "she made a Sign to him to retire . . . But . . . he was quite unacquainted with these Sorts of dumb Commands" (36–37). However, this language system only confuses most who come into contact with it; other characters, having long abandoned the language system associated with the private discourse between mother and child, often find Arabella impossible to decipher:

> Arabella, supposing he meant to importune her still more, made a Sign with her Hand, very majestically, for him to be gone; but he, not able to comprehend her Meaning, stood still with an Air of Perplexity, not daring to beg her to explain herself; supposing as she, by that Sign, required something of him. (256)

Arabella believes that as a woman, and as the "true" subject and object of romance, she has absolute power over language production in both public and private spaces. Romance has taught her that a romance heroine provokes and controls discourse. The romance heroine's lover dares not speak, for example, until she gives her permission. She can command her servants, as Arabella commands Lucy, to write the story of her glorious life. In the texts that Arabella reads, moreover, a queen or princess appears to acquire vast kingdoms and political power through her ability to manipulate the behavior of the subjects who desire her. As a romance heroine, Arabella imagines herself owning a language which gives her the power of life and death (she asks at one point: "shall I . . . make myself the author of his death?" [210])

She resists only that discourse which might compromise her power and authority. In particular, she avoids exchanges with all would-be suitors: "she took all opportunities of avoiding [Glanville's] conversation; and seemed always out of temper when he addressed anything to her; but was well enough pleased when he discoursed with [her father]; and would listen to the long conversations they had together with great attention" (33). As did Anna Howe in *Clarissa*, Arabella sees unchaperoned conversation between the sexes as a transmitter of sexual desire. When Glanville seeks a private conversation with her, she responds angrily: "What Intercourse of Secrets is there between you and me, that you expect I should favour you with a private Conversation? An Advantage which none of your Sex ever boasted to have gained from me; and which, haply, you should be the last upon whom I should bestow it" (31).

Arabella's refusal to speak privately to Glanville seems at first prideful, and to assume a power of language unbecoming to a woman:

> What a horrid Violation this, of all the Laws of Gallantry and Respect, which decree a Lover to suffer whole Years in Silence before he declares his Flame to the divine Object that causes it; and then with awful Tremblings and submissive Prostrations at the Feet of the offended Fair! (32)

Nonetheless, Arabella does not seek to elevate herself so much as she seeks to elevate the language system she has learned from reading romances. Arabella insists that romance heroines deny men the authority to transform the physical language associated with the body—they must show literally how they feel rather than verbally expressing their emotions. Unfortunately, Arabella's desire for the discourse of romance increases her vulnerability; it paves the way for Sir George to be able to deceive her with the fictions he constructs.

While hyperbolic, Arabella's desire to restrict men's correspondence with her, a desire she has internalized from reading romances, has some justification. If only Clarissa had felt similarly! In a fashion similar to that of the *Female Spectator*, Lennox both reminds the reader that a woman's privacy has its advantages and implies that reading romances does not necessarily make women the dupes of men.

Even while Mr. Glanville despairs at the way she experiences the world, then, Arabella arouses in him the passions associated with the lover of the romance heroine. He resists reforming her, perhaps, because he realizes that to change Arabella will be to change the nature of his love for her. When Arabella's father wants to burn her library because her books are causing her to behave so excessively, Glanville prevents him from doing so in order to gain her approval, despite Arabella's father's warning that to save the books from the fire is to encourage his daughter in her folly (63).[21] Glanville's desire for Arabella prevents him from properly carrying out his role in society. His infatuation with her threatens to change his value system, to cause him to give priority to the language of emotion rather than to the discourse of economics, politics, and bourgeois morality that normally shapes his actions and motivates his behavior. Moreover, his infatuation also eventually leads him to disobey patriarchal law. When he resists reforming Arabella, when he is seduced by her though she behaves like a romance heroine, and when he behaves as her romance lover, Mr. Glanville recapitulates romance. He begins himself to read and then eventually to rewrite the world in romantic fashion. For instance, when Arabella calls upon Glanville to take on the role of the romance hero, to defend her against Hervey, one of her former suitors, he is angry at her. But when Glanville encounters him, Hervey begins to ridicule Arabella, enraging Glanville. Glanville winds up defending her anyway and strikes Hervey, eschewing the role of gentleman assigned him by society and acting instead the part of a romance hero.

The most dangerous instance of Glanville's recapitulation of romance occurs when Arabella refuses to see him after she hears that he is an unfaithful gigolo. As I noted above, Mr. Glanville is not himself a very skillful reader and has not been any more capable of reading Sir George's artifices than anybody else, despite his superior posturing throughout the novel. Imagine his outrage, then, when told of this romance plot: he finally realizes that all along, Sir George has been conspiring to usurp his place in Arabella's heart. Lennox makes it clear that it is not Arabella's romance which incites Glanville but Sir George's:

> Sir George's behavior to her rush'd that Moment into his Thoughts. He instantly recollected all his Fooleries, his History . . . probably done with a View to some other Design upon her.
> These Reflections . . . convinc'd him [Sir George] was the Author of their present Mis-understanding . . . he stamp'd about his Room, vowing Revenge upon Sir George, execrating Romances, and cursing his own Stupidity, for not discovering Sir George was his Rival, and knowing his plotting Talent, not providing against his Artifices. (354)

Sir George, not Arabella, as previous critics have tended to imply, "authors" the romance plot that causes Mr. Glanville to seek revenge. This reinforces society's need to restrict *men's*, as well as women's, access to and production of romance.

Glanville himself erroneously constructs a romance between Sir George and Arabella where none exists. In an attempt to catch Sir George in the act of romantic deception, he looks out his window into the garden. There, "he thought he saw his cousin [Arabella], cover'd with her Veil as usual," romancing Sir George. Instead of making sure that Arabella is in fact the person he sees with Sir George, Mr. Glanville, "[t]ransported with Rage at this sight . . .

snatch'd up his Sword, flew down the Stairs into the Garden, and came running like a Madman up the Walk in which the Lovers were" (357). He "penetrates" Sir George with his sword, and almost kills him before he realizes his mistake; Sir George is talking to Glanville's sister.

Interestingly, he wants to lay part of the blame on her: "Mr Glanville, with a Heart throbbing with Remorse for what he had done, gaz'd on his Sister with an accusing Look . . ." (357). Time and again, men use language to deceive women in *The Female Quixote*, and yet when they are themselves the dupes of other men's language (or their own), they invariably blame it on the women. Existentially speaking, the male characters of this novel have trouble accepting responsibility for their own behaviors and actions. And with this scene Lennox suggests that their guilt over reading romances and being taken in by them leads many male writers of the period to blame women for the continued popularity and production of romances. A case in point is Samuel Johnson, who enjoyed reading romance "while blaming them [in private] for 'that unsettled turn of mind which prevented his ever fixing in any profession.'"[22] In periodicals like *The Rambler*, Johnson spent a good deal of time decrying romance as producing corruption in women.

With this incident, Lennox implies that what men fear most is not female, but male, desire. Glanville recapitulates middle-class critics' desire to "reform" or rewrite the romance, their desire to obliterate them as texts—a desire which arises because romance novels have the power to seduce men into believing these texts possess truth. When Glanville literalizes the romance, he obeys Arabella's romantic maxim that "the Law has no Power over Heroes" (129). In almost murdering Sir George, he disobeys the Christian, moral code of culture, as well as the law of the King. Those who have power in culture fear that any material reproduction of romance ideology will lead to anarchy. The language associated with women, the language that patriarchy associates with the erotic discourse of the romance, must be repressed so that the language of middle-class patriarchy, the order that maintains control within the socio-economic and political spheres, may remain intact.

Until the penultimate chapter of *The Female Quixote*, Lennox shows no man capable of completely understanding how to use language properly, even though the men all seem to understand the nature of men's relationship to language within their own society.

In contrast, she presents two women, Arabella's maid, Lucy, and the Countess, who understand as women their proper relationship to language and also how they ought properly to use it. Lucy figures as the proper woman who understands that within this culture women's relationship to patriarchal language remains extremely limited. She can carry the word from one place to another without implicating herself in its production, as she frequently does in her capacity as Arabella's messenger between would-be suitors. But she cannot herself generate stories.[23] She initially refuses to "write" Arabella's history when commanded to because she has been trained to perform domestic duties; she has not the proper training needed to carry out such a literary task. "Indeed," said Lucy, "I must beg your Ladyship will excuse me. I never could tell how to repeat a Story when I have read it; and I know it is not such simple Girls as I can tell Histories; it is only fit for Clerks, and such Sort of People, that are very learned" (121).

The proper writer of "histories," factual accounts of the lives of heroes or heroines, is he or she who has been trained for it professionally: the "clerks" and those people who have received a good education. And that means many women of the upper as well as lower classes will be excluded because they lack the classical learning and the experience in the world that prepares the clerks and other learned professionals to write, and to publish those writings in the public sphere.

The Countess best exemplifies the woman who makes proper use of her education, an education that denies her access to a language that has any real power within this culture, and one that has trained her to believe that women's discourse belongs only in the private sphere. The Countess enters the story when Glanville decides that before he can marry Arabella, she must be educated out of reading the romances. He chooses the Countess to reform, to "rewrite" Arabella in the image of woman that this society values. The Countess appears to be an apt choice because "This Lady, who among her own Sex had no Superior in Wit, Elegance, and Ease, was inferior to very few of the other in Sense, Learning, and Judgment" (322).[24] She finds Arabella worthy of admiration:

> A Person of the Countess's nice Discernment could not fail of observing the Wit and Spirit, which tho' obscur'd, was not absolutely hid under the Absurdity of her Notions. And this Discovery adding Esteem to the Compassion she felt for the fair Visionary, she resolv'd to rescue her from the ill-natur'd Raillery of her Sex . . . to abate the Keenness of their Sarcasms, acknowledg'd, that she herself had, when very young,

been deep read in Romances; and but for an early acquaintance with the World, and being directed to other Studies, was likely to have been as much a Heroine as Lady Bella. (323)

As the Countess has knowledge of the world, and because she has been directed to other types of books, her learning produces a woman whose intellect and understanding outshine those of many men. It is she who reinforces the judgment that, paradoxically, Arabella's isolation and lack of guidance in her early years are responsible for her romantic turn, for her desire for a public power.

The Countess is among the most positive figures in the text for Lennox because, as a woman, she knows how to negotiate between the language of the romance and that of the novel. It is her ability to speak the romance that causes the males discomfort at first. When she first visits Arabella, she expresses herself in a language that conforms to Arabella's:

> The Favour I have receiv'd from Fortune, said she, in bringing me to the Happiness of your Acquaintance, charming Arabella, is so great, that I may rationally expect some terrible Misfortune will befall me: seeing that in this Life our Pleasures are so constantly succeeded by Pains, that we hardly ever enjoy the one without suffering the other. (325)

Arabella is "quite transported," but the Countess's language here "greatly confound[s]" Mr. Glanville, and Sir Charles is "within a little of thinking her as much out of the way as his niece" (363). Neither man really understands the language the Countess speaks because neither man reads romances; Lennox here implies what both Richardson and Fielding also imply in their novels: only an individual acquainted with both the "immoral" romance *and* "moral" fiction is capable of reforming the behavior of society. The best author/critic of fiction helps to reform the behavior of society when he or she first reads, and then reforms, immoral into moral discourse. Lennox believes that such an individual can be a woman very much like the Countess—or Arabella for that matter. Nevertheless, she is well aware that power in literary culture lies in the hands of a few men. She must tread lightly.

The Countess's own initiation into the world of the moral discourse of culture has taught her that within the lives of women who "have a moderate Share of Sense, Prudence, and Virtue" (327), there are "few and natural Incidents which compose [their histories]" (327). That is, her experience as a woman in culture has taught her that romances improperly relate women's histories because they focus more on women's "adventures" with men, i.e., their journeys and their love affairs, rather than on heroic virtue. To tell her story in the style of the romance would be an immodest gesture. Since, moreover, women have no active role in political or economic society, they have very little worth relating. The Countess has internalized patriarchy's mandate to limit her experience and her access to a language with which to describe it. As a woman, her proper duties ordinarily keep her within the domestic sphere, silent and serving.

Using the language of romance, the Countess begins to instruct Arabella on the ways in which romance language inadequately describes present-day experience: "Tho' the Natures of Virtue and Vice cannot be changed, . . . yet they may be mistaken; and different Principles, Customs, and Education, may probably change their Names, if not their Natures" (328). The essence of things may not have changed, but in a patriarchal culture, "custom" makes it possible for those who control the symbolic order to change what may symbolically represent vice and virtue from one day to the next. By initially conforming her language to Arabella's, then, the Countess intends to initiate the young would-be heroine into the symbolic order which has gained dominance over that of the romance.

Paradoxically, her own role in society as the symbolic mother figure for Arabella, and as the literal daughter of her own ailing mother, means that before she can achieve Arabella's reformation, she must become literally the absent referent of whom Homans speaks. More specifically, the Countess cannot reform Arabella because the place of the literal within this society is in the home—it is a language that allows for intimate relationships, for equality within relationships, because difference doesn't exist. In public society, the hierarchic order demands that the literal accede to the symbolic. In order for Arabella to be reformed, the Countess's literal language must be vanquished, and she herself must accept the place of the literal—she must herself disappear from the text. She therefore loses the power to reform Arabella; to reform, or rather to "rewrite," one must use language. Thus "her good Intentions towards our lovely Heroine were suspended by the Account she receiv'd of her Mother's Indisposition, which commanded her immediate Attendance on her at her Seat in ___ " (330).[25]

Arabella must be reformed to accept the place of the literal as the Countess does, which means that she too must eventually disappear from the text. Lennox's implicit emphasis on the economics of reading uncovers another reason why it is necessary for Arabella to be reformed. The anxiety shown by the male characters in this text is directed toward the power of women's language to reform their own behavior, and by extension to reform the power structures by subverting the laws of patriarchy.[26] Once women are allowed to speak their judgments, to read productively like Arabella, rather than as passive consumers, men's control of positions of power may very well change. The men of this text believe that reading is part of the labor of writing. To allow women to be productive readers would also give them some measure of power within the economic world of work, and by extension within the political sphere. Arabella must be reformed so that she reads only books, such as *Clarissa*, which will teach her the value of the silent moral exemplar, and to see reading as a contemplative, meditative, but silent activity of consumption.

The only figure who can reform Arabella, then, is the learned divine—a nameless symbol of what the culture sees as best in patriarchy. Mr. Glanville's earlier speech, in which he railed against writers like Sir George, foreshadows Lennox's vision of the ideal literary critic, and also prepares us for the shift in style within the novel's penultimate chapter, a shift to a more pedantic and ponderous language. In order to establish her own moral credentials, Lennox transforms the secularized, cosmopolitan, and aesthetically elite cultural critic that Mr. Spectator embodied into a more literal symbol of morality when she creates this clergyman. The ideal reader Mr. Glanville defined in his earlier speech was the learned divine, whose language might be described, like the criticism of a Young, a Richardson or a Johnson, as "stiff, laboured and pedantic"; because he preaches a moral system of reading, his discourse contains "the finest System of Ethic yet extant . . . for over propping Virtue" (253). Lennox perhaps places the responsibility for Arabella's reform in the learned divine's hands because his position has exposed him to both the poor and ignorant, and the wealthy and knowledgeable. His reading of scholarly texts gives him the ability to write and rewrite, a skill that, as Arabella's maid, Lucy, points out to the reader early in the novel, lies primarily within the realm of an individual like the learned divine.

The character called the learned divine reforms Arabella by echoing the words—almost verbatim—of such middle-class critics as Samuel Johnson, inheritors of Mr. Spectator's critical legacy. Romances, he asserts are dangerous, and "if they are at any time read with safety, owe their Innocence only to their Absurdity"(374).[27] He recommends that Arabella read *Clarissa* because it conveys "the most solid Instructions, the noblest Sentiments, and the most exalted Piety in the pleasing dress of a Novel, and . . . 'Has taught the Passions to move at the Command of Virtue' " (377). What separates the learned divine from other characters in the text is that he reads fiction for moral instruction as well as diversion, viewing the language of these texts as "Truth" or as "Lectures of moral and domestic Wisdom." He thus represents those in society who argue that their novels are reformative. Just as importantly, the learned divine is asexual. Like dry moral conduct books, the learned divine can teach Arabella to adopt the role of the "tasteful consumer" because she will never make the mistake of reading him as a romance hero.

One cannot forget at this point that the antecedent text for Lennox's novel is *Don Quixote*: Lennox rewrites Cervantes to give an account of the romance's influence on female experience. In the earlier novel, Don Quixote poses a real physical danger to those whom he encounters—characters get hurt because Quixote literalizes the romance as heroic battle in encounters with ordinary and often defenseless contemporaries. Like Quixote, Arabella threatens other characters, but the danger she poses is articulated as the ability to transform other characters into literal readers who restore the legitimacy of romance as a discourse of power and authority.

One of the saddest incidents in Cervantes' novel is when Don Quixote falls ill, repents and reforms, and dies. Lennox offers a parallel structure: Arabella falls ill, is reformed by a learned divine, but then marries. Don Quixote's reformation causes sadness; Sancho Panza begs him not to give up his romantic illusions. Arabella's reformation produces great joy in the men, but shame in her. If we read Lennox's transformation of the final scene of *Don Quixote* ironically, we can read Arabella's marriage as a form of death. Like the Countess, Arabella no longer has a history beyond being born, being raised and educated in solitude, living without incident, and getting married. Glanville's silent partner, she must give up all autonomy and access to the public realm; she must retreat into obscurity. Arabella's reformation can only be successful when she can correctly interpret her own behavior within the context of the society within which she lives: "Arabella . . . continued, for near two hours afterwards, wholly absorbed in the most disagreeable reflections on the absurdity of her past behaviour, and the contempt and ridicule which she now saw plainly she had exposed herself" (423). That correct interpretation leads to her silencing. Hence, "the cure of Arabella is as much to be mourned as the death of Don Quixote."[28]

Ros Ballaster argues that in idealizing the figure of morally superior women, authors such as Fielding and Richardson helped to diminish the "possibilities of female self-representation for the women writers that succeeded and imitated them." Specifically, she claims that women writers of the novel were "forced ... to encourage ... an identification between themselves and their morally upright heroines."[29] Laurie Langbauer embraces this perspective when she asserts that Lennox identifies with Arabella; both are romance heroines whose hopes and desires are denied by the end of the novel: "Just as Arabella, once in this sphere, loses her voice, when Lennox calls on the male sphere in the penultimate chapter of *The Female Quixote*, so does she."[30] While Lennox's women characters, including Arabella, are clearly defined outside the public sphere of literary criticism by the end of the novel, I would argue this is not true of Lennox herself. After all, by revealing her own critical acumen in her treatment of the romance and its misreaders, Lennox gains a certain positive critical reputation among established critics, men like Johnson. Her allegory of reading gives her the power and authority to produce the first full-length critical study of Shakespeare ever written by a woman: *Shakspear Illustrated, or the novels and histories on which the plays of Shakspear are founded* (1753). And interestingly enough, in that text, she examines Shakespeare's debt to the romance writers of his time and then critically evaluates his use of those authors. Those who argue that Lennox loses her power and authority as a writer when she silences Arabella ignore that she herself never gave up either her romances or her voice.

Lennox subverts the imposed silencing of women's critical voices in another way. Notably, of the women she creates who do not seek the power to write or judge, neither Lucy nor the Countess is a middle-class woman. True, Arabella becomes a model of the middle-class wife when she marries Glanville, but her reform is predominantly one of class. She moves from the superior aristocracy to innocuous middle-classdom. She is primarily silenced because she espouses aristocratic values. By failing to represent a middle-class woman who adheres to society's ideal model of women's relationship to language, Lennox keeps open a public space within which a middle-class woman like herself, who espouses the values of her class, can speak. Therefore, rather than reading the novel as escaping the control of its female author, it may be more useful to read *The Female Quixote* as a novel that exposes the primarily economic motivations behind the eighteenth-century literary profession's attempts to devalue romance for certain groups of writers and readers.

In addition, in having a learned divine "reform" Arabella, Lennox could in fact be subversively arguing for a reformation in critical practice. As I argue above, the novel's male characters in particular see criticism as a political language—remember that, according to her uncle, Arabella's demonstrations of her superior judgment might have resulted in a book *and* won her a seat in parliament, if she had been a man. At this moment in history, women cannot hold political office. By the definition of writers such as Henry Fielding, the Office of English Critic is a political one. Women who wish to be critics, as Lennox does, need, then, to redefine the office of "critic" if they are to be allowed to practice it with any power or authority—or indeed, in Henry Fielding's eyes, if they are to practice it at all. Lennox recognizes that women have a socially ascribed role of educating their children to be moral adults, a role very similar to that of the learned divine. Moreover, the moral education of children and the fictional reformation of Arabella both occur in the private space of the home. Like Eliza Haywood, then, Lennox validates the fictional domestic sphere as an intermediate zone within which women's public, critical discourse can be authorized. Like Haywood, Lennox could be attempting by this means to give herself and other women better access to the occupation of literary critic. Furthermore, in implicitly emphasizing criticism's moral function, rather than its strictly political agenda, she identifies it as a language and profession that negotiate between the private and public spheres.

As my next chapter demonstrates, she is not be the only woman to do so. In *The Cry: A New Dramatic Fable*, published in 1754, Sarah Fielding, with Jane Collier, creates a narrative more radical in style and content than virtually any other eighteenth-century narrative in its explicit and forthright insistence that women be allowed to practice criticism.

5
Friendship, Equality, and Interpretation in *The Cry*

> Strength and honour are her clothing; and she shall rejoice in time to come. She openeth her mouth with wisdom; and in her tongue is the law of kindness. She looketh well to the ways of her household, and eateth not the bread of idleness. Her children arise up, and call her blessed; her husband also, and he praiseth her.
> —31 Proverbs 25–28

> Speak, woman, sacred lifegiver!
> —Leopold Bloom

IN *THE CRY: A NEW DRAMATIC FABLE*, SARAH FIELDING AND JANE COLLIER try to alter the politics of criticism in the same way that Lennox does in *The Female Quixote*; that is, they attempt to do away with the socio-political and economic hierarchies that exclude certain individuals, most particularly women, from entering this profession.[1] However, they go one step further than Lennox does in her choice of a learned divine, when they choose to have a woman character, Portia, articulate their agenda as she herself performs the labor of a critic.

The Cry deals with the proper nature of female identity and its relation to the arts, education, the economy, and particularly to the practice of literary criticism; the narrative embodies the refusal of Sarah Fielding and Jane Collier to be denied the opportunity to strive for the level of literary authority enjoyed by their male contemporaries.[2] Like Samuel Richardson and Henry Fielding, Sarah Fielding and Collier proclaim their originality and desire to be innovative, to "strike a little out of a road already so much beaten."[3] To do so, they remark, "'tis necessary to assume a certain freedom in writing, not strictly within the limits prescribed by the rules" (I: 14). They organize their experimental narrative as if it were a play, what they call a dramatic movement, because its characters enact processes which demonstrate those qualities of mind necessary for the production and reproduction of morally instructive texts and readings. In doing so, they make the spectator-as-critic not a dispassionate observer of the action of texts, but an active participant whose choices and actions matter to the final outcome of their story.

As authors of *The Cry*, Fielding and Collier argue that a superior critic views language as the means by which humans communicate, and it is the possession of a dialogic, communal language that forms stable communities. They suggest that "the dramatic form of expression—the dialogue" best represents language as a system that can potentially build a moral society.[4] *The Cry* becomes a network of voices that emphasizes the need for a discourse generated from a desire for equality and friendship among all human subjects. This narrative creates a theater of expression within which Portia, its primary actor-orator, vocally expresses her indignation, her compassion, her mercy. In the space opened by this vocalized text, women regain the power to be active, public social critics, and thus by extension gain the power to be literary critics.[5] Women can become authoritative figures in criticism, both because their spiritual education teaches them how to moderate their passions, and because their practical experience as managers of the domestic economy schools them to negotiate the network of human relationships.[6]

Today we depend on men for Sarah Fielding's and Jane Collier's stories; most of what we know of either of them is contained in the biographies of Samuel Richardson and Henry Fielding, with their stories told in relation to those of men.[7] Like many other single, untrained gentlewomen, both women either depended solely upon male relatives for financial assistance or turned to writing as a means of supporting themselves. "Lively and learned,"[8] Jane Collier was the daughter of the Reverend Arthur Collier and sister to Dr. Arthur Collier, who was, like Henry Fielding, "a lawyer who practiced as an advocate at Doctors' Commons, the ecclesiastical court" (*HF* 392) and Sarah's tutor. She apparently collaborated on a number of projects with Sarah, most notably on *The Cry*, but also on *The Governess*, and she provided the preface to *David Simple: Volume the Last* (1753).[9] In 1753, she anonymously published *On the Art of Ingeniously Tormenting*. The reviewer for the *Monthly* assumed a male author, saying of this "humorous" work that "tho' no extraordinary genius for satyr appears in it, [it] is far from being a contemptible performance."[10] Readers apparently agreed that it was a solid performance; it went into several editions, the last of which was published in 1811. Collier's literary career was cut short by her death in 1754.

We know not much more than this of Sarah Fielding, although we do know that like her brother Henry, she was born into the gentry class.[11] The chronology of Sarah's life included in the Kelsall edition of *David Simple* illustrates a central problem in twentieth-century scholarship about her: it begins not with her birth, but with her brother Henry's, some two years prior.[12] Such a chronology implies that without Henry, Sarah the writer would not have existed—that Henry-the-writer gave birth to Sarah-the-writer. This may or may not be true. As has been the case with Charlotte Lennox, however, Sarah Fielding has by and large been denied any status as an author.[13]

A tendency to replicate, often unwittingly, eighteenth-century literary culture's propensity to marginalize female authors has also prevented the inclusion of works such as *The Cry* in recent histories of eighteenth-century novels and criticism. For example, in *The Fame Machine*, Frank Donoghue bemoans that the critical double standard at work in the reviewing apparatus "all but disabled the hopes any woman author [such as Sarah Fielding] might have of achieving a level of success comparable to that enjoyed by the best male writers," and concludes that "the literary career [as defined by the narratives contained in the major *Review*s] was an exclusively male form of social practice."[14] Because the major *Review*s do not narrate for women a "literary career," neither does Donoghue. With regard to Sarah Fielding, for instance, he only discusses the preface written for the second edition of her first novel, *The Adventures of David Simple*, a preface authored by her brother, Henry.[15]

Sarah's literary career did not end, however, with that first novel, nor did her attempts to achieve fame or to claim publicly her authority as a writer. Her literary career spanned almost two decades, ending with her translation, *The Memoirs of Socrates* (1762). *The Monthly Review*, a periodical that grew increasingly influential during the latter part of her career, positively assessed whatever of her work it reviewed.[16] By the end of this career, moreover, she had apparently grown comfortable enough with her own identity as an author to assert it publicly: according to a note attached to the review of *The Cry*, printed one month after its publication, the author of *David Simple* claimed it as her own.[17] She more explicitly acknowledged authorship (in the dedication) of *The History of Cleopatra and Octavia* (1757), and, on the title page, of *The Memoirs of*

Socrates.¹⁸ That she disclosed her identity also suggests that Sarah Fielding felt she had achieved a respectable level of fame and authority as a writer among professional and amateur readers alike. That she was at least partially correct in this assumption seems also to be evidenced by the fact that *The History of Cleopatra and Octavia* had 491 subscribers, while *The Memoirs of Socrates* had "an astonishing 611."¹⁹

Sarah Fielding's interactions with her brother Henry and Samuel Richardson during the early part of her career can be interpreted as both beneficial and constraining. Henry encouraged her to write; she apparently wrote the Leonora chapter of *Joseph Andrews*, and he was supportive of her project to write *The Adventures of David Simple*. Martin Battestin in fact implies that Henry may have actually written parts of the first draft as well as the second: "When drafting *David Simple*, Sarah naturally sought her brother's advice" (*HF* 379). Malcolm Kelsall argues, however, that Henry Fielding was extremely busy traveling on the Western circuit during the period when Sarah was probably composing the novel.²⁰ Moreover, much of his free time was spent tending a very sick wife. Those more contemporaneous to her seem to concur. In a letter to the Reverend Mr. Leonard Chappelow, Hester Thrale Piozzi wrote that, "Miss Fielding was totally unassisted by her Brother whatever She Wrote."²¹ In the Preface to the second edition, Henry himself insisted that "indeed the strongest Reason which hath drawn me into Print, is to do Justice to the real and sole Author of this little book."²²

Richardson was supportive of Sarah Fielding's writing as well, and brought to print a number of her works. He also, nevertheless, made sure that she bowed to his authority. Battestin relates an anecdote of Sarah "struggling with the revisions Richardson required in *The Governess*," revisions, he goes on to say, that she did not really wish to make: In *The Governess*, Sarah again submitted to Richardson's influence; as Edward Young put it "prettily to the master, it was one of the several pieces 'which, like beautiful suckers, rise from [Clarissa's] immortal root' " (*HF* 445).

Both Richardson's and Fielding's biographers seem to imply, then, that Sarah's interpersonal relationships with these men actually influenced her literary productions in subtly negative ways. As I pointed out in Chapter 3, Battestin asserts that the relationship between Richardson, Henry, and his sister "[was] a fascinating, intensely personal triangular [one] in which all three authors, jealously interacting, spurred each other on to their best work, as well as to less appealing displays of pettiness and spite" (*HF* 379). Notably, however, the displays of pettiness and spite seem to have erupted only from the men. Richardson's biographers admit the mean-spiritedness of Richardson, noting, for instance, that "[Richardson's] remarks on *Tom Jones* and *Amelia* are not admirable" (*HF* 296).[23]

Sarah Fielding's distaste for the nastiness that Richardson displayed in the privacy of his home and in his private correspondence may well have led to what Eaves and Kimpel refer to as the cooling of the three authors' friendship. Her relationship with Richardson seems to have settled into a distantly professional acquaintanceship not too very long after the publication of *The Governess*. Richardson was not, for example, Fielding and Collier's printer for *The Cry*.[24]

There is also some evidence to suggest that Henry was jealous of Sarah's turning to other men for intellectual support. While pointing to Sarah's skill as an author, Hester Thrale Piozzi also wrote that Henry openly resented Sarah's pursuit of a classical education, and "[teized]" her mercilessly about it.[25] Importantly, neither Battestin nor anyone else provides any evidence that brother and sister ever wrote fiction together again after 1747—a year that marked Sarah's meeting and development of a friendship with Samuel Richardson, Henry's public scandal, and Sarah's move out of her brother's house. Sarah Fielding's designation of Jane Collier to write the preface for the last volume of *David Simple* also seems to me an explicit statement that she has disavowed all jealous, censorious, or immoral male authority.

Critics have tended to view Sarah Fielding as a conservative author, constrained by male authority.[26] This in turn has led them to read *The Cry* as they often do Eliza Haywood's *The Female Spectator*: as a typical and didactic example of an eighteenth-century work about courtship, female friendship, and marriage. As an obvious attempt to engage Fielding and other powerful literary critical voices in the ongoing debate about issues of authorship and criticism, *The Cry* calls those conservative readings into question. This narrative focuses on issues of interpretation and judgment, both social and textual, and it is within this context that one can find explicit evidence of Sarah Fielding's struggle to shape and to actively partake in that social practice called a literary career.

The narrators of *The Cry* seem to be directly speaking to Henry Fielding in their description of its action: "the puzzling mazes into which we shall throw our heroine, are the perverse interpretations made upon her words" (Introduction 13). This assertion harks back to the Preface to *David Simple* wherein Henry Fielding claimed that "the Merit of this little work consists in a vast Penetration into human Nature, a deep and profound Discernment of all the Mazes, Windings and Labyrinths, which perplext the Heart of Man to such a degree, that he is himself often incapable of seeing through them."[27] Sarah Fielding and Jane Collier's statement of purpose categorizes the private sensibilities of popular criticism's reviewers as those mazes that perplex the heart of their protagonist Portia. But because Portia can claim a "vast Penetration into human Nature," she will solve the labyrinth, and expose the foundations for the condescension toward women writers and critics that male writers and critics such as Henry Fielding exhibit in their prefaces and reviews.

This narrative's characters gather in a spacious hall, and because Fielding and Collier borrow names and dialogue from the stage, most readers assume that it is a theater. Within this theater, Fielding and Collier articulate the plight of female authors who strive to gain admission to the elite literary critical establishment. The stage becomes a battleground on which a war to determine the rules of critical practice is waged. Thus, *The Cry* carves out a unique position in the history of authorship and criticism in its depiction of the relationship between the institutions of authorship and criticism. Fielding and Collier self-consciously wage a battle to set the terms in which women's fiction will be discussed, and to urge that the literary establishment give women equal voice in the determination of refined taste.[28]

The Cry was not Sarah Fielding's first foray into the field of criticism. Unlike Sophia Western, who failed to respond when Blifil publicly criticized Tom Jones, Sarah Fielding was unable to hear her favorite author so criticized without in some way responding in kind, and so in January of 1749, she published, albeit anonymously and apologetically, the pamphlet *Remarks on "Clarissa."*[29] Its protagonist, Miss Gibson, proves that not all women read in the unsophisticated manner described by Richardson in his Postscript to *Clarissa*. For one thing, she supports Richardson's decision not to accede to demands for a happy ending for Clarissa and Lovelace. While this pamphlet depicted women as capable of proper moral judgment, however, its ultimate purpose was to judge the moral and aesthetic worth of Richardson's novel.

By 1754, however, Sarah, her collaborator, and their spokeswomen characters are much less deferential and self-deprecating than was Sarah when she wrote either her first novel or that critical pamphlet. A comparison of two scenes from *Remarks on "Clarissa"* and *The Cry* respectively shows an evolution in Sarah Fielding's authorial persona; she has become, paradoxically, a more self-sufficient, independent, and feminist writer by the time she collaborates with Collier on this narrative. In *Remarks on "Clarissa,"* Fielding creates a character, Mr. Dellincourt, "who found great Fault with the Liberties [Richardson took] with the English Language, and said, [he] had coined new Words, and printed others as if [he] was writing a Spelling-book, instead of relating a Story." Sarah Fielding's alter-ego, Miss Gibson, self-deprecatingly defends Richardson by asserting, "Indeed, Sir, I do not pretend to be any Judge of the Accuracy of Stile, but I beg to know, if in the writing familiar Letters, many Liberties are not allowable, which in other kinds of writing might perhaps be justly condemned" (*Remarks* 41).[30]

The Cry's narrator Portia figuratively follows in Richardson's footsteps by similarly "coining a new term," "turba." In contrast to Miss Gibson, however, Portia unapologetically justifies her own practice by citing Horace—one of the many writers and critics from whom she has learned superior writing and interpretive skills. She demonstrates her fluency in language when she quotes him in the original Latin and then elsewhere translates his words: "Horace . . . shews that the change of words, and the adapting them to new purposes, doth make language follow the fate of all nature. He says, that it is, and always will be, lawful to produce new words" (I: 196). About her own new word she declares "that it [needs] no apology for its novelty. . . . Those . . . who understood the meaning of the word perturbation, or a perturb'd mind, [cannot], except through wilful ignorance, be at a loss for the full idea of what she intended to express" (I: 197).

In a pamphlet entitled, "An Inquiry into the Causes of the Late Increase in Robbers, etc.," Henry Fielding once argued that when people break the law, "examples of justice are more merciful than the unbounded exercise of pity"—in other words, that convicted felons should be denied leniency or clemency.[31] Similarly, in the cases of such literary offenders as Colley Cibber, he showed himself to be as merciless in his literary as in his juridical judgments. Sarah Fielding and Jane Collier take issue with critics such as him and their propensity to be combative and censorious, as well, toward women. Just as Henry Fielding metaphorically depicted his own literary war against Cibber and popular taste in his periodicals, Fielding and Collier render explicitly in their narrative the battle between eighteenth-century female authors and their reviewers via the characters of Portia and the Cry.

As an audience whose sentiments are not unlike those of Henry

Fielding, the Cry behaves as those "morose" professional critics do who, seeing themselves as judge and jury, long to pronounce harsh sentences on the stories they hear or read.[32] As its numbers suggest, the Cry owns a discourse, albeit an immoral one, of Power. Its discourse is that of the popular culture, that discourse most often found in the periodicals of the century. It represents the published work of those who help to reproduce those powerful prejudices held by members of various classes, and by members of both genders: "for composing critical essays (not like the ingenious Dr. Swift to amuse and entertain but in order to vent the highest malignity) is one of the favourite employments of the Cry" (III: 230). The discourse of the Cry might be labeled ideological, supported by and supporting the stereotypes created by the institution of literary production to control access to power within the writing profession. Portia's story is viewed by the Cry as both alien and subversive because she actively resists and undermines these stereotypes. The Cry frequently tries to intimidate Portia, and accuse her of abusing language, often claiming that it does not understand the words she uses.

Una, in a role similar to that of Spenser's Una in *The Faerie Queene*, provides Portia with spiritual, emotional, and moral support, which protects her from the slander of the Cry as she recounts her story. While in the company of this mortal form clothed in the light of truth, Portia might be said to enjoy the same "state of grace" that Spenser's Red Cross Knight often enjoyed in Una's presence. While the Cry represents a multitude of voices, the chaos of bad judgment, Una is one, the clear voice of truth. She functions as an embodiment of the judgment of the "candid reader," a tasteful member of the general reading public who eschews popular criticism's vituperative discourse.

The Cry picks up where *Remarks on "Clarissa"* left off when it focuses on the practice of criticism itself. It defends women's right to practice literary criticism in the face of society's tendency both to interpret women's stories negatively and to hold up male interpretations as always valid and correct: "[we endeavor to rescue women from] the perverse interpretations made upon her words . . . [by] the spiteful and malicious tongues of her enemies" (I: 13). Fielding and Collier articulate their desire for greater political equality and a more public forum for their ideas and speech by having Portia tell her story of courtship and marriage in a public forum, rather than locating it only within the private sphere.

Early in his career, Henry Fielding used the stage as a forum to air his social criticism publicly, particularly as a means of dramatizing his political grievances against Walpole, a practice that ultimately helped to end his career as playwright. By writing themselves as dramatists, Fielding and Collier use the stage for similar purposes, though the narrative provides a safer space within which to air their views.

Portia metaphorically speaks in the intermediate zone that the theater provides in a text that is nevertheless meant to be consumed within the private space of the home.[33] Her creators thereby provide a bridge between the private sphere in which society normally attempts to confine the discourse of women, and the public sphere of the political and socio-economic world at large. While popular criticism argued that women owned only a discourse of relationships, it also acknowledged that the rules by which those relationships should be negotiated could also be publicly represented by the behaviors and language of actors on the stage.

By appropriating Shakespeare's Portia, Fielding and Collier remind *The Cry*'s audience that as spectators and readers, women have played a central role in "rescuing the admirable, yet almost forgotten Shakspear, from being totally sunk in oblivion."[34] The authors echo Eliza Haywood's point that women have already achieved some critical authority within the public sphere of eighteenth-century letters. And, they argue, women deserve even more.

Locating Portia's story in the theater initially appears to be a fairly conventional stratagem given that Fielding and Collier's audience is familiar with the Portia that Shakespeare brought to life in the theater—for them, she has always existed in that space. But Fielding and Collier recognize and make use of Portia's associations not only with the physical space of the stage but also with the metaphysical concepts of law and justice. While Shakespeare's Portia spoke in a court of law disguised as a man, however, *The Cry*'s Portia makes no attempt to disguise her feminine identity in order to speak.

In this novel, Portia attempts to gain access to the Law of the Father (language) and to the public realm by representing herself as a moral woman—one who maintains her ability to act roles of both the proper wife and mother and the moral interpreter of texts. Portia does not seek to be a politically powerful figure within criticism, she merely wishes to be an authoritative member of a reformed and less politically motivated profession. Hers is an enterprise doomed to fail, some might with reason argue, but one that has always existed within criticism (witness Addison and Steele's attempts in *The Spectator*, and that of the twentieth-century New Critics, for example).[35]

In Henry Fielding's novels, women who aspire to literacy or the power to articulate their judgments publicly are caricatured like Mrs. Western, represented as physically and mentally "masculine." Though she has both literary and critical aspirations, Portia is all woman.

For an audience well-acquainted with Shakespeare, the current legal status of married women, and the place of women as readers and spectators (as described by *The Female Spectator*), Fielding and Collier's refusal to disguise Portia holds a great deal of significance, particularly when Portia discloses that she has been married for two years. As a married woman, Portia exemplifies that moral criticism need not require the complete repression, as it did for Clarissa, of a woman's body. The creation of a Portia who will always be read as feminine by others, who has no need or desire to represent herself as "masculine" when she interprets, provides a welcome antidote to poisonous depictions of eighteenth-century women critics. Portia demonstrates why women readers such as Sophia ought to be given a voice.

Portia's connection to the literary world of law and the courtroom is not unlike that of Henry Fielding, who wrote not only fiction but legal essays in his capacity as magistrate. One of these essays, the pamphlet mentioned above, "An Inquiry into the Causes of the Late Increase of Robbers, etc.," examines the causes of and possible solutions for the increase in crime. In his introduction, Fielding divides the people of Britain into three classes: the nobility, the gentry, and the commonality. The increase in trade, he argues, has greatly altered the condition of the commonality; they have gained an "[a]lmost unbounded liberty, or rather licentiousness," whereas the law's power has decreased.[36] This greater liberty has led members of this commonality to drink and gamble too much (among other things), which in turn has led them to commit felonies. One of Fielding's solutions is to apprentice or indenture the children of this class, so that they might stay out of trouble. And, as noted above, he supports harsh punishments for those who fail to do so. Interestingly, he never mentions education—literacy—as a solution to the problems of either idleness or criminal misbehavior, despite its being a standard tool used by those of the upper classes for inuring self-discipline.

Evaluating Fielding's pamphlet for the *Monthly Review* in 1751, the anonymous reviewer begins by acknowledging the level of fame Fielding has achieved up to this point in the literary world: "If he has been heretofore admired for his wit and humour, he now merits equal applause as a good magistrate, a useful and active member, and a true friend to his country." He then links Fielding's skill in writing to the experiences he has encountered in his public life: "As few writers have shown so just and extensive a knowledge of mankind in general, so none ever had better opportunities for being perfectly acquainted with that class which is the main subject of this performance; a class of all others the most necessary and useful to all, yet the most neglected and despised; we mean the labouring part of the people."[37]

Within the literary world, the class prejudice revealed by Fielding's pamphlet and described by the *Review* in its account of it, is compounded by gender prejudice. As a group of literary laborers, Sarah Fielding and Jane Collier argue in *The Cry*, women are likewise the "most necessary and useful to all, [and] yet the most neglected and despised." Their protagonist Portia argues that it is in fact a lack of education that gives rise to the kinds of uninformed prejudices and biases to which *The Monthly Review* calls attention.

In their narrative, Fielding and Collier uncover how the language of capitalist economics can give rise to prejudicial views of an individual's authority to speak in terms of both class and gender. Through their women characters, Fielding and Collier argue that it is not only important to develop one's judgment as a writer and reader, it is also crucial for people to develop the ability to judge properly in their everyday lives so that they may become productive members of society. In order to develop proper judgment in an increasingly literate society, in a society where language is power, one must be allowed a proper education. Unfortunately, most citizens remain self-interested because society has failed to provide them with an education that will help them to relate well to one another and to develop properly their moral natures, their private sensibilities. Conflicts between the haves and have-nots fester in such a society.[38]

Fielding and Collier also explore a related problem: in its failure to provide an adequate education to women and members of the lower classes, society attempts to yoke both groups to the private sphere and to a private language. As a woman, Portia speaks primarily of society's attitudes toward the female population, and from her own standpoint, she sees that society has in various ways denied women access to language. Society has attempted to define women's position within culture too narrowly, and has also yoked them to a privatized female sexual identity as a means of controlling their literary output. In asserting that women speak primarily the language of emotion while men speak primarily the language of reason, the culture of letters provides itself with a rationale for denying women access to the kind of education provided to men.

Along with parents and teachers, literary critics were held partly responsible for providing a moral education during this period, particularly when it came to teaching the general public to choose its reading material wisely. Portia purposes to prove her mettle as an educator as she occupies all three roles—parent, teacher, critic. Via her interpretations of literary texts and the problems she faces in her experiences with her husband Ferdinand's family and others, she proves that one's relationship to language either empowers or disenfranchises one within society.[39]

Portia asserts ruefully that the desire to deny some members of society an education arises from the need of the well-educated to assert their superiority. For example, the rich often elevate themselves by boasting of their superior learning compared to those who cannot so easily afford it. She criticizes society's attitude toward those classes who have not the money or, sometimes, the aptitude, for university learning:

> As this world is at present constituted, what we call the lower part of mankind work for pay, and by that means support themselves and families; yet their assistance by the means of their labour, is as necessary to the rich, as the pay of the rich is to the labouring man. Did not this dependence for common subsistence oblige the lower class of men to sell their labour; if the gentleman whose birth and fortune had enabled him to have had a literate education, was to despise his cook for his ignorance; the cook in my opinion would then have a very reasonable pretence for withdrawing his labour, and forcing the learned insulter to employ some of that time in preparing food for his body, which he (by the help of his cook) hath now leisure to employ in pampering the pride of his heart, by first inquiring, and then applauding his own acquired learning. (I:140)

Like the language of women, the language of the illiterate laboring class is denigrated. But both laborers and women are necessary to the operation of society. Each portion of the population provides knowledge; each has a language which must interact with all other languages if society is to run smoothly:

> 'Tis the application alone which gives value to any sort of knowledge and renders it either useful or agreeable . . . It must be current coin before he can be the better for it. He must see useful knowledge contained in the most vulgar language, as well as admire it in a fine writer: . . . otherwise, let him be ever so profuse or eloquent in his admiration

of them, yet by refusing to own their acquaintance when they are unembellished and unadorned, he denies himself the utility of their friendship. (I: 182–83)

The narrators of *The Cry* act as a chorus, relating "such matters as are necessary to be known, and 'which we could not prevail on any of our actors to tell for us'" (I: 16). Mirroring their image of the good critic who is both candid and modest, like Portia they modestly instruct the reader about proper judgment. In their role of chorus, the narrators echo much of Portia's argument; they too bemoan that within this society all values rest on individualistic goals (II: 4). They argue against a vision of knowledge as a kind of economic power base, as property that raises one individual above another:

> Men look on knowledge which they learn, or might learn from others, as they do on the most beautiful structures, which are not their own: in outward objects they would rather behold their own hogsty than their neighbor's palace; and in mental ones, would prefer one grain of knowledge, gain'd by their own observation, to all the wisdom of a thousand Solomons. (II: 6)

Society raises one language above another, and then denies particular groups access to those it values most highly, believing that those languages retain value only insofar as their owners limit the production and reproduction of them (a typical supply-and-demand economic stance). Those valued languages therefore must be wielded against others to prevent their own value from diminishing as pieces of property. The narrators and Portia argue that to treat knowledge as a static commodity meant only for the use of one individual, or one class, or one gender, will result in the breakdown of all modes of production. Knowledge—language—is only useful insofar as it is applied, reproduced by all members of a community who depend on one another for support and maintenance.

During the course of Portia's appeal for equal access to education, the Cry continually interrupts and often willfully misinterprets her words, her judgments about love, knowledge and language. It abhors, in particular, Portia's refusal to acknowledge its critical superiority or to "allow the authority which they brought from their reading; and declared, that she was the most perverse, obstinate, arrogant, self-sufficient woman, that ever yet was born" (II: 87). The Cry attacks her judgment on the basis of her gender:

> Then [the Cry] opened all at once full-mouthed against woman's understanding logic: . . . they abused female logicians, and cast forth sly

reproaches against every woman that knew any thing of the matter. First, all the feminine part of the Cry utterly disclaim'd all knowledge of it themselves; and whatever they thus disclaim, they not only insinuate is of no value, but labour also to shew that the possession of it is attended with shame. Then they unanimously pronounced that logic was a man's business; and they were certain that a woman would never be married who pretended to such high learning. (I: 122–23)

Various members of the Cry define logic as a language or a form of discourse and deny that women should have any access to it. They conclude as a body "that for a woman to pretend to understand logic, or any other kind of learning, which was properly a man's business, it must and would subject her to deserved contempt, and she would be despised and neglected by all mankind" (I: 126). Interestingly, the women of the Cry are some of the most vociferous opponents of women's education. The authors demonstrate that the right to language is not simply a gender issue; women are part of the Cry, and therefore part of the ideology that the Cry upholds. The female members of the Cry unwittingly replicate that ideological position which seeks to exclude them from acquiring a certain kind of knowledge and authority.

Portia believes that society should provide all its members with an education that will teach them to use language as a tool to discover and achieve common goals. She recommends that they be taught to read those texts which will instruct them about the moral use of language so that their relationships with others will flourish. Real knowledge is "connected with such a regulation of the mind, and animate[s] the heart with such a degree of goodness, as will be a recommendation to the God of truth and wisdom." The intelligent and moral man wants a wife of good judgment and lively conversation, because without equality in language, there can be no love, no social intercourse: "A man who chuses a companion whose capacity doth not reach high enough to comprehend any of his ideas, might be as well struck dumb; for the utility of language is to him entirely vanished" (II: 227). Likewise, those who would teach should communicate knowledge clearly for "the good and happiness of" their students.

The authors of *The Cry* recognize that a culture's value system must be grounded in the language system it uses, and in order to change its values, one must not only change the language itself, but the culture's relationship to that language. Society constructs difference through language in its definitions of male and female sexuality as well as its definitions of class, and then transforms that difference into conflict. *The Cry* enacts interpretation as a war of languages, and seeks to neutralize that conflict by creating a discourse in "which no language prevails over any other, where the languages circulate."[40]

Portia advocates, then, a moral use of language based on the proper negotiation of human relationships. An inability to use language to form bonds with other members of society leads to alienation and isolation (I:39). Portia explains to Una and the Cry that her own happiness depends upon her experiencing "conversation in which I could, without any painful reserve, open my whole heart; and where I could be understood, and not have my words misinterpreted, and tortured into meanings I never thought of" (II: 45). She has such a relationship with Ferdinand's sister Cordelia, and needs not fear that Cordelia will misinterpret her, because Cordelia's readings are always motivated by love and friendship. As with Cordelia, Ferdinand's behavior mirrors his use of language: "his humanity and compassion . . . was in his practice, as well as in his discourse" (I: 113; I: 78). Furthermore, Ferdinand freely converses with Portia, "ready at all times to give [Portia] information concerning any thing, in which [she] had a curiousity to be inform'd" (I: 80). He willingly and properly instructs her because he "has a candour in his mind which gives him a capacity of perceiving when ignorance is not willful, and a generosity and communicativeness of disposition, which makes him delight in the informing of his companions" (I: 82).

Portia argues that the best judge, in both the public arena of critical judgment and in the domestic arena, is motivated by the love and friendship he or she feels for an author's words, and for an individual's thoughts and deeds. As Portia discusses issues such as interpretation and knowledge, she also tells her audience a story that appears to be little more than a domestic romance: the story of her own courtship and marriage. The authors of *The Cry* construct this tale in order to demonstrate more forcefully that they see the role of the critic and the duty of women as the same: to instruct society how to behave morally in both the private and public spheres.

Portia seeks the same qualities in written texts that she finds in Ferdinand and Cordelia, and because she has learned the moral use of language in her relationships with others, she has become a moral literary critic as well. In her textual criticism, Portia points to critics who have called the public's attention to other writers' inferior learning. For example, Ben Jonson, a writer whom Sarah's brother Henry greatly admired (see the preface to *Joseph Andrews*), called attention to his own exalted learning and Shakespeare's comparative ignorance in order to raise himself in the public's eyes (I: 163), just as Henry was dismissive of both Sarah's and Samuel Richardson's lack of a classical education.[41] Like Jonson and Henry Fielding, many critics claim that classical languages like Greek and Latin have especial value, and refuse to see in the more "vulgar" writings any knowledge which they can apply in their daily lives—even as they control access to classical education.

As a moral reader, Portia demonstrates the art of literary criticism as it should be practiced, showing a balance in her discussion of what Jonson lacked as a writer and critic. She gives him proper credit by discussing the ways in which his characters, plots and scenes "are such proofs of genius as have often pleased [her] fancy, and claim'd [her] admiration" (I: 166). However, she suggests that Jonson's envy and malice in his criticisms of Shakespeare (an immoral use of language) lessen the possibility that he or his writings will achieve immortality:

> Had Ben Johnson known the insignificancy of genius in comparison with a benevolent heart, he had been contented with himself, had borne to have taken the second rank, had loved his friend Shakespear instead of abusing him, had therefore been a happier man whilst he lived, and left behind him posthumous fame . . . Sufficient to have gratified the wishes of any reasonable man. (I:167)

For Portia, the ways in which individuals like Jonson and collectives like the Cry interpret texts demonstrate not love, but self-interested Desire. Portia attempts to create a more democratic, less hierarchical, form of discourse, one that includes terms like "turba," "dextra," and "sinistra," so that all members of society can communicate with one another. In her attempt to reinvent her relationships with society, "new words [spring] from the very woman [Portia] who refuses to appropriate" the Cry's words and its implicit founding values.[42] In effect, she tries to reform language itself. This new discourse invests her with an authority the Cry cannot dispute. Her terms make sense—and they are terms which in other forms all mankind is so familiar with that she excludes no one when she uses them. Portia uses this new discourse not to elevate herself, but to develop a discourse which allows all members of society to acquire the same knowledge.

The narrators agree that the immortality of the best writers stems from a quality they all share, "judgment directed by modesty and candor, which will not suffer the poet to think there is a magic in his touch which immediately brings all things to perfection." The best authors act as their own critics; moral authors' modesty "engages [them], before [they vent their] thoughts, to examine and reexamine them . . . before [they bring their] productions into the public view" (II: 9).

To illustrate that one cannot be a good writer unless one is a moral critic, a good judge of texts, the narrators point, as did Richardson and Fielding, to Aristotle, Homer, Virgil, and Horace. Unlike Richardson and Henry Fielding, though, Sarah Fielding and Collier emphasize that these authors shared critical rules and practices that were themselves communally generated (II: 11). Fielding and Collier domesticate the ancients, reading in their rules of epic poetry and in their criticism a domestic power, an economy of relationships. These early critics belonged to a family who supported each other's judgments, and who attested to the equality of others by re-inscribing the rules of those writers who preceded them. As the descendants of this family of critics, the narrators and Portia read their world in terms of kinship structures and relationships, and their rules of criticism are similarly—and systematically— founded upon the motives of friendship and community.

In their novels, Richardson and Henry Fielding implied that a superior critic must not only recognize, but be capable of resisting, an immoral text's seductive message. Portia proves her critical mettle when she analyzes and criticizes romance discourse, and calls upon society to restrict its consumption. She insists that readers of immoral fictions acquire from them and internalize improper economic and political motivations for their behavior; she suggests that romances have encouraged their readers to commodify the language of the private domain.

Portia examines historically the ways in which romance narratives have represented a woman's behavior during courtship, and how that behavior is reproduced by contemporary romance readers. In romance, authors draw women who think "it the highest breach of modesty to give the least hint of having one sentiment for [their] lover[s]" (I: 60). From the time they are small, little girls "are taught by [their mamas], that [they] must never speak before [they are] spoken to" (I: 62). Portia speculates that such a repression of language, because it leads to isolation and neglect, leads to a buildup of passion within the child's mind. As she grows older, motivated by passions like envy, jealousy, and vanity, a young woman expects to be persuaded with the excessively erotic discourse of love found in the romance.

Cylinda's story, as told to Una, the Cry, and Portia, can be called a romance, because in it, she relates the history of her "adventures," primarily her immoral romantic liaisons. But the story also demonstrates the dangers of an improper education. When Cylinda was a child, her father chose to tutor his motherless daughter "just in the same manner as if [she] had been a boy" (II, 254). As a woman educated like a man, Cylinda grows into a highly individuated woman, one who thinks not in terms of a network of relationships, but in terms of power and hierarchies. She learns to compete with her cousin, Phaon, "a spritely boy . . . [whom] . . . I did not suffer . . . to outrun me in any sort of learning; and by the time I was sixteen I became an exceedingly good *latin* scholar, and was pretty far advanced in *greek*" (II, 254). She has a series of immoral relationships, including one with Ferdinand's father. Because she has not received a proper education, because she has not had a mother like Portia's to guide her education, and because she has not been given the appropriate texts to read as a child, Cylinda's relationships with men are flawed: "In short I made wives of them; I first admired them, then made them my own property, and if they would not submit to my will, I again turned them off and divorced them" (II: 312). She believes that "the loss of liberty which must attend being a wife, was of all things the most horrible to my imagination" (II: 320).

Like other women, Fielding and Collier imply, Cylinda has been misdirected to immoral texts by men. When it suits their purpose, men encourage women to read romances—in the privacy of their homes. *The Cry* establishes, as did Lennox's *The Female Quixote*, that erotic desire is no more an exclusively female emotion than it is an exclusively male emotion—and that language very often gives rise to desire. Cylinda's story, which mirrors that of *Joseph Andrews*'s Mr Wilson,[43] faults male education as productive of false and misplaced desire, and even more subversively attacks the educational system for denying to men an education (in human nature) which women like Portia readily receive.

Importantly, Cylinda's story establishes also that poor judgment is not innate in—or confined to—women. The type of education one receives either develops or inhibits one's ability to judge, no matter the gender of the individual. As she tells her story, Cylinda comes across as a likable, intelligent, but misguided woman. Fielding and Collier create Cylinda to affirm that *any* improperly educated person will travel the wrong road.

As did Lennox, Portia implicates men equally in this reproduction of improper discourse. She argues that in order to flatter a woman's vanity, to ensnare this female commodity, the male lover "profusely pours forth his angels and his goddesses," his "strange language" of adulation (I: 68, 70). Unschooled in language, the romantic young woman fails to see that her lover means, "madam I like you . . . and . . . [desire that] you will bind yourself before God and man to obey my commands as long as I shall live. And should you after marriage be forgetful of your duty, you will then have given me a legal power of exacting as rigid a performance of it as I please" (I: 70).

Society has used the language of the romance to blind women to the very real economic and political implications of this particular kind of discourse. In a world where one's survival depends on one's economic power, language itself has become saturated with economic connotations. Teaching women to focus on the erotic component of the language of romance helps to disguise its political nature. The erotic discourse of the romance has become the language of exchange, a language which endows its user, typically a man, with the political power of master over slave. When Cylinda falls in love with a married man, Eustace, she seeks books that will feed and foster her passion:

> No reading could I now attend to with pleasure, but such as presented me with the image of my own thoughts. The tumultuous conflicts of Medea's passions, the mad love of Phaedra for her husband's son Hippolytus, and the raging flame of Dido's bosom, sympathizing with what dwelt within my own breast, served at once to soothe and inhance my inclination for Eustace. (III: 71–72)

As improperly trained readers, women like Cylinda who consume erotic discourse allow themselves to become material objects of exchange, mistakenly seeing this discourse as giving them a certain kind of power within that exchange (III, 79).

In teaching their readers how to recognize romance discourse, whether in written texts or in conversation, Fielding and Collier have in the process also transformed romance from a form which focuses on the erotics of relationships or heroic achievements of men in the public realm, to one that focuses on the transformative and reformative powers of a superior private sensibility to affect the behavior of others. That is, they reform romance into criticism.

Criticism becomes here a type of narrative that focuses on the private thoughts and motivations deriving from the world of texts read in the private space of the home; Fielding and Collier insist that society acknowledge the expression of those thoughts to have a very public and moral utility. In the final section of the novel, Portia literalizes, through her behavior and words, the transformative and reformative process termed by eighteenth-century men and women of letters literary criticism.

To suggest at this moment in history that women should be given access to the political, economic, and social realms required a strategy even more radical than simply allowing a woman actor/orator to speak in the public space of the theater. Part the Fourth of *The Cry* ends with Cylinda realizing that the text from which she should have learned judgment as a child was the Bible. Collier's and Fielding's use of the Bible as the authoritative text which empowers Portia and themselves as women to be literary and social critics may be the most subversive of all the strategies they use in their narrative.

On the surface, making use of the Bible seems instead relatively conservative, especially given patriarchal interpretations of the Bible's teachings by such influential writers as Samuel Richardson. Indeed, until this point, the Bible had been a favored tool for teaching women to be properly submissive to authority. After all, in *Clarissa*, Clarissa Harlowe's reading of Scripture helped her abdicate her authority to speak, even as it showed her how to be a moral exemplar. But Fielding and Collier recognize the radical nature of what the New Testament teaches; in recognizing everyone as equal in the sight of God, the Bible makes inequality hard to justify. In *The Cry*, then, Portia's reading of the Bible teaches her that in order to be a moral exemplar, she must have the authority to teach this lesson publicly and verbally.

The moral instructors of society should be those who read the text(s) which contain the values, ethical laws, and precepts that society propounds. But Portia indicates that although the proper rules for Christian behavior are contained in the Bible, ironically the most educated people—the men—of the culture do not read it.[44]

And so in a particularly subversive and radical move in Part the Fifth of *The Cry*, Fielding and Collier have their protagonist Portia literally become the Word of the Lord, a female Savior figure, in order for her to help to reform the moral behavior of characters like Cylinda. They interpret the Scriptural notion of the Word of the Lord to mean more than simply the semantic units on the pages of the Bible; unlike Richardson, Fielding and Collier do not limit their heroine's reading of the Bible to the more patriarchal and authoritarian Old Testament. They adopt and adapt instead the New Testament's connotation of the covenant of God with his people. They assume the "Word made flesh" to be Christ as the literal embodiment of the covenant that God made when He sent this, His only son to redeem and to save His followers. Christ as the Word made Flesh was an embodiment of God's promise that if humans loved one another, and did unto others as they would have done unto them, i.e., if they reformed their behavior, they would be saved. Moreover, in the New Testament, St. Paul makes no distinction among people who accept and are baptized into the covenant. All have the ability to embody Christ-as-Word.[45]

Literalizing this message, Fielding and Collier turn Portia into a Christ Figure—she embodies, in her acceptance of Christ's Word, Christ himself; that is, she embodies the Word made Flesh as well. Thus, just as Belford, Fielding-as-Narrator, and the learned divine became the best critics of their texts because of their superior judgment, Portia can become the best writer/critic in this work. As wife, mother, and Savior figure, Portia demonstrates superior judgment in her management of the domestic economy of relationships, and in her interpretations of the world of texts. This superior judgment gives her, within the text she inhabits, a public power that no other eighteenth-century female character—or female-proper—experiences.

As the final section of the novel opens, trouble between brothers Ferdinand and Oliver leads to Ferdinand's temporary emigration, for business reasons, to one of the colonies. For some time after Ferdinand first leaves home, Oliver intercepts all his letters and tells Cordelia and Portia that Ferdinand is reported to be living a decadent and debauched life, has ruined a woman, and is squandering all his money. When Portia receives evidence to support these charges, she reluctantly acknowledges that "Ferdinand had put it out of [her] power to become his lawful, his faithful wife" (III: 214). Portia retires to the countryside both to dissuade Ferdinand from pursuing her, and to restore her mind to tranquillity.

Ferdinand follows her, however, and finding her alone in a garden, tries to convince her to marry him. She refuses, and absconds to France. On her journey, she is "seized with a fever, and is perfectly insensible for twenty one days." During her illness she falls into a fit "so strongly resembling death," that her servant brings the news to London that she is in fact dead (III: 242).

Nonetheless, she recovers from her illness. Ferdinand's temptation of Portia in the garden, her three-week illness and subsequent "rising from the dead," are all events which too closely resemble events in the life of Christ to be ignored (although the similarity in the two stories has in fact been missed by the few critics who have discussed the novel). The narrative unmistakeably figures Portia as a female Christ figure, the female Word whose power as Text to reform is all-encompassing.

Like Clarissa, Portia "seriously [endeavors] to conquer a Passion for a Man who proves himself unworthy her Love" (*Remarks*, 22). She accomplishes, however, what Richardson refuses to allow Clarissa to accomplish. Portia reforms the immoral rake, Ferdinand, so that he will make a good husband. As the "book" which Ferdinand reads, Portia's actions and behaviors before and after her illness teach him to reform his own immoral conduct, to stop his deception. In fact, Ferdinand confesses his sins to her:

> Portia, (said he) you are now risen from the dead; and as faithfully as I would speak to one of those blessed spirits before whom no falshood can remain undiscovered, will I lay open to your view every action, every thought that hath passed in this unhappy breast . . . (III, 249)

Her reported death leads to Ferdinand's repentance and reformation, his conversion.

In contrast to Fielding's Judge in his Censorious Court of Literature, Portia judges Ferdinand—who has sinned against both the laws of family and literature with his immoral fictions—mercifully:

> no sooner did I see the once loved bosom of my Ferdinand free from those deformed demons which had crept in and filled up the vacant space, than beholding my natural home once more the seat of innocence and truth, my heart joyfully danced into its delightful abode. (III: 277)

Portia also proves herself to be the author of a moral and improving narrative: her story of how she reformed Ferdinand leads Cylinda, who has joined the Cry and Una as a member of Portia's audience, to repent and redeem herself, as well:

> O Portia . . . My life hath been . . . a tale told by an idiot, and my imagination a strutting player, full of sound and signifying nothing. . . . I now too plainly see that I was inviting cruel tyrants into my bosom. . . . My life may properly be called the triumph of the imagination, as yours, Portia, is of the judgment. (III: 279–80)

Realizing that her life has been little more than an immoral fiction, a romance, Cylinda renounces her past life, and "reforms" her life from "immoral romance" to moral history as well when she promises to seek "the lost and true path to peace and tranquility." Like the good Savior figure that she is, Portia judges Cylinda mercifully;

she embraces her, and warmly welcomes her, as Christ did Mary Magdalene ("I came not to judge the world but to save the world," 12 John 47), into her family, so that she and Ferdinand can provide Cylinda with the compassion and forgiveness which they believe sincere penitents such as she deserve.

Portia's story, then, not only reforms, but redeems its listeners, and all those ready to accept her Word—which is nothing more than a translation of Christ's Word into her everyday thought and deed. Portia's story in *The Cry* becomes a version of the Gospel. Like Christ's parables, her story teaches moral behavior to those who are willing to listen. Her story is a testament to the power of the human love that Christ preached as it is expressed in and through language. Portia's story does not merely exemplify good moral and social judgment, it enacts it.

Portia acquires access to the public realm of discourse by virtue of her profound ability to judge, and because she admits to wanting no other power but that of judging to whom she should be subject, and that of instructing others in the moral use of language, so that they might find similarly satisfying mates and friends. Unlike Clarissa, Cylinda does not have to die because of her excessive desire for her own critical language. Sophia's refusal to judge made her a superior mate for Tom; in this narrative, Portia's ability to judge morally and her articulation of those moral judgments makes her a superior mate for Ferdinand. And, unlike Arabella, Lennox's silenced heroine, Portia has not lost the power of language by marrying. At the time she relates this story, she and Ferdinand have been married for two years. Since she is the head of the domestic economy, responsible for the education of the children, and an equal part of the family of humankind, she has equal access to a language by which to achieve reform in social behavior and mores.

The Cry was not popular in its own time, and has received very little critical attention in the twentieth century, perhaps because it differs so radically in form and content from many eighteenth-century novels. Richardson felt "that though the book had natural strokes and a knowledge of the heart, its end was poorly managed"(SR 203).[46] *The Monthly Review*'s critic opined:

> The stile is sometimes heavy; the action too much interrupted by the Cry; and the plan we fear, too abstracted from the present taste, to procure the work as many readers as it deserves. The sentiments are, generally, just; the passions drawn from nature; and the whole performance contains more literature and good sense, than, a few only excepted, all our modern novels put together. We write this with the

more pleasure, as we believe we are doing justice to the production of a lady.[47]

Concurring, Hester Thrale Piozzi wrote, "[T]he Cry contains more good Sense and true Knowledge of Life than many a popular Work of its own Sort, but being odly put together never had any sale."[48] In the end, Sarah Fielding and Jane Collier's lack of success with this novel seems to lend some credence to Frank Donoghue's implication that only the *Review*s had the power to tell the official story of the working female writer's professional self, that unlike the career of an eighteenth-century male subject, that of an eighteenth-century female subject's was entirely authored by the institutions that constrained her.[49] Whereas the Cry ultimately fails in its attempts to victimize and to silence Portia, popular criticism and culture apparently succeeded in silencing these literary women who sought authorial status in such an unconventional way.

Nonetheless, *The Cry* urges its readers to resist being seduced by popular criticism's narratives about women's and men's roles in language usage in the mid-eighteenth century. Portia's story illustrates that women's language can no longer be confined to the private realm of the home, or denied power and authority, since without it, society as a whole, including the political and socio-economic realms of the public sphere, will break down. The most radical reformation of romances that Fielding and Collier's narrative carries out, then, is that unlike those romances that tell their readers the hero and heroine live happily ever after in wedded bliss, *The Cry* makes clear that for women, living happily ever after depends upon equality in language, a reciprocal relationship motivated by love and sympathy.

6
Privacy, Privilege and "Poaching" in Austen's *Mansfield Park*

PORTIA'S STATUS AS A PUBLICLY AUTHORIZED CRITIC WAS SO SUBVERSIVE because the vast majority of discourse in this period represented proper women as extremely private; in other words, silent. What, of course, was not unusual by this time was the emphasis on a critic's responsibility to ensure the moral health of society, in and through language. Belford and Allworthy have power and status in the public realm, but they also demonstrate superior morality—either by virtue of their reading of the Bible, like Belford, or by virtue of their belief in secularized Christian doctrine, like Allworthy.

Given society's suspicions about women writers in particular, women writers struggling to be seen as moral often created characters whose moral stature would not normally be questioned by their readership. Lennox's learned divine is a much more literal symbol of morality than Belford and Allworthy, but like them, he is a paternal one. Like most women authors, then, Lennox acceded, in some measure, to societal norms in order to achieve some measure of economic success.

Significantly, Lennox's learned divine achieves critical authority by repeating almost verbatim the review of *Clarissa* that Samuel Johnson published in *The Rambler*. When Lennox has the learned divine re-educate Arabella to read novels like *Clarissa* instead of romances as a means to achieve her moral reformation, she demonstrates how close in function the professions of clergyman and literary critic are seen to be. Further, she demonstrates why clergymen become such apt symbols of the ideal literary critic for writers such as herself and Jane Austen.

In terms of the history of criticism, Lennox's character of the learned divine and Fielding and Collier's character of a woman who teaches a moral program of reading foreshadow a figure of the critic as pedagogue that has a good deal of currency not only in the world of fiction but in the material eighteenth-century world, and on into the nineteenth century. This figure has not been adequately accounted for in such histories as *The Function of Criticism*, an entirely male-driven history. Previous historians of literary criticism have considered only the relation between the male critic and the public sphere over time, and then, once that critic enters what they consider to be the privatized world of the university, rue his loss of public status.[1] If we include female authors in our history of literary criticism, however, we find them, like Lennox and Fielding and Collier, highlighting the pedagogic aspect of the critic's role; therefore not only her role within the public space of business is important, but her role within the more private spaces of society. For women novelists, the critic who sees his or her role as properly being that of a teacher is to be praised rather than mourned.

Terry Eagleton makes an astute point, though, when he argues with regard to the nineteenth century that "the most searching, invigorating social critic was the writer [herself]."[2] One of the reasons that early nineteenth-century author Jane Austen has remained part of today's eighteenth-century canon is because, as the omniscient narrator in her novels, she continues to convince scholars that she is not merely a writer but also a critic.[3] She is a critic, however, who does not ignore the critical wisdom of her female ancestors. Like Lennox and Fielding and Collier, she believes that an author best serves his or her society in the profession of critic by teaching, first of all, which texts to read and how to read them morally.

In novels such as *Mansfield Park*, Austen explicitly draws our attention to issues of interpretation and gender when she calls into question society's propensity to invest individuals with moral and critical authority purely on the basis of their institutional and/or professional affiliations. In particular, she treats as suspect the tendency in the field of letters to represent men (especially men of property or men of the cloth) as the moral guardians of the public domain, and therefore best suited to the profession of literary criticism.

As did the other authors studied in this book, Austen-as-narrator, in *Mansfield Park*, adopts a Spectator-like persona; she also apparently shares Charlotte Lennox's position that the professions of clergyman and literary critic are very similar, both in form and in function.[4] Her private writings certainly suggest as much. Austen once noted that "[a] classical education, or at any rate a very extensive acquaintance with English literature, ancient and modern, appears to me quite indispensable for the person who would do any justice to your clergyman."[5] But she does not believe that education alone makes a person a suitable social critic, any more than she believes that a woman's education ought to force her to develop such an intensely private sensibility that she has no power, or is of no public use to the society within which she moves. Austen creates Fanny Price, a version of the Female Spectator, as a means to uncover shortcomings of cultural metaphors of both male and female readers.

In *Mansfield Park*, Austen examines the power relationships that develop between women-as-writers and women-as-readers, and the institutions that reduce their options and make them marginal, especially in the field of letters. In particular, Austen scrutinizes exchanges between authors and their publics—both amateur and professional readers—and the critical discourse that structures the eighteenth-century project of moral education. *Mansfield Park* uncovers the ways that education can shape women as readers, but implies as well that they have the power to resist being wholly determined by that education.

This chapter focuses on the relationship between education and literary criticism that Austen develops in the novel. I address the ways in which protagonist Fanny Price makes use of the education she receives from her cousin Edmund Bertram to achieve autonomy as a reader. Initially, this education appears to form her into a reader who, some critics have charged, refuses to act.[6] Despite the conventional interpretation of her as a passive consumer, Fanny actually becomes an active producer who moves across the Bertram landscape, across linguistic and moral fields written most particularly by Edmund Bertram. To borrow Michel de Certeau's term, Fanny becomes a "poacher" when she learns to use for her own ends the education she is provided.[7] Although her education is meant to teach Fanny her proper role and place as an upper-middle-class female reader, it ultimately leads to her achieving a critical authority, and therefore a public power and status within the society of Mansfield Park, that the literary culture of the period is reluctant to afford to women.

JANE AUSTEN: PROFESSIONAL AUTHOR/CRITIC

Jane Austen was "a professional author who [was] acutely conscious of her sales and eager to increase her profits."[8] While her audience was an intimate one, composed, argues Jan Fergus, of "like-minded members of her own social group,"[9] Austen also wanted to be taken seriously by a broader audience, one that included professional readers and other authors. She therefore took a great deal of interest in all aspects of the publishing of her novels. When she was halfway through the writing of *Mansfield Park*, for instance, she made the often-quoted remark with regard to *Pride and Prejudice*:

> Upon the whole . . . I am quite vain enough and well satisfied enough. The work is rather too light, and bright, and sparkling; it wants shade; it wants to be stretched out here and there with a long chapter of sense, if it could be had; if not of solemn specious nonsense, about something unconnected with the story; an essay on writing, a critique on Walter Scott, or the history of Buonaparte . . . [10]

Fergus reads Austen's tones as completely ironic here. She asserts that "Austen clearly had no real wish to include essays and critiques into her work . . . The passage reflects her own sense that her style had changed and deepened since she had first written *Pride and Prejudice* more than fifteen years earlier."[11] What is just as likely, if not more so, however, is that this passage reflects Austen's awareness of what is at stake in the struggle for status among eighteenth-century novelists in the field of letters. Long chapters of "solemn specious nonsense, about something unconnected with the story," essays on writing, and critiques of rival authors are the sorts of discourse her contemporaries often include in their novels as a means of elevating themselves in the eyes or reviewers and ordinary readers. It is writing designed to demonstrate a writer's superior, classical education, a kind of education usually denied to women. In fact, it is the sort of writing that those reviewers, and indeed some academic critics of our own century, will designate "masculine" (read "good") writing. It is likely then that Austen refers to the critical double standard of judgment in the publishing world when she points to a criterion meant to exclude certain writers from the literary canon of her era.

Fergus provides some evidence that Austen had reservations about the practices of the literary establishment when she discusses Austen's frustration with powerful members of the publishing world: "She evidently had learned to prefer her own judgment of the value of her work to [her publisher] Egerton's . . . Publishing *Mansfield Park* for herself would once again give her brother Henry the task of supervising the printers, but Henry probably urged her not to sacrifice her profit to his convenience."[12] Notably, because of her involvement and business sense, the novel *Mansfield Park* reaped for Austen her greatest profit, despite the fact that it was not reviewed.[13]

Austen's attitudes about women writers were said to be fairly traditional: "In accordance with feminine dutifulness and deference, she generally hid her work and kept silent about it."[14] This seems a problematic statement, however, given that "in 1809 Jane Austen aggressively renewed her attempts to publish"[15] and given Austen's niece's reminiscence that when

> Austen stayed with the Knights in Kent, she shared her manuscripts with Fanny, Marianne's eldest sister, and probably with Lizzy . . . As Marianne tells it, 'I remember that when Aunt Jane came to us at Godmersham she used to bring the MS of whatever novel she was writing with her, and would shut herself up with my elder sisters in one of the bedrooms to read them aloud. I and the younger ones used to hear peals of laughter through the door, and thought it very hard that we should be shut out from what was so delightful.'[16]

While this scene demonstrates that Austen appeared to be keeping her work private by retreating to an even more private realm within the domestic sphere in order to share it, reading aloud one's writing is not keeping silent. Deborah Kaplan herself admits that "by sharing work in progress, [Austen] was not only acknowledging the fact of her products but the labor of creating them, and she was welcoming her female audience's participation in that labor. They laughed, but they also offered suggestions and criticisms."[17]

A better explanation for Austen's reading aloud behind closed doors is that Austen made use of the privilege of privacy afforded her in the domestic sphere, as an intermediate zone within which to prepare her words for public consumption. First, in the privacy of this space Austen's novels became a private hunting reserve for these women as socially unauthorized readers, who by their laughter and jesting, introduced "plurality and difference into the written system of a society and text."[18] The bedroom, that is, constituted a secret, discursive space within which the women could themselves poach upon Austen's writing, and alongside her, resist for a time the rules of the field of letters. We might see these women as reading outside of the law given by socially authorized professionals and intellectuals.

Second, despite her desire to keep her identity as a writer private, she wished her writing to be public; remember that she "aggressively [attempted] to publish" her novels. In fact, she was annoyed enough about the lack of critical notice for *Mansfield Park* that she wrote a letter in protest.[19] At best, Austen seems to have been torn between desires for privacy and for publicity; thus her attitude toward women's reading and writing must be described as more complex than recent critics have allowed.

As a general characterization of the novel, Jan Fergus writes that, "power is central to *Mansfield Park*."[20] To be sure, Fergus refers primarily to domestic power, but Austen also considers the power of texts, and more specifically, texts as tools of education, within that domestic space. As Austen's bedroom readings demonstrate, literary criticism plays an important role in the private sphere. The home is where children, particularly female children, learn to behave publicly. Books are often a part of that domestic education.

This study has provided a good deal of evidence to show that a standard premise of eighteenth-century literature was that all professionals who wrote as part of their labor, including those in the new profession of literary criticism as well as those who were members of the clergy, must convince their respective audiences that they could author morally instructive texts. Austen suggests that in order to enter either the profession of criticism or the profession of the clergy, individuals must not only write moral texts, such as the ones she herself writes, but also demonstrate a consistency in their ability to read morally. She treats ironically the notion that men of the upper classes are better prepared as readers to take on the role of moral arbiters than women or members of the laboring classes. Hence, Austen insists that her audience consider whether clergy or critic should have sole authority for deciding how society ought to receive and interpret texts.

The Learned Divine Revisited

In *Mansfield Park*, Austen reacts in part to cultural restrictions on women's linguistic production when she creates Fanny Price, a protagonist whose perspective appears to other characters (as well as to extratextual readers) to be that of a detached and tasteful reader[21]:

> In a way there is a little of the artist about her: she speaks for the value of literature, of memory, of fancy; she alone reveals a true appreciation of nature. More important, [Fanny] is in a way the supreme consciousness of the society she moves in. Like many Jamesian figures, she does not fully participate in the world but as a result she sees things more clearly and accurately than those who do.[22]

Indeed, Fanny's gaze recalls the gaze of such earlier eighteenth-century social critics as Addison and Steele's Mr. Spectator and

Eliza Haywood's Female Spectator. For example, as the Female Spectator recommended to her readers, Fanny has made the study of Nature one of her primary activities. As Eliza Haywood suggested it might, such a study has in fact helped to shape Fanny's aesthetic sensibility: "When I look out on a night such as this, I feel as if there could be neither wickedness nor sorrow in the world; and there certainly would be less of both if the sublimity of Nature were more attended to, and people were carried more out of themselves by contemplating such a scene."[23] As such she can be read as Austen's reaction to and appropriation of—her "poaching" of, in Michel de Certeau's terms—that popular trope of "spectator." Austen brings her novel into dialogue with these earlier representations of readers both as a means to reveal the shortcomings of the spectator trope and to transform it into an image that gives women better access to the critical authority it has come to represent for men.

She casts the soon-to-be-ordained clergyman Edmund Bertram in the role of Fanny's primary instructor and socially sanctioned critic for the novel's society. Importantly, in doing so Austen yokes education and literary criticism. Edmund is provided a literary education at Oxford like the one Austen described as needed to "do justice to your clergyman." At least initially, therefore, Edmund seems the most logical choice to be Fanny's teacher and Mansfield Park's moral and aesthetic arbiter.

Austen is interested, however, not only in issues of the literariness or interpretability of texts but in the professionalism of the field. Eagleton argues that the intensely political nature of the late eighteenth century eventually gave birth to "the nineteenth-century sage," a critic whose relation to his audience was now "transcendental, his pronouncements dogmatic and self-validating, his posture towards social life chillingly negative."[24] Austen's examination of the critical profession portrays the debate over who can best perform the labor of critic as one that pits the cleric against the self-absorbed and elitist aesthete. She makes clear which side of this debate she favors when she looks closely at the motivations for choosing the clerical profession of both Edmund and Henry Crawford (who, however whimsically, considers taking vows).

As a second son who will not inherit a fortune, Edmund needs to "do something for [himself]" (MP 92); he needs a profession in order to provide himself with an income. While the popular opinion of many (as expressed by Mary Crawford) is that those in the upper classes seek a literary education because of their "indolence and love of ease—[and their] want of all laudable ambition" (MP, 110), Edmund believes that only an education like the one he receives at Oxford can prepare him for work that will be "of the first importance to mankind, individually or collectively considered, temporally and eternally—which has the guardianship of religion and morals, and consequently of the manners which result from their influence" (*MP*, 92). When Edmund uses the term "manners," he means moral conduct. He sees his duty as a member of the clergy as to "teach and recommend" good principles of living, rather than to be an arbiter of "good breeding, [a regulator] of refinement and courtesy, [a master] of ceremonies of life" (*MP* 93). Edmund chooses this profession because it will allow him to serve others. As an individual whose "strong good sense and uprightness of mind, bid most fairly for utility, honour, and happiness to himself and all his connections" (*MP*, 21), Edmund sees this profession as providing him with more than money or leisure.

In contrast, when Henry Crawford considers the profession of clergy, he considers how it will allow him to serve himself. He believes that the qualifications for the clergy are not unlike those for other aesthetic or artistic enterprises. If he were to join the professional ranks of the clergy, he would do so in order to show off his superior education and aesthetic sensibility, and his ability to serve as an arbiter of good breeding:

> A thoroughly good sermon, thoroughly well-delivered, is a capital gratification . . . There is something in the eloquence of the pulpit, when it is really eloquence, which is entitled to the highest praise and honor . . . I never listened to a distinguished preacher in my life, without a sort of envy. But then I must have a London audience. I could not preach but to the educated; to those who were capable of estimating my composition. (*MP*, 341)

Henry Crawford assumes that a clergyman's goal is not unlike that of many a literary professional: to write beautiful and entertaining texts for an elite audience who can praise and honor him for his skills, rather than to write—as reputable clergy or literary men would admonish—beautiful and moral works whose primary purpose is to instruct, even as they entertain. In this sense, he becomes an exaggeration and parody of that figure Eagleton describes as "sage": "the Romantic critic is in effect the poet ontologically justifying his own practice, elaborating its deeper implications, reflecting upon the grounds and consequences of his art." Henry Crawford has no real urge to ensure the morality of his audience; instead, he is one who views the role of clergyman as giving him the opportunity to be "at once [a] source of sagelike authority and [as well as a] canny popularizer, member of a spiritual clerisy but plausible intellectual salesman."[25]

Given his ethics, then, Edmund seems a far more worthy spokesman for his society's moral values, and so he plays a large role in Fanny's education. Early on, he "[recommends] the books which [charm] her leisure hours, he [encourages] her taste, and [corrects] her judgment." Over time he "[makes] reading useful by talking to her of what she read, and [heightens] its attraction by judicious praise" (*MP*, 22). As an adult, Fanny attributes her aesthetic appreciation of Nature to Edmund: "you taught me to think and feel on the subject [of Nature]" (*MP*, 88). In other words, his purpose and labor as Fanny's teacher mirrors that of the period's literary critic: to shape her aesthetic sensibility in order to help her to become a better person. But Edmund begins to lose his status as teacher/critic when he fails to understand the value of consistency in his readerly behavior.

A central incident in the novel involves the inappropriate attempt of the Bertrams, the Crawfords and Mr. Yates to stage *Lovers' Vows* in the Bertram home, an act which goes against all the rules of polite society. One of Edmund's initial objections to their group's performance of the play is the impropriety of his sisters acting, though he hedges by deferring to patriarchal authority: "[His father] would never wish his grown-up daughters to be acting plays" (*MP*, 127). Knowing that the play signals "the end of all . . . privacy and propriety" (*MP*, 153), and still apparently eager to uphold Spectator-like principles of proper aristocratic decorum, Edmund goes to Fanny's room to ask her opinion of his joining in the action. Mary Crawford has coyly suggested that only Edmund is suited to play the role of Anhalt in the play. Edmund's infatuation with Mary makes him willing to do just about anything that will give him the opportunity to get closer to and to please her. Edmund plans therefore to renege on his initial refusal to act in such an inappropriate drama.

Fanny stews:

> To be acting! After all his objections—objections so just and so public! After all that she had heard him say, and seen him look, and known him to be feeling. Could it be possible? Edmund so inconsistent. Was he not deceiving himself? Was he not wrong? Alas! it was all Miss Crawford's doing. She had seen her influence in every speech, and was miserable. (*MP*, 156)

Edmund loses credibility as a critic because he fails to repress his emotions and instead allows his passions to interfere with his ability to author and to interpret texts properly. In acting the part of Anhalt, he reproduces an immoral text, one which he *knows* to be immoral. The best clergy and the best critics of the day would not set such a bad example for their respective congregations. It is important to point out at this juncture that not one member of the Bertram circle who behaves badly in the novel ultimately changes his or her ways due to Edmund's influence. Because Edmund fails as a reader he also fails to achieve the ultimate goal of both clergy and critics alike: the moral reformation of society. Through her characterization of Edmund Bertram, Austen challenges the ideology that a clergyman's education and professional affiliation alone grant power and authority in literate and literary culture.

By contrast, when she first arrives at Mansfield Park as a young girl, Fanny "could read, work and write, but she had been taught nothing more" (*MP* 18). Her lack of knowledge in languages, geography and music distances her from her cousins. Her marginal status as a poor relation to the Bertrams often means she has "no share in the festivities of the season" (*MP*, 35). She spends most of her time watching and listening—a mere spectator.

In Addison and Steele's *The Spectator*, Fanny's position as female spectator would have simply been that of an outsider, a passive consumer of texts, but in *Mansfield Park*, it is in her position as outsider and apparently passive spectator that Austen first reveals Fanny's aptitude for poaching. One way that Fanny becomes an outsider is in her refusal to learn either music or drawing, in the sense that she refuses to be a "producer" of either form of art. Like Eliza Haywood's Female Spectator, she does not, however, refuse to learn how to "consume" the arts. Clever, quick, full of good sense, and fond of reading, Fanny capitalizes on the education Edmund provides her, consuming and discussing all of the books he recommends.

On an aesthetic level, she learns as well to appropriate and make her own the world of Mansfield Park she encounters. In fact, she literally "poaches" what was once the girls' schoolroom: "gradually, as her value for the comforts of it increased, she had added . . . her possessions, and spent much of her time there; and having nothing to oppose her, had so naturally and so artlessly worked herself into it, that it was now generally admitted to be her's" (*MP*, 151). Not even Mrs. Norris's insistence that she be denied a fire can dampen her sense of ownership—particularly when Sir Thomas orders the fires to be lit regularly. When the Bertrams decide to join Yates in his plan to stage *Lovers' Vows*, Fanny becomes a spectator by choice and makes of the world of texts that surrounds her something different from what those most anxious to regulate her behaviour have intended.

As a spectator who "poaches," Fanny travels across the linguistic and moral fields of the Bertram circle of actors, "always walking from one room to another and doing the lookings on" (*MP*, 166) at her ease. She "derive[s] as much innocent enjoyment from the play as any of them" (*MP*, 165) because in refusing an active part in it, she escapes from the pressures it exerts upon the other actors. "Emancipated" from the Bertram stage, Fanny's body as reader is "freer in its movements."[26] It was "a pleasure to her to creep into the theatre, and attend the rehearsal of the first act" (*MP*, 165). She reads the play's scenes and then "creates something unknown in the space organized by their capacity for allowing an indefinite plurality of meaning."[27] The other characters begin to recognize her capacity, as cultural consumer, to perform that activity of "reading" normally reserved for the literary critic or professional intellectual (cleric).

To repeat Tony Tanner's estimation of Fanny, "in a way there is a little of the artist about her: she speaks for the value of literature, of memory, of fancy; she alone reveals a true appreciation of nature,"[28] and her fellow characters in the novel seem to recognize as much. During rehearsals, all of the players in *Lovers' Vows* turn to Fanny for directorial guidance, which requires not only knowledge of the lines but an ability to interpret how they should be delivered. Austen remembers what many critics would forget: "a director is the author of [a play's] production."[29] Although Fanny never literally takes the position of the author,[30] she does become an active producer of meaning.

Furthermore, at several junctures in the text, Austen alludes to Fanny's "delicacy of taste, of mind, of feeling" (*MP*, 81). Fanny admires "all that was pretty . . . [in] nature, inanimate nature" (*MP*, 80–81). "As far as she could judge, Mr. Crawford was considerably the best actor," (*MP*, 165) and she greatly appreciates his skill at reading speeches from Shakespeare's *Henry VIII*: "in Mr. Crawford's reading there was a variety of excellence beyond what she had ever met with" (*MP*, 337). It is Fanny, rather than Edmund or Henry Crawford, who demonstrates better than any other character proper aesthetic appreciation for all sorts of texts.

Keeping Private, or How to Privilege Repression

Nina Auerbach argues that Fanny refuses stubbornly to act, both in the play *Lovers' Vows* and in general.[31] I have suggested, above, however, that Fanny plays a very active role in the drama by guiding other characters, as well as a very active role in the rest of the novel—if only as an interested listener. Fanny Price's education as reader and spectator in *Mansfield Park* has appropriately produced in her the kind of interiority—or private sensibility—that the *Spectator* approves. It often impels her to her tiny room where she takes refuge from the world. Fanny's refusal to act a more public part in the various dramas of the novel seems a predictable outcome of her education.

A case in point: when Edmund seeks Fanny's advice prior to his accepting the role of Anhalt in *Lovers' Vows*, he does so because, presumably, he knows her to be a good and proper judge of what she reads and witnesses. But while Edmund solicits Fanny's judgments, he does not necessarily take them very seriously. When he sees that Fanny's "judgment is not with [him]" (*MP*, 154), for instance, he immediately interrupts her and rationalizes that "if I can be the means of restraining the publicity of the business, of limiting the exhibition, of concentrating our folly, I shall be well repaid." Fanny is not convinced; Edmund allows "if you are against me, I ought to distrust myself—and yet . . ." (*MP*, 155). He then proceeds to try to pressure Fanny into supporting his decision to contradict himself. He implies that Fanny is being selfish: "I thought *you* would have entered more into Miss Crawford's feelings" (*MP*, 155). Like many people of the period, Edmund believes that women like Fanny should be seen and not always heard, particularly in a public forum. Hence, as his pupil, it is little wonder that Fanny plays so well the role of a proper eighteenth-century woman reader, that she takes the part, to quote Marylea Meyersohn, of a "quiet auditor of the whole."[32]

Rather than being a reader who passively absorbs texts, however, Fanny ultimately rewrites the trope of woman spectator that Edmund has recommended. She becomes instead the sort of reader who insists upon independent thinking, who does not look to others—as do Edmund or Henry Crawford—for approval, but finds the authority for her interpretations within: "We have all a better guide in ourselves, if we would attend to it, than any other person can be" (*MP*, 412). Much of her new sense of her own critical authority develops in Portsmouth.

After she refuses Crawford's offer of marriage, Sir Thomas sends her to Portsmouth because he believes "that a little abstinence from the elegancies and luxuries of Mansfield Park, would bring her mind into a sober state, and incline her to a juster estimate of the value of that home of greater permanence, and equal comfort, of which she had the offer" (*MP*, 369). Fanny's trip to Portsmouth teaches her, however, not so much the value of elegance and luxury as the value of the kind of education that members of the upper class typically receive:

> The living in incessant noise [in Portsmouth] was . . . an evil which no superadded elegance or harmony could have entirely atoned for . . . At Mansfield, no sounds of contention, no raised voice, no abrupt bursts, no tread of violence was ever heard; all proceeded in a regular course or cheerful orderliness, everybody had their due importance; everybody's feelings were consulted. If tenderness could be ever supposed wanting, good sense and good breeding supplied its place. (*MP*, 392)

As this quotation illustrates, Austen certainly shares some of the biases of the educated class to which she belongs. One of the privileges of polite society is that one moves in a circle where others have learned to edit themselves, to keep certain emotional responses private and the expression of others restrained. In Austen's mind or, at the very least, in Fanny's mind, although the inhabitants of Mansfield Park may suffer severely from moral malaise, at least their expression of it is tastefully subdued.

But while in Portsmouth, Fanny learns to put these prejudices in perspective. In particular, she comes to realize that Edmund is not solely responsible for her own good sense when she develops a strong relationship with her sister Susan: "the intimacy thus begun between them was a material advantage to each" (*MP*, 398). With surprise, Fanny realizes that even though Susan has been deprived of an education like her own, she has "so much better knowledge, so many good notions." Moreover, having been "brought up in the midst of negligence and error, [Susan has] formed such proper opinions of what ought to be—she, who had no cousin Edmund to direct her thoughts or fix her principles" (*MP*, 397–98). Acknowledging that despite her lack of patriarchal education, Susan has innate good judgment, Fanny must also acknowledge that Edmund cannot be totally responsible for her own proper opinions and notions.

Her material distance from the patriarchal authority that Mansfield Park represents allows Fanny to evaluate this knowledge in light of Edmund's moral inconsistency. Edmund's inconsistency undermines his status as a representative of the clerical and educational professions; "the creativity of the reader grows as the institution that controlled it declines."[33] Fanny seeks books on her own without Edmund's help or sanction: "She became a subscriber—

amazed at being anything in *propria persona*, amazed at her own doings in every way; to be a renter, a chuser of books" (*MP*, 398). In selecting books for herself, she also serves as a literary reviewer for Susan: "Susan had read nothing, and Fanny longed to give her a share in her own first pleasures, and inspire a taste for the biography and poetry which she delighted in herself" (*MP*, 398).

Fanny reforms Susan, to be sure, but it is not so much a moral reformation as it is an aesthetic one. Susan has already "proper opinions of what ought to be"; what she lacks is a private sensibility like Fanny's. Education trains Susan to repress her emotions properly, to behave with more decorum. A literary education can be a "useful influence, [can have] a moral effect on the . . . understanding and manners," but only if an individual has learned first "the necessity of self-denial and humility" (*MP*, 463). *Mansfield Park* suggests that in Austen's view, children's dispositions are their parents' responsibilities, rather than those of authors, critics, or the clergy. Ordinary people, that is, play as important a role, if not a more important role, in the moral education of society as those in the profession of moral education, be it literary or religious. This means that a self-denying and humble disposition as well as a literate education give one authority as a reader. Only Fanny, in *Mansfield Park*, fits the bill.

Whereas Charlotte Lennox's novel ends with the woman reader being reformed by the clergyman so that she can marry the middle-class man chosen by her father, Austen's novel ends with the woman reader marrying the reformed clergyman, her cousin, a match initially considered by all to be "impossible" (*MP*, 6).[34] Fanny thereupon acquires as her home the Parsonage, a discursive space within which Edmund will prepare morally edifying texts for the public consumption of his parishioners—with Fanny acting, presumably, as his best reader and critic. The novel ends by constricting circumstances not unlike those in which Austen herself prepares her texts. Fanny and Austen both accomplish the "impossible" by poaching, by their making use of the privileges of privacy in order to earn the sanction of their respective societies as readers.

Historically, authors and critics have often figured women-as-readers as passive consumers, unable to make powerful use of their reading by their writing, and unable to use their experience as readers to transform their experience as people. I have argued here that our characterizations of women-as-readers depend upon twentieth-century understandings of the terms "private" and "privacy," twentieth-century understandings of eighteenth-century distinctions between private and public spheres, and our belief that eighteenth-century education inculcated in women a proper understanding of their roles or lack thereof in each sphere, an assessment that many women quietly and whole-heartedly accepted. But although Austen's gender and class certainly influenced her writing, as an "ordinary" person, so too did her idiosyncratic experiences. Like other ordinary people, she was as capable of resisting the institutions she examined as she was of reproducing them.

Furthermore, Austen, like the other women novelists I have discussed in this book, should be read, as Addison and Steele and Richardson and Fielding are read, as an author and as a critic, rather than as a professional-but-female author. Like any other author writing at that social moment, male or female, she was engaged in an ongoing struggle with other writers for authority and status. Austen's literary career depended as much on male novelists as it did on other female novelists; likewise it depended as much on male readers as it did on female readers. Like many literary professionals, male and female, Austen felt society's bias against novelists strongly enough to wish to keep her identity private, but saw too that privacy was one of her rights and privileges as a member of the educated classes.

Austen disliked many of the practices of professionals within the field of letters, perhaps particularly their treatment of women authors. So while Austen appears at times to have been traditional, deferential, and intensely private, I interpret her as a writer who takes the role of female author imposed on her and makes something quite different from what those in power in the literary field had in mind. To cite de Certeau once more, Austen's use of the dominant literary critical order, represented by Edmund Bertram in *Mansfield Park*, deflects its power.[35] Fanny escapes Edmund's power without leaving Mansfield Park. In fact, she acquires better access to it. In *Mansfield Park*, Austen capitalizes on the private zone to which women have been consigned, and depicts criticism as a viable activity and profession for women.

Conclusion

This book has traced the contribution of novelists to the development of literary criticism in the eighteenth century, and more specifically, women's relation to and role in criticism in that period. Women's representations of themselves and their characters as readers provide evidence that women were capable of creating for themselves powerful authorial subjectivities as critics.

These women's novels help to enrich, expand, and transform our narrow and received vision of the history of criticism. Lennox and Austen create as the professional best suited to the practice and labor of criticism—best suited to recommend moral literature for an audience to read—a literarily educated clergyman. And, with regard to the material circumstances of the history of university English departments, this character seems to reflect more accurately the dominant view as to whom should be responsible for education. Laurence Veysey reminds us that "in nineteenth-century America, educational and theological orthodoxy almost always went together"; its concept of literary cultivation was one "which promised to reconcile moral and intellectual training."[36] That is, the story of criticism we find in these women's narratives seems to reflect more accurately than does Eagleton's story in *The Function of Criticism* the displacement of criticism to university English departments. As Gerald Graff notes, "to reconcile moral and intellectual training" pedagogically was an ideal that held sway until the last decades of the nineteenth century: "As late as the turn of the century at some colleges, there remained only a faint line separating professors of English from the clergy and men continued to move freely between the two professions."[37]

Historically, society has provided the means for literacy to empower some individuals more than others, depending on one's class and gender as well as profession. It is also true that literary culture has tried to hierarchize both texts and ways of reading them. But finally, it is true as well that ordinary people, like the disenfranchised voices I have included in this study, successfully maintain an ability to resist and evade the manipulations of the institutions of literary production and thereby exert a not inconsequential influence on the world around them. Lennox's and Fielding and Collier's arguments about the role that women do have, or should have, in society because of their unique position in language may have been too radical for their own time. Jane Austen nevertheless seems to have felt the same way; she offers a means by which women, though denied professional training of the sort that Edmund Bertram receives, can participate in that professional enterprise as wives and therefore as primary readers and editors of their husband's texts. Because of such things as *The Cry*'s radical structure and the innovative way in which all of these women authors discuss women's ownership of a discourse of power, it is time that we as critics begin to take their work more seriously, and accept the necessity of using these novels pedagogically, alongside those of such male authors as Samuel Richardson and Henry Fielding. The women's novels that I have examined are texts that not only uniquely discuss women's experience in the eighteenth century, but speak directly to the writings of Richardson, Fielding, and other male authors. Their novels reveal the contradictory quality of writers' lived experience that has since been codified only in terms of the current male-dominated canon.

Lennox, Sarah Fielding and Jane Collier, and Jane Austen themselves author criticism that calls into question the structures and ideologies upheld not only by the male-authored texts that I have examined here, but those structures and ideologies that we continue to propagate in the criticism of the twentieth century. Contemporary literary criticism has heretofore ignored that strand of argument these female authors develop in their respective novels that speaks to women's abilities to participate in the profession of criticism. This critical double standard has been used in the twentieth century to exclude eighteenth-century women critics as well. The stereotype of the woman critic whose readings are flawed because she cannot control her sexuality has carried over into the writings of such influential critics as Lawrence Lipking.[38]

The twentieth-century world of literary criticism has also overlooked these female critics' argument positing a practice of literary criticism that keeps as its primary and most public function the moral reformation of society. Part of the reason for this may be that all three novels locate moral reformation in the private space of the home. The learned divine reforms Arabella and her reading habits as she lies ill in bed; Portia carries out what she considers to be her most important reformations of Cylinda and Ferdinand in that same space. Edmund Bertram's reformation is achieved within the private world of Mansfield Park. For all four women authors, it is in the family, after all, that a moral education begins. But they thereby argue for a reformation in society's perception, from considering the public and private spheres as autonomous and independent spaces to one acknowledging the interrelationship between the two—and a reformation in criticism that will establish it as a discourse that negotiates the relation between all manifestations of private and public in the human experience.

While the criticism contained in the novels of Lennox and Fielding and Collier is meant to serve a very public function, society's perception of their novels as private discourse results in this criticism paradoxically becoming a private matter altogether. Still, and as crucially, these novels' representations of critics and criticism presage critical discourse's passage into the academic sphere. Novels like *Mansfield Park* suggest, moreover, that the ideological turn away from Edmund and Fanny Bertram's practice of criticism toward the aesthetic, self-absorbed critical practice of Crawford has helped to render, in many people's eyes, this passage to the academy as a withdrawal or a displacement. In much of society's opinion, the discourse of literary criticism is extremely privatized; Terry Eagleton describes it as, "a domestic one . . . within an institution [where] the critic's voice . . . is effectively inaudible to the society as a whole."[39] Novels as I have discussed here continue to reveal to us the ways in which the study of literature, the practices of interpretation, can serve a public function.

I have attempted to uncover the ways in which these novels have constructed and put readers into place so that I might help students begin to examine more closely how they too resist or connect with cultural texts. The literary critical environment of the eighteenth-century novel stressed debate and dialogue. So, too, can the environment of our classroom if we structure our syllabi to include both canonical and noncanonical texts, and foreground a view of authors within any particular historical era as members of a community, however competetive that community might be.

My readings of these novels also suggests that, as Fanny Price discovers is true of her sister Susan, students already have the potential to perform literary interpretive acts, to make "socially progressive" uses of texts that raise, among others, issues of gender, marriage, work, and literacy in a capitalist society. Particularly in terms of the issue of women's authority to read, my assumption is that my students already have the ability, as did Charlotte Lennox and Sarah Fielding, Jane Collier, and Jane Austen in the eighteenth century, to resist becoming totally disempowered. My task will be to help students to recognize better their autonomy as readers, and their power to effect positive change in the world of cultural texts around them.

Notes

Chapter 1: Introduction

1. See for example Terry Eagleton's *The Function of Criticism* (New York: Verso Press, 1984) or Brian McCrea's *Addison and Steele are Dead: The English Department, Its Canon, and the Professionalization of Literary Criticism* (Newark: University of Delaware Press, 1990).

2. Eagleton, *Function*, 33.

3. "Territorial Disputes in the Republic of Letters: Canon Formation and the Literary Profession," *The Eighteenth Century: Theory and Interpretation* 31, no. 1 (Spring 1990): 4.

4. *The Fame Machine: Book Reviewing and Eighteenth-Century Literary Careers* (Stanford: Stanford University Press, 1996), 1, 2. Donoghue examines the relationship between periodicals and the concept of authorship, specifically the ways in which authorship was defined in popular criticism, and the institution of criticism's share in the making of literary careers. It differs from my study in at least two ways. First, my aim is to reveal how the novel itself functions as literary criticism. Donoghue confines his attention to examining both the critical narratives of the major *Reviews* and authors' responses to these polemics, be they letters, prefaces, plays or novelistic discourse. Second, he argues that women were "denied a means of participating in the dialectic that generated narratives of professional achievement" (161), and only briefly examines the strategies by which such women as Sarah Fielding, and playwrights Elizabeth Griffith and Frances Sheridan, and Frances Burney attempted to achieve fame. In trying to reveal the ways in which women's novels speak to the novels of men and respond to the polemics of the two *Spectator* journals, I argue here that whether or not their participation was publicly acknowledged in journals such as the *Monthly* or *Critical Reviews*, women did publicly participate in that dialectic within their novels.

5. See Ruth Perry's much-cited "The Veil of Chastity: Mary Astell's Feminism," in *Sexuality in Eighteenth-Century Britain*, ed. Paul Gabriel Bouce (New York: Barnes & Noble, 1982), 141–58, and *Women, Letters and the Novel* (New York: AMS Press, 1980). This study follows her lead to compare the ways in which male- and female-authored texts speak to each other (See also her "Bluestockings in Utopia," in *History, Gender and Eighteenth-Century Literature*, ed. Beth Fowkes Tobin (Athens: University of Georgia Press, 1994), 159–78). Too, in my refusal to read women authors as victims, I, like Mitzi Meyers, try to draw attention to "the subtleties and ambiguities of belief systems generated by the culturally inarticulate" ("Reform or Ruin: A Revolution in Female Manners," *Studies in Eighteenth-Century Culture*. Vol. 11, ed. Harry C. Payne [Madison: University of Wisconsin Press, 1982], 202). Besides the work of Perry and Myers, there are any number of critics who have done and continue to do important work on the issues of gender and eighteenth-century writing, including Janet Todd (*Bibliography of*

Women and Literature [New York: Holmes & Meier, 1989] and *The Sign of Angellica: Women, Writing and Fiction 1660–1800* [New York: Columbia University Press, 1989], to name just two), Felicity Nussbaum and Laura Brown (see especially Nussbaum and Brown's "Revising Critical Practices: An Introductory Essay" in *The New 18th Century: Theory, Politics, English Literature*, ed. Felicity Nussbaum and Laura Brown [New York: Methuen Press, 1987], 1–22), and Margaret J. M. Ezell, *Writing Women's Literary History* (Baltimore: The Johns Hopkins University Press, 1993).

See also Cheryl Turner's *Living by The Pen: Women Writers in the Eighteenth Century* (New York and London: Routledge Press, 1994), Kristina Straub's *Divided Fictions: Fanny Burney and Feminine Strategy* (Lexington: The University Press of Kentucky, 1987), and Catherine Gallagher's *Nobody's Story: The Vanishing Acts of Women Writers in the Marketplace, 1670–1820* (Berkeley, Los Angeles: University of California Press, 1994).

6. Turner, 3. We have, for example, critical studies exploring *The Origins of the English Novel 1600–1740* (Baltimore: The Johns Hopkins University Press, 1987), by Michael McKeon, and *The Rise of the Woman Novelist: From Aphra Behn to Jane Austen* (New York: Basil, 1986), by Jane Spencer, but there is little or no overlap in the way that male authors and female authors are discussed. Note, for example, the distinction made in their respective titles: McKeon focuses on genre—and designates, as did Ian Watt before him (*The Rise of the Novel* [Berkeley: The University of California Press, 1957]), Richardson and Fielding as primarily responsible for the emergence of the novel. In contrast, Spencer looks at the novels of several women writers in order to make more general conclusions about their individual achievements as authors.

7. Ibid., 5.

8. J. Paul Hunter, *Before Novels* (New York: Norton, 1991).

9. Coincidentally, twentieth-century women critics' interest in eighteenth-century women-as-professional-readers appears to be quickening. In "Shakespeare's Novels: Charlotte Lennox Illustrated," (*Studies in the Novel* 19, no. 3 [Fall 1987]: 296–310), and "A Cultural Reading of Charlotte Lennox's *Shakspear Illustrated*" (*Cultural Readings of Restoration and Eighteenth-Century English Theater*, ed. J. Douglas Canfield and Deborah C. Payne [Athens: University of Georgia Press, 1995], 228–57), Margaret Anne Doody and Susan Green, respectively, have attempted to recuperate for study Charlotte Lennox's "neglected and maligned" *Shakspear Illustrated* (Green, 229). Green argues that her study "[offers] material for a history of the female textual subject" (250). Mine offers material for a history of the female textual and extratextual reader/critic subject.

More recently, in a chapter of her book called, "Aristotle's Sisters: Behn, Lennox, Fielding, and Reeve," Laura L. Runge investigates "two critical 'truths' that devolve from the initial gendered conditions of criticism in the eighteenth century: first, that there are no female critics from the period, and, second, that the female critics we do recover from the era represent a universal and monolithic female perspective on literature" (*Gender and Language in British Literary Criticism, 1660–1790* [Cambridge University Press, 1997], 123). Runge's examination of the ways in which "aesthetic discourse . . . [adopts] prevalent notions of gender to explain and defend literary standards" (37) makes an important contribution to scholarship on gender and the history of literary criticism; like other scholars, however, she believes that novel-as-criticism is a strategy adopted by women, a "masquerade for the subversive role of female critic." She does not, that is, address the issue that there are male writers, such as Henry Fielding and Samuel Richardson, who use the same strategy.

10. Maximillian Novak, introduction to *Educating the Audience: Addison, Steele, and Eighteenth-Century Culture*, ed. Edward A. and Lillian D. Bloom and Edmund Leites (Los Angeles: William Andrews Clark Memorial Library, University of California 1984), iii.

11. November 1692, *The Gentleman's Journal, or the monthly miscellany* (London: R. Baldwin, 1691-93), 23.

12. February 1693, *The Gentleman's Journal*, 61.

13. Robert Newton Cunningham, *Peter Anthony Motteux 1663–1718: A Biographical and Critical Study* (London: Basil Blackwell, 1933), 36.

14. January 1691, *The Gentleman's Journal*, 26.

15. See also Jean Bethke Elshtain, *Public Man, Private Woman: Women in Social and Political Thought* (Princeton: Princeton University Press, 1981), for an examination of the ways in which "we are, each of us, shaped to and for a way of life whose public and private forms, linked to or embodied within a grammar of basic notions and rules, either nourish or distort our capacities for purposive activity, either strengthen or rob us of the power (potentia) to love and to work" (xiv).

16. Hunter, *Before Novels*, 171.

17. See Armstrong and Tennenhouse's Introduction to *The Ideology of Conduct: Essays in Literature and the History of Sexuality* (New York: Methuen Press, 1987), 1-24, and Armstrong's "The Rise of the Domestic Woman," *The Ideology of Conduct: Essays in Literature and the History of Sexuality*, ed. Nancy Armstrong and Leonard Tennenhouse (New York: Methuen Press, 1987), 96-141.

18. J. Paul Hunter discusses society's desire to keep women readers under surveillance in "The World as Stage and Closet," *British Theatre and the Other Arts*, ed. Shirley Strum Kenny. (Washington: The Folger Shakespeare Library, 1984), 271-87. Hunter notes: "Seventeenth-century guidebooks largely assume that closets are places for devotion, self-examination, prayer, and devout reading, but not long into the eighteenth century one observes a sharp tonal shift. Instead of the commendation of certain exercises and the recommendation of certain appropriate books, there are warnings about the misuses of private time and space. Assumptions that people come to their closets to pray now shift into assumptions that closeted individuals titillate themselves with novels and romances" (282).

19. 19 October 1667, *The Diary of Samuel Pepys: A New and Complete Transcription*, ed. Robert Latham and William Matthews (Berkeley: University of California Press, 1970), 8: 487.

20. 23 October 1667, ibid., 498.

21. See for example, Allan Richard Botica, "Audience, Playhouse and Play in Restoration Theatre 1660-1710" (Ph.D diss., Oxford University, 1985); Laura Brown's *English Dramatic Form, 1660-1760. An Essay in Generic History*, (New Haven: Yale University Press, 1981); Robert D. Hume's *The Development of English Drama in the Late Seventeenth Century* (Oxford: Oxford University Press, 1976); and Judith Milhous's *Thomas Betterton and the Management of Lincoln's Inn Fields, 1695-1708* (Carbondale: Southern Illinois University Press, 1979).

22. Deborah C. Payne " 'And Poets shall by Patron-Princes Live': Aphra Behn and Patronage," in *Curtain Calls: British and American Women and the Theater, 1660-1820*, ed. Mary Anne Schofield and Cecilia Macheski, (Athens: Ohio University Press, 1991), 105.

23. Addison, of course, had tried his hand at playwrighting and Steele had taken over as one of the managers of the Drury Lane theater company in 1711.

In *Transparent Designs: Reading, Performance and Form in the Spectator Papers* (Athens: University of Georgia Press, 1985), Michael G. Ketcham argues that

The Spectator essays teach a generation of theatergoers how to become better interpreters within that space "through the observation of manners: the private thoughts of the social actor become public in his outward gestures; the social observer looks outward toward the behavior of others and turns inward toward his own reflections, which are his attempt to understand the actor's inward motives" (9). I argue that Mr. Spectator also intends that theater audience to employ those same interpretive practices outside that space when they read the textual world.

24. Joseph Addison and Richard Steele, *The Spectator*, edited with introduction and notes by Donald F. Bond (New York and London: Oxford University Press, 1987), vol. 1, 18. Further references to this edition will be cited parenthetically in the text.

25. Daniel Cottom, *The Civilized Imagination: A Study of Ann Radcliffe, Jane Austen and Sir Walter Scott* (Cambridge: Cambridge University Press, 1985), 18.

26. Eagleton, *Function*, 22.

27. Cottom, 3.

28. Eagleton, *Function*, 17.

29. *Women and Print Culture: The Construction of Femininity in the Early Periodical* (London and New York: Routledge, 1989), 15. As Shawn Lisa Maurer also notes, Mr. Spectator "is narratively distinguished by his public silence" ("Reforming Men: Gender, Sexuality, and Class in the Early English Periodical" [Ph.D. diss., The University of Michigan, 1991], 18); he communicates only in the privacy of his club or within the literary space of the periodical. Given that those who have no access to literacy have no access to the discourse of literacy either, the space of the periodical becomes, then, like that of a private club.

30. Ros Ballaster similarly argues that Addison and Steele represent "Woman" as the object or consumer of polite discourse, rather than its subject (*Seductive Forms: Women's Amatory Fiction from 1684 to 1740* [Oxford: Clarendon Press, 1992], 39).

31. Some of those women who were writing and/or publishing at this time included Susannah Centlivre and Mary de la Rivière Manley, who was reportedly the editor of *The Female Tatler* during the period in which Addison and Steele wrote *The Tatler* (See Fidelis Morgan's Introduction to the Everyman's Library edition of *The Female Tatler* [London; Rutland, Vt.: J. M. Dent & Sons Ltd. and Charles E. Tuttle Co., Inc., 1992]). Moreover, Delarivier Manley's *Secret memoirs and manners of several persons of quality, of both sexes, from the New Atalantis, an island in the Mediteranean* (1707) was so popular that by 1736 it had been reprinted seven times (See Rosalind Ballaster's edition [New York: New York University Press, 1992]).

32. [Charles Gildon], (1702; reprint, New York: Garland Press, 1973).

33. Interestingly, the play it fails to mention was one that "was acted with great Applause; the Rules of Aristotle being observ'd, and the Metaphors and Allegories [being] just" (Giles Jacob, *The Poetical Register: or, the Lives and Characters of the English Dramatic Poets* [1719; reprint, New York: Garland Press, 1970], 169).

34. [Gildon], 26.

35. Landes, 3. In terms of the eighteenth century's construction of a public sphere and twentieth-century scholars' discussion of its formation, Landes reminds us that "if we think about the public sphere at all, it is difficult to ignore its gendered meanings": "the early Latin *poplicus*—from the feminine *poplus*, later the masculine *populus*, 'people'—appears to have given way to *publicus*, 'under the influence of *pubes*,' in the sense of 'adult men,' 'male population.' . . . Stated baldly, the early modern classical revival—with its political, linguistic, and stylistic

overtones—invested public action with a decidedly masculinist ethos." (*Women and the Public Sphere in the Age of the French Revolution* [Ithaca and London: Cornell University Press, 1988], 3). In *The Transformation of the Public Sphere*, trans. Thomas Burger (Cambridge: MIT Press, 1989), Jurgen Habermas had argued that as Britain became an increasingly capitalistic society, the public sphere became more egalitarian. Landes refers especially to his work and that of Eagleton when she examines the sexism of the bourgeois sphere, and what motivated the specifically modern varieties of masculinism in the public sphere of France during the age of the Revolution. See also Elshtain, who argues that Hobbesian theory not only deprived women of a public-political voice but of their traditional role in moral education through the activity of mothering. Similarly, Elshtain asserts, Lockean epistemology requires a public/private split that results in two spheres of existence, one of public minds, the other of private desires: "The fact that women were denied a public voice within seventeenth- and eighteenth-century liberalism meant that the 'voice' of woman was necessarily that of privatized, irrational desire."

36. There are a number of good sources on how playwrights made a living during this period, among them Milhous.

37. See the introduction to *Female Playwrights of the Restoration: Five Comedies*, ed. Paddy Lyons and Fidelis Morgan (London and Rutland, Vt.: J. M. Dent & Sons, 1991).

38. *Before Novels*, 72–74. Hunter notes that "The rate of increase [in literacy rates] late in the seventeenth century and through most of the eighteenth was, all scholars agree, very minimal indeed" (67).

39. [Gildon], 27–28.

40. If, as Ros Ballaster suggests, the primary reader of *The Spectator* was male and the category of reader called "Woman," functioned primarily as "substitutive sign for masculine subjectivity" (40), it is easy to see how the potential subversiveness of this message would go unnoticed for so long by readers of this periodical.

41. Aphra Behn, Preface to *The Lucky Chance*, in *The Other Eighteenth-Century*, ed. Robert Uphaus and Gretchen M. Foster (East Lansing, Mich.: Colleagues Press, 1991), 65.

42. This study, of course, owes much to Cottom's and Shevelow's discussions of the issues of private sensibility and aesthetic taste. I am arguing, however, that we can see *The Spectator*'s influence on the literary imagination much earlier than Cottom sees it in his examination of late-eighteenth- and early nineteenth-century novels and that women make more subversive use of their association with the private than Shevelow suggests that they do in her examination of women's relationship to print culture

43. Quoted in Cottom, 8.

44. In " 'As Sacred as Friendship, as Pleasurable as Love': Father-Son Relations in the *Tatler* and *Spectator*," Shawn Lisa Maurer looks at their development of "a nonpartisan, noncompetitive and familial masculinity" (in *History, Gender & Eighteenth-Century Literature*, ed. Beth Fowkes Tobin [Athens and London: The University of Georgia Press, 1994], 15). See also, for their discussions of ways in which certain men were discouraged from pursuing certain professional ambitions, Beth Fowkes Tobin, "Arthur Young, Agriculture, and the Construction of the New Economic Man," ibid., 179–97, and Maurer's dissertation, "Reforming Men."

45. Eagleton, *Function*, 13.

46. I borrow Judith Fetterley's term here to describe Haywood's practice; my

own interpretations of the texts I examine here will likewise be those of a resistant reader. See *The Resisting Reader: A Feminist Approach to American Literature* (Bloomington: Indiana University Press, 1978).

47. The work of twentieth-century women critics suggests that Eliza Haywood, the daughter of a shopkeeper, was a savvy professional who after suffering much public abuse for her writing in the first quarter of the century, went underground for a time. She apparently kept her foot in the door, however; "During her six year silence, Haywood tried her hand at publishing; not only did she print *The Busybody* and *Anti-Pamela* at the "Sign of Fame in Covent Garden," but, according to Schofield, she attempted to write moral conduct books in the guise of *The Fortunate Foundlings*, and in the two novels attributed to her, *Dalinda* and *The History of Cornelia* (*Eliza Haywood*, [Boston: Twayne Publishers, 1985], 7). Schofield is actually a little fuzzy on her dates; later in her book, she asserts that *The Adventures of Eovaii* (1736) "was the last of Haywood's productions for almost ten years." Alison Adburgham says her "silence" lasted sixteen years (*Women in Print: Writing Women and Women's Magazines from the Restoration to the Accession of Victoria* [London: George Allen and Unwin Ltd., 1972], 95). Neither Schofield nor Adburgham seems aware of the ambiguity of her respective definitions of "silence."

48. Haywood, *The Female Spectator*, (London: A Millar, W. Law and R. Cates, 1744–46), vol. 1, 2. Further references will be cited parenthetically in the text.

49. Shevelow, 167.

50. For an alternative perspective on Haywood's domestic ideology, see Deborah Nestor's "Representing Domestic Difficulties: Eliza Haywood and the Critique of Bourgeois Ideology" in *Prose Studies* 16, no. 2 (August 1993): 1–26. Nestor argues that in *The Female Spectator*, Haywood calls into question the notion that "women who follow the patterns of virtuous behavior established by social authorities will be rewarded with positions of authority and power within their own households" (1). Nestor also notes that eighteenth-century readers themselves apparently held this periodical in high regard (22n).

51. See J. G. A. Pocock, *Virtue, Commerce, and History: Essays on Political Thought and History, Chiefly in the Eighteenth Century* (Cambridge: Cambridge University Press, 1985). Catherine Gallagher examines the ways in which the ideology of civic humanism, whose growth Pocock traces in the eighteenth century, helped to aggravate "anxieties about the possible independence of language from reality and women from men" in *Nobody's Story* (92).

52. *Seductive Forms*, 208.

53. *Desire and Domestic Fiction: A Political History of the Novel* (New York and Oxford: Oxford University Press, 1987), 97.

54. Janice Haney-Peritz, "Engendering the Exemplary Daughter: The Deployment of Sexuality in Richardson's *Clarissa*," in *Daughters and Fathers*, ed. Lynda E. Boose and Betty S. Flowers. (Baltimore and London: The Johns Hopkins University Press, 1989), 204.

55. Ibid., 186.

56. For a theoretical discussion of readerly desire, see, for example, Roland Barthes' *The Pleasure of the Text*, trans. Richard Miller (New York: Hill, 1975) or *Criticism and Truth*, trans. and ed. Katrine Pilcher Keuneman (Minneapolis: University of Minnesota Press, 1987).

57. See Foucault's *The History of Sexuality*, vol. 1, trans. Robert Hurley (New York: Pantheon Press, 1980).

Chapter 2. A Will to Read: Intellectual Property and Critical Practice in *Clarissa*

1. Mark Rose, *Authors and Owners: The Invention of Copyright* (Cambridge, Mass. and London: Harvard University Press, 1993), 59–60.

2. "The Author in Court: *Pope v. Curll* (1741)," in *The Construction of Authorship: Textual Appropriation in Law and Literature*, ed. Martha Woodmansee and Peter Jaszi (Durham and London: Duke University Press, 1994), 214.

3. Gallagher, 157.

4. Ibid., 153.

5. T. C. Duncan Eaves, and Ben D. Kimpel, *Samuel Richardson: A Biography* (New York: Oxford University Press, 1971), 84. Hereafter all quotations from this text will be cited internally and use the abbreviation *SR*.

For more information on the publishing world in general, see also John Feather, *A History of British Publishing* (New York: Routledge, 1988) and Alvin Kernan, *Printing Technology, Letters and Samuel Johnson* (Princeton: Princeton University Press, 1987). Prior to the eighteenth century, The Stationer's Company legislated the book trade and maintained copyright privileges. When the Statute of Queen Anne, or The Act of 1710, shifted jurisdiction of literary property debates from the guild to the public courts and gave authors legal rights of ownership, the ground was prepared for the Stationer's Company to lose a good deal of their economic and political power (Feather, 73–74). Despite the Act's potential to revolutionize the printing industry, though, for years after its passage, "no one seems to have recognized the radical change of ownership from printer to writer that had occurred in the statute, and ... all went on, as they had before, selling and purchasing what the booksellers and authors still assumed to be perpetual rights in books old and new" (Kernan, 99). Authors remained at the mercy of their publishers and sometimes their printers until well into the century: "unless a writer sold his copyright he had very little hope of success, and stood but little chance of combatting piracy, if his book was worth pirating" (Kernan, 100). Serious challenges to the practice of an author selling his copyright to the bookseller or publisher "came later along in the century" (Kernan, 101). The end result, particularly for women, was that until late in the eighteenth century, publishers continued to have most of the power; "having paid the author for a manuscript, they owned it" (Gaye Tuchman, with Nina E. Fortin, *Edging Women Out: Victorian Novelists, Publishers, and Social Change* [New Haven: Yale University Press, 1989], 36).

6. Terry Eagleton writes: "Richardson was printer to the House of Commons, and later in life statute and law printer to the king, with a half-share of an exclusive right to print all books dealing with common law. Nor were the academic institutions omitted: Richardson was one of three printers employed by the Society for the Encouragement of Learning, and was later to become printer to the Royal Society (*The Rape of Clarissa: Writing, Sexuality and Class Struggle in Samuel Richardson* [New York: Oxford University Press, 1982], 9–10).

7. Glen M. Johnson, "Richardson's Editor in *Clarissa*," *Journal of Narrative Technique* 10, no. 2 (Spring 1980): 99. See also Everett Zimmerman, "*A Tale of a Tub* and *Clarissa*: A Battling of Books," in *Critical Essays on Jonathan Swift*, ed. Frank Palmeri (New York: G. K. Hall & Co., 1993), 143–63.

8. See Gallagher's discussion of nobody protagonists, such as Clarissa, in *Nobody's Story*. There, Gallagher argues that "in the middle decades of the century, fictional nobodies [such as Clarissa] became the more popular and respectable

protagonists": "that the story was nobody's made it entirely the author's; that it was nobody's also left it open to the reader's sentimental appropriation" (159). Because most authors did not own the copyright to their texts until late in the century, Gallagher finds a universal "theme of dispossession in the rhetoric of authorship [also implied by the concept of 'nobody's story']"; "male authors also frequently stressed that their work and their authorial personae could circulate only because they sold them" (xxi). As both author and publisher of *Clarissa*, Richardson becomes a curious permutation to this rule.

9. *Epistolary Bodies: Gender and Genre in the Eighteenth-Century Republic of Letters* (Stanford: Stanford University Press, 1996), 2.

10. See Michel Foucault's "What is an Author?" in *The Foucault Reader*, ed. Paul Rabinow (New York: Pantheon Books, 1984): 101–20.

11. See Katharine Rogers, "Sensitive Feminism vs. Conventional Sympathy: Richardson and Fielding on Women," *Novel* 9 (1976): 256–70. Rogers argues, "While Richardson was a radical feminist, Fielding accepted the male chauvinism of his culture" (257) To this end, Angela Smallwood asserts, "feminist criticism of Fielding has remained relatively small-scale and undeveloped, whilst Richardson's novels seem to have attracted ever-increasing volumes of absorbed attention" (*Fielding and the Woman Question: The Novels of Henry Fielding and Feminist Debate 1700–1750* [New York: St. Martin's Press, 1989], 4). That could be changing, however. Jill Campbell has since produced the provocative *Natural Masques: Gender and Identity in Fielding's Plays and Novels*, (Stanford: Stanford University Press, 1995).

12. As an example of Richardson's supportive attitude toward women-as-writers, Lady Bradshaigh once wrote to Richardson, complimenting Balzac, who had written, "I could more willingly tolerate a woman with a beard, than one who pretends to learning. In earnest, had I authority in the civil government, I would condemn all those women to the distaff, that undertook to write books, that transform their souls be a masculine disguise, and break the rank they hold in the world." Richardson responded to this sentiment thus: "To say truth, I never can esteem your author for the passage you have quoted from him. It is, I will venture to say, a rash, a silly, an unjust passage in him; and written in the security of a man's heart, who thought he might write anything. I am no enemy to the distaff; but the woman who writes a book, breaks not thereby the rank she holds in the world. The pen is almost as pretty an implement in a woman's fingers, as a needle. He might have said, of a Thalestris armed with a spear, and falchion, and equipped with a breast-plate, helmet, and shield, that she transformed her soul by a masculine disguise; but were I to chuse the attitude that I would have one of the dearest of my lady-correspondents drawn in, it should be with a pen in her hand, in the act of writing, and I know to whom. Madame Sevigne, Madame Dacier, the Marchioness of Lambert, three of that writer's countrywomen, wrote more to the purpose a great deal than Balzac" ([1751], *Selected Letters of Samuel Richardson*, ed. and with an introduction by John Carroll, [London: Oxford University Press, 1964], 183–84).

13. Ibid., 184.

14. Contemporary scholarship has not yet fully addressed the means by which authors such as Richardson responded to women authors' success in the literary marketplace. While scholars such as Cheryl Turner have discussed the ways in which male authors, printers, and publishers have helped, or failed to help, women in publishing or selling their novels, as Linda Zionkowski's essay reveals, they have not yet examined how male novelists engage women authors-as-readers in the ongoing literary debate about canon formation.

15. Eagleton, *Rape*, 9–10.

16. He therefore argued that women needed men, either a good father or father figure, to help them to make judgments, in his eyes: "Would I marry a young Woman you ask, meaning would I have a young Woman married who is incapable of judging for herself?' Would I! Yes I would; and for that very reason should Rejoice, were She my Daughter, that she was in better and surer Protection, than otherwise I should dread such an injudicious Girl would be in . . . Which is most likely to be right, the Parent, who has lived twice the Time in ye World, or the Daughter" (To Frances Grainger, 21 December 1749, *Selected Letters*, 141). In her essay, "Engendering the Exemplary Daughter," Janice Haney-Previtz likewise argues that Richardson's deployment of feminine sexuality was a means to keep all women subject to parental, and then spousal, authority.

17. See also Mona Scheuermann, *Her Bread to Earn: Women, Money, and Society* (Lexington: University Press of Kentucky, 1993), in which she persuasively argues that: "Richardson shows not only that money does not give women power, but that it should not: Clarissa could enter into litigation and be free, but good girls die first . . . While the author is allowed to be critical of the way Clarissa's parents treat her, Clarissa herself may not be" (78).

18. Samuel Richardson, *Clarissa, or The History of a Young Lady*, ed. with an introduction and notes by Angus Ross (New York: Penguin, 1985), preface, 35. While Margaret Anne Doody and Florian Stuber argue that the Penguin text is not ideal as it does not contain "the many passages and letters Richardson restored to the second and third editions" ("*Clarissa* Censored," *Modern Language Studies* 18, no. 1 [Winter 1988]: 87n.), I have chosen to use it primarily because it is more readily available and affordable; as such, it is the edition I would most likely ask my students to use. Moreover, as a version of the first printed edition, it demonstrates that Richardson's desire to control literary critical practice was always inherent in Clarissa's history and in the apparatus of the novel itself. Further references to both the letter (L) and page number will be cited parenthetically in the text.

19. In the *Pope v. Curll* decision, Hardwicke had ruled that Pope's letters were valuable commodities precisely because "no works have done more service to mankind, than those which have appeared in [letters], upon familiar subjects, and which perhaps were never intended to be published" (quoted in Rose, *Authors*, 63–64).

20. Richardson wrote to Aaron Hill, "But how have I suffered by this from the Cavils of some, from the prayers of others, from the Intreaties of many more to make what is called a Happy Ending! Mr. Lyttleton, the late Mr. Thomson, Mr. Cibber and Mr. Fielding, have been among these (7 November 1748, *Selected Letters*, 99).

21. For further support of the idea that Richardson worried about women gaining public power as critics or editors, see Martin C. Battestin, with Ruth R. Battestin, *Henry Fielding: A Life* (New York: Routledge, 1989), hereafter cited parenthetically in the text as *HF*. Richardson delayed the publication of Sarah Fielding's immensely popular *The Governess*, the first full-length children's novel, by troubling her with trivial and petty suggestions for revision (*HF*, 445–46). One reason that he might have done so is because, as April London has demonstrated, this work's purpose was to provide rules of judgment and interpretation—a sort of instruction manual for teaching children how to read properly ("Sarah Fielding," *Dictionary of Literary Biography: British Novelists 1660–1800*, vol. 37, ed. Martin Battestin [Detroit: Bruccoli, 1985], 201).

While Peter Sabor argues, in his introduction to Sarah Fielding's *Remarks on "Clarissa"* (no. 231–32, Augustan Reprint Series [Los Angeles: William Andrews Clark Memorial Library, University of California 1985]: vi), that Richardson revised his novel with this pamphlet in mind, it is worthwhile to note that Richardson did not publicly acknowledge his debt to her.

22. Alexander Pettit similarly argues that Anna Howe reads Clarissa's letters as fiction, arguing that she constructs "her friend in accordance with conventions of comedy discredited elsewhere in *Clarissa*" ("Wit, Satire, and Comedy: Clarissa and the Problem of Literary Precedent," *Studies in the Literary Imagination* 28 [Spring 1995]: 38).

23. To Sarah Chapone, 2 March 1752, *Selected Letters*, 199.

24. To [Lady Bradshaigh?], n.d., ibid., 168.

25. Symbolically, Judy M. Cornett reads Clarissa as a symbolic potential juror, but I suspect that Richardson would not have wished to put that much ambition into his female readers' heads. See "The Treachery of Perception: Evidence and Experience in *Clarissa*," *University of Cincinnati Law Review* 63 (1994): 165–93.

26. Christina Marsden Gillis notes that Clarissa's "letters are not 'premeditated.' Rather they are merely 'scribbled,' ostensibly the products of a private activity with Anna Howe" (*The Paradox of Privacy: Epistolary Form in* Clarissa [Gainesville: The University of Florida Press, 1984], 8). As Marlon B. Ross would argue, therefore, Clarissa and Anna cannot be considered "authentic authors" because of their "scribbler" status. In his provocative essay, Ross asserts that for the eighteenth-century writer "scribbling is both positive and negative, both necessary and impossible. It is positive in the sense that . . . [t]o scribble is to make a mark on the world that ties the private mind to public realities in a literally tangible way. . . . It is what we must do in order to make sense of ourselves and our worlds, but it should be done only in those moments of leisure, while reflecting on the central business of managing life, and should be done only by those who are leisured, those in the leisured class who have no other pressing obligations.

"On the other hand, scribbling is temporary madness. It represents yielding to the temptation of individual whims at the expense of commonsense understanding. In this negative sense, the scribbler is always self-deluded" ("Authority and Authenticity: Scribbling Authors and the Genius of Print in Eighteenth-Century England," *The Construction of Authorship: Textual Appropriation in Law and Literature*, ed. Martha Woodmansee and Peter Jaszi [Durham and London: Duke University Press, 1994], 237).

This begins to explain Richardson's suspicion, as an individual with a strong middle-class work ethic, toward men like Lovelace—who should have more pressing obligations than to scribble fictions. Willed Clarissa's correspondence, Belford becomes its "authentic author" when he ushers the manuscript into print, whose uniform script "reminds the reader of the difference between soul and body, between substance and instance, between public authority and private apprehension of that authority" (Ross, 234).

27. See Habermas, who writes that until the eighteenth century, "even letters which before all else declared 'married love and faithfulness' to the spouse . . . still had its mainstay in the dry communications, the news report. . . . Subjectivity was always already oriented to an audience." He notes, furthermore, that letters by strangers were borrowed, copied and sometimes published (49). Clarissa's attitude toward the correspondence assumes this type of "public" orientation toward letter writing with Lovelace.

28. 2 March 1752, *Selected Letters*, 200.

29. Roland Barthes has proposed that literary production is concerned with the desire of the subject in language, and his work provides a useful context within which to understand the types of desire that motivate Lovelace and Clarissa to correspond. He discusses the erotics of reading, positing a difference between reading for pleasure and reading as a critic that involves a shift in the objects of desire. Reading for pleasure arises from desire for the text, while the critic moves from desiring the work to desiring his or her own language: "there is a third adventure of reading . . . : that of Writing; reading is a conductor of the Desire to write. . . . In this perspective, reading is a veritable production: no longer of interior images, of projections, of hallucinations, but literally of work: the (consumed) product is reversed into production, into promise, into desire for production, and the chain of desires begins to unroll, each reading being worth the writing it engenders, to infinity . . ." (*The Rustle of Language*, trans. Richard Howard [New York: Hill and Wang, 1984], 40–41). See also *Criticism and Truth*, trans. and ed. Katrine Pilcher Keuneman, (Minneapolis: University of Minnesota Press, 1987), and *The Pleasure of the Text*, trans. Richard Miller, with a note on the text by Richard Howard (New York: Hill and Wang, 1975) for a discussion of Barthes' theory of the erotics of reading.

30. Barthes, *The Pleasure of the Text*, 14.

31. Both Carol Houlihan Flynn, in *Samuel Richardson: A Man of Letters* (Princeton: Princeton University Press, 1982), and Janet Butter, in "The Garden: Early Symbol of Clarissa's Complicity," *Studies in English Literature* 24, no. 3 (1984): 527–44, argue that Clarissa has trouble reading herself (Flynn, 24), that she is a study in self-deception (Butter, 539). My contention is that she begins to deceive herself about Lovelace only after she has left her father's house, and only after she has symbolically rejected her father's patriarchal authority. Although Terry Castle argues that others are responsible for Clarissa's misreadings (*Clarissa's Ciphers: Meaning and Disruption in Richardson's "Clarissa"* [Ithaca: Cornell University Press, 1982]), we must look to what Clarissa herself tells us: "I hope . . . I do not deceive myself, and instead of rectifying what is amiss in my heart, endeavor to find excuses for habits and peculiarities which I am unwilling to cast off or overcome. The heart is very deceitful: do you, my dear friend, lay mine open (but surely it is always open before you!) and spare me not, if you find or think it culpable . . . This observation, once for all, as I said, I thought proper to make, to convince you that to the best of my judgement my errors in matters as well of the lesser moment, as the greater, shall rather be the fault of my understanding than of my will (L185, 596).

32. Bond, vol. I, 18.

33. It is only at this point that Clarissa, as Terry Castle suggests, begins to read Lovelace in terms of Nature rather than in terms of Art (57). See especially Castle's introduction and the chapter titled, "Interrupting Miss Clary." Unfortunately, Castle never interprets Clarissa as a sophisticated reader, but only a victim of others' readings. She argues that "Clarissa's basic linguistic assumption is that words embody, absolutely and transparently the inner life of the speaker" (67), and assigns this as a cause for Clarissa's misreading of Lovelace. She also holds Anna Howe culpable for Clarissa's being unable to read properly Lovelace's "Art." Anna, she says, contributes "as much as anyone else to Clarissa's mistakes of reading, and to the greater peril into which she falls" (76). Castle believes that Clarissa tends to consume others' interpretations, and to let those interpretations penetrate her. This seems somewhat naive in light of evidence that indicates, at least

in the early stages of the novel, that Clarissa correctly reads Lovelace's hypocrisy. Such an interpretation also denies that Clarissa has any agency.

34. See, for example, Castle; Terry Eagleton, *Rape*; William Beatty Warner, *Reading "Clarissa": The Struggles of Interpretation* (New Haven: Yale University Press, 1979); and Patricia McKee, *Heroic Commitment in Richardson, Eliot, and James* (Princeton: Princeton University Press, 1986). Although McKee, like the former critics, believes power is at issue in the novel, she argues that it is "not because Lovelace and Clarissa are both struggling to gain it, but because only one character regards it as a possession from which others must be excluded" (101). The character to whom she refers is of course Lovelace, but as I argue here, the editor certainly struggles to gain power—and in fact, unlike Lovelace, he comes to possess it legally.

35. Elizabeth Heckendorn Cook examines the ways in which letters "became [emblems] of the private," and argues that in the eighteenth century they became "intimately identified with the body, especially a female body, and the somatic terrain of the emotions, as well as the thematic material of love, marriage and the family" (*Epistolary Bodies*, 6). The proper subject of the Republic of Letters, the citizen-critic, is a public person, "divested of self-interest, discursively constituted and functionally disembodied" (8). Noting, similarly, that "the sexed body in literature and art is perhaps most notoriously female," Tassie Gwilliam asserts that "Clarissa's exemplarity . . . relies on her eventual departure from the body that threatens to deny her difference" (*Samuel Richardson's Fictions of Gender* [Stanford: Stanford University Press, 1993], 82). In all three scenarios—Cook's, Gwilliam's, and Richardson's—to become a proper subject of the Republic of Letters, Clarissa must literally deny that which makes her a woman—her body. Her repression of her body does not help her to achieve the critical authority associated with Mr. Spectator—since she'll be dead without it.

36. One can argue, a la Margaret Homans, that Clarissa "bears the word" of her own exclusion from linguistic practice. See *Bearing the Word: Language and Female Experience in Nineteenth-Century Women's Writing* (Chicago: University of Chicago Press, 1986).

37. Along with Janice Haney-Previtz's examination of Richardson's representation of Clarissa as daughter, see Florian Stuber's "On Fathers and Authority in *Clarissa* (*Studies in English Literature* 25, no. 3 [1985]). Stuber argues that in *Clarissa*, "Richardson presents . . . a society with a weakened and a weakening sense of and respect for 'authority.' It is authority itself which is weak" (560). For Stuber, Clarissa's father represents this weak type of authority. However, unlike Janice Haney-Peritz, Stuber fails ultimately to see how closely related the ideas of authority and authorship are in the novel's images of patriarchal authority figures who write letters. He asserts that "fundamentally [Richardson] is not a paternalist . . . his book is presented without any authority, without an author . . ." (570). Perhaps one major reason why Clarissa's father is a "weak authority" in this novel is because he does not write; there are only two letters written by him contained in the novel. For Clarissa, what appears to make a man attractive or respectable is very much connected to erudition—the ability to be at once both author and authority.

38. See Foucault's discussion of the attempt to repress the body in the discourse of the eighteenth century in *The History of Sexuality*, vol. 1.

39. As the pamphlet advises, for example, Belford learns not to neglect his duty to God and adopts the view that "A good Dramatick Writer is a Character that this Age knows nothing of" when he comes to censure Lovelace's dramatic plots and

intrigues (*The Apprentice's Vade Mecum* [1734], no. 169–70, Augustan Reprint Series [Los Angeles: William Andrews Clark Memorial Library, Univeristy of California 1975]: 12).

40. Michael McKeon discusses the eighteenth-century debate over the Bible as an authoritative (or not) text in *Origins*, and helps to explain why the Bible, considered a mere "romance" by many seventeenth-century scientists, might have fallen out of the educated eighteenth-century man's canon.

41. As I noted earlier, since Belford echoes many of the sentiments which the editor expresses in the preface and postscript, some readers might assume that Belford is the fictional editor who provides us with these volumes of letters per Clarissa's final request. For further evidence to support the notion that, as this editor, Belford is the most authoritative reader and critic in this text, see Glen M. Johnson and Zimmermann.

42. Eaves and Kimpel note that "throughout his career as a novelist [Richardson] was anxious to demonstrate that honesty is the best policy and will lead to wealth and popularity" (*SR*, 96). Hence, Belford's reform and ability to reform others' behaviors and texts increase his business and his wealth considerably. There is no question that Richardson saw himself as a type of moral guardian, and thought that the duty of the man of letters was a moral one of instruction, but that role was still very firmly tied to the world of business. Eaves and Kimpel call what Richardson practices "the religion of a tradesman—God is good business" (*SR*, 52).

43. See Brenda Bean's "Sight and Self-Disclosure: Richardson's revision of Swift's 'The Lady's Dressing Room'," *Eighteenth-Century Life* 14 (February 1990): 1–23. Bean argues that both Swift and Richardson "describe for instructive purposes the sight that confronts the male observer as he ventures into private female space," but she is more interested in how they represent "woman's moral and physical nature and of man's relationship to woman as observer and interpreter" (1). Her essay actually emphasizes Swift's and Richardson's attitudes toward female virtue and vice rather than examining issues of interpretation or critical authority. Thus, she concludes that "Swift empties the conventional content from traditional images of female perfection; Richardson constructs his tragedy upon them" (18).

44. *Mother Midnight: Birth, Sex, and Fate in Eighteenth-Century Fiction* (New York: AMS Press, 1986), 180. Richardson's self-identification with the publishing industry may be the reason Tom Keymer finds that "there is no . . . 'Richardson' to supervise the reader's experience of *Clarissa* . . . the author remains almost an absence" (*Richardson's "Clarissa" and the Eighteenth-Century Reader* [Cambridge: Cambridge University Press, 1993], xiv).

45. Rose, "The Author in Court," 214.

46. In essence, after the rape, Clarissa no longer uses experiential language; instead, she allegorizes. Of those who examine the role of allegory in *Clarissa*, see Jonathan Loesberg's "Allegory and Narrative in *Clarissa*," *Novel* 15, no. 1 (1981): 35–59, where he posits that Clarissa turns to allegory because she has learned that writing is seduction, a type of intercourse which creates a relationship of subjection. Clarissa creates allegory to represent her loss of subjectivity. Says Heckendorn Cook in *Epistolary Bodies*, "Signifying allegorically, Clarissa is herself transformed into a personification, one circumscribed by the more powerful narrative of eighteenth-century male literary authority and thereby stripped of any transgressive potential of its own" (112). Similarly, John Richetti argues that in the end Clarissa loses her human, material voice, and in the process, any identity

within the real social world of the novel: "After her brutal rape, she may be said to lose her [powerful and articulate] voice, but she quickly assumes another sort of eloquence and specifically marked voice that promotes her new identity as violated Christian virgin-martyr, speaking now in strange and sublime accents as she sheds mortal encumbrances and passes from moral argument to religious homily and allegory" ("Voice and Gender in 18th-Century Fiction: Haywood to Burney," *Studies in the Novel* 19, no. 3 [Fall 1987]: 269). By using this more spiritual language, Clarissa shows that she has moved outside of the "real" world of the novel. Clarissa has become, in William Warner's terms, an "elusive spiritual presence" ("Reading Rape: Marxist-Feminist Figurations of the Literal," *Diacritics* 13, no. 4 [Winter 1983]: 12–32.). Hence, she has lost her critical voice as a critic; she has become purely written, a symbol pointing to something else, a "religious homily and allegory." Because Clarissa has lost the power to interpret, as John Preston points out, "[Belford] is really present on the scene [of Clarissa's dying to *read* it for us" (*The Created Self: The Reader's Role in Eighteenth-Century Fiction* [New York: Barnes, 1970], 60).

47. See, for example, Heckendorn Cook, Gwilliam and Haney-Previtz for some astute examinations of Richardson's attitudes toward gender.

Chapter 3. No Jury of his Peers: Reading *Tom Jones*

1. See John Zomchick (" 'A Penetration which Nothing Can Deceive': Gender and Juridical Discourse in Some Eighteenth-Century Narratives," *SEL: Studies in English Literature, 1500–1900* 29, no. 3 [Summer 1989]: 535–61), who argues along similar lines that Tom and Blifil's rivalry represents a struggle for power.

2. See relevant passages in biographies of both Richardson and Fielding. Eaves and Kimpel note that Richardson revealed his belief that Fielding wrote *Shamela* around the time that *Clarissa* was published. He mentioned it to Lady Bradshaigh with regard to the popularity of *Tom Jones*: "the Pamela, which [Fielding] abused in his Shamela taught him to write to please . . . ([1749] Carroll, 133).

3. In alluding to economic and political sanctions suffered by Fielding, I refer especially to the end of his playwrighting career, one whose success was abruptly cut short by the Licensing Act of 1737.

4. Henry Fielding, *The History of Tom Jones, A Foundling*, ed. Fredson Bowers (Middletown: Wesleyan University Press, 1975), book XI, chapter i, 568. Further references will be cited parenthetically in the text.

5. To understand how little evidence of this inner life he did leave, see *The Correspondence of Henry and Sarah Fielding*, ed. Martin C. Battestin and Clive T. Probyn (Oxford: Clarendon Press, 1993). Nonetheless, in terms of what we do know of Fielding's private life, those who have examined it in relation to his art still downplay its significance. See, for example, Battestin's discussion of the issue of incest in regard to Henry and Sarah's relationship in both the biography (23–30) and in "Fielding and 'The Dreadful Sin of Incest,' " *Novel* 13 (1979): 6–18.

6. See Richardson's letter to Ann Donnelan, 22 February 1752, *Selected Letters*, 197.

7. As a journalist, for example, Fielding was embroiled in the nasty political backbiting waged in the world of print during Walpole's administration; he often found himself the object of "virulent personal attacks leveled against him by the ministerial writers" who supported a prime minister he frequently and openly crit-

icized. See Battestin's discussion of the gossip surrounding Fielding's marriage in *HF*.

8. See Zionkowski, John Richetti, "The Old Order and the New Novel of the Mid-Eighteenth Century: Narrative Authority in Fielding and Smollett," *Eighteenth-Century Fiction* 2, no. 3 (April 1990): 183–96; "Class Struggle Without Class: Novelists and Magistrates," *The Eighteenth Century: Theory and Interpretation* 32, no. 3 (Autumn 1991): 203–18; and Katharine Rogers.

9. Zionkowski, 4.

10. Joseph F. Bartolomeo, *A New Species of Criticism* (Newark: University of Delaware Press, 1994), 10.

11. Nicholas Hudson, "Signs, Interpretations, and the Collapse of Meaning in *Tom Jones* and *Amelia*," *English Studies in Canada* XVI: 17–34. See also Malinda Snow's "The Judgment of Evidence in *Tom Jones*," *South Atlantic Review* 48, no. 2 (May 1983): 21–36 and Zomchick. Like John Bender (*The Mind as Penitentiary*, [Baltimore: The Johns Hopkins University Press, 1990]), Zomchick associates Fielding's juridical approach with his attempts to "discipline" narrative form, and astutely reads Fielding's use of the narrative process as one designed "to construct a juridically-subordinated female—it required the concomitant en-gendering of a juridically-empowered and naturally-sanctioned (masculine) conscience" (536).

12. Kernan, 4.

13. Robert Chibka views *Tom Jones*'s characters as the kinds of readers that Fielding describes in the prefatory chapters and establishes "the connection to Tom's life story that [Wayne] Booth expected but failed to locate" ("Taking 'The Serious' Seriously: The Introductory Chapters of Tom Jones," *The Eighteenth Century: Theory and Interpretation* 31, no. 1 [Spring 1990]: 30). In effect, his essay serves as a jumping-off point for my argument that Fielding is as concerned with the business of reading as he is with the business of writing.

14. Katharine Rogers paved the way for twentieth-century readings of Fielding's attitudes toward women. Since then essays have formed the bulk of writing on the issue of Fielding and gender. Among those, April London has, for instance, examined Fielding's use of the "key metaphor" of property as "an explanatory model of the relations that especially interested" eighteenth-century authors ("Controlling the Text: Women in *Tom Jones*," *Studies in the Novel* 19, no. 3 [Fall 1987]: 323–33). See also Margaret Lenta's "Comedy, Tragedy, and Feminism: The Novels of Richardson and Fielding," *English Studies in Africa* 26, no. 1 (1983): 13–25. Using a Lacanian model in *The Novel as Family Romance: Language, Gender, and Authority from Fielding to Joyce* (Ithaca: Cornell University Press, 1987), Christine Van Boheemen argues that in *Tom Jones*, Fielding presents his fiction as a quest for the symbolic, "to the place from which he can speak." Tom Jones-as-text is a "text born outside the patriarchal law that governs literary culture and understanding" (50). Finally, Mona Scheuermann argues, "Fielding is entirely comfortable with women only when they stay within traditional limits of discourse and behavior" (96).

Angela Smallwood's is the first book-length treatment of Fielding and gender; her book primarily addresses twentieth-century interpretations of Fielding's feminist tendencies, or lack therof.

More recently, Jill Campbell examines Fielding's complicated engagement with the nature and consequence of gender terms, arguing that in his representations of men's and women's struggle for a gendered identity, he calls attention to the way that changes in the largely public forums of male identity—the institutions of government, the economy, high literature—shape and are shaped by changes in the conventionally female realms of home, virtue, and feeling" (*Natural Masques: Gender and Identity in Fielding's Plays and Novels* [Stanford: Stanford University Press, 1995], 7–8). With regard to *Tom Jones*, Campbell focuses predominantly on the socio-political events that shape Fielding's representations of gender in the novel, such as the rebellion of 1745 and the clash between Whig and Jacobite ideology (See part 3, chapters 5–7).

15. Rose, "The Author in Court," 169.

16. See the Introduction to Armstrong and Tennenhouse's *The Ideology of Conduct*, wherein they discuss the ways in which conduct books made clear distinctions between the public and private spheres and men's and women's roles within each.

17. Donoghue, 33.

18. *Authors and Owners*, 65–66.

19. Cornett, 193. Cornett's argument about "metaphoric jurors" in *Clarissa* seems particularly relevant to Fielding's representations of "readers" in *Tom Jones*.

20. *Natural Masques*, 1.

21. See Eaves and Kimpel, *SR*, Battestin, *HF*, and Sabor, who all point to Fielding's glowing review of *Clarissa* and his personal letter to Richardson as evidence of friendship between the two men. A skeptic might not entirely trust such an outpouring of comraderie from a man who wrote such a scathing satire of Richardson's first novel and who, as Campbell points out, could be inconsistent in his criticism.

22. Jill Campbell argues that "he consistently treats problems of male identity and of female identity together, as necessarily interlocking parts of a single economy of system . . . [and] treats the definition of one gendered identity as inextricably bound up with the definition of the other" (7–8). One might argue that Tom cannot learn how to become properly masculine without penetrating all variations of those who are female, including those, like Bridget, whose "masculine" qualities Tom must learn to emulate.

23. "The Mitigated Truth: Tom Jones's Double Heroism," *Studies in the Novel* 19, no. 4 (Winter, 1987): 400. Carlton's choice of words here is unfortunate. While he seems unconscious of the political implications of his sexual metaphors, he also overlooks that, early in the novel, Tom reads in a way similar to the women.

24. See my discussion of women and romances in chapter 1.

25. See Battestin's biography of Fielding, and Eaves and Kimpel's of Richardson, for their discussion of Sarah Fielding's professional dealings with both. Hester Thrale Piozzi suggests that Henry and Sarah had a falling out at about the time that *Tom Jones* was written, not only because of Henry's marriage but because of his attitude toward Sarah's learning Latin and Greek from Arthur Collier. See relevant passages in *The Piozzi Letters: Correspondence of Hester Lynch Piozzi, 1784–1821 (formerly Mrs. Thrale)*, vol. 2 (1792–1798), ed. Edward A. Bloom and Lillian D. Bloom (Newark: University of Delaware Press, 1991), and *Thraliana: The Diary of Mrs. Hester Lynch Thrale (Later Mrs Piozzi) 1776–1809*, ed. Katharine C. Balderston, 2nd ed., vol. 1. *1776–1784*, (London: Oxford University Press, 1951), 78–79.

Battestin does not put much stock in Hester Thrale Piozzi's anecdotes, and rather angrily denounces her as a "reckless gossip who rarely troubled to distinguish truth from falsehood." He provides no evidence to justify this comment, except to argue "[t]hat Sarah's mastery of the classics could have spoiled her relationship with her brother to this degree is, however, unlikely," and to insist that "[a]ll other evidence available to us suggests that there existed between [Henry and Sarah] nothing but love and mutual respect" (*HF* 380–81). The evidence to which he points is her praise of Fielding's novels within her later writings, but in *The Cry* she also praises the writing of Ben Jonson while casting aspersions on him as a person. That is, her respect for an author's ability to write does not mean that she respects or loves him personally or vice versa.

On another note, see William McCarthy, who examines the " 'double bind' or double standard that has continued to operate in twentieth-century critical discussions of [Piozzi] as an author" ("The Repression of Hester Lynch Piozzi: or, How We Forgot a Revolution in Authorship," *Modern Language Studies* 18, no. 1 (Winter 1988): 99–111.

26. "Engendering the Exemplary Daughter," 203. Haney-Peritz refers to Clarissa in her essay when she makes this remark, but it applies as well to Sophia.

27. In a chapter titled, " 'When Men Women Turn': Gender Reversals in Fielding's Plays," Jill Campbell argues that "women's appropriation of male 'empire', the threat of 'petticoat government', is the most general and persistent topic of sexual satire" in Fielding (*Natural Masques*, 21). Interestingly, she feels that Fielding's relation to patriarchal power is ambivalent. She asserts that while Fielding wants "to clothe phallic identity in the outward authority of political, financial and moral power, he is not blind to the ways in which, put to such uses, the phallus becomes a part of impersonal trappings of power" (59).

28. See Battestin's discussion of the issue of incest and Henry and Sarah's relationship in both the biography (*HF*, 23–30) and in "Fielding and 'The Dreadful Sin of Incest.' "

29. From "Soliloquy: or Advice to an Author," *Eighteenth-Century Critical Essays*, ed. Scott Elledge, vol. 1 (Ithaca: Cornell University Press, 1961), 209–10.

30. See J. F. Burrows and A. J. Hassall, "*Anna Boleyn* and the Authenticity of Fielding's Feminine Narratives," *Eighteenth-Century Studies* 21, no. 4 (Summer 1988): 427–53. Burrows and Hasall note that Fielding "usually appropriates the virtuous lives of his heroines to his own authorial discourse, while relegating minor characters with racier pasts to the 'other' discourse of self-portrayal" (447). Hassall goes on to suggest that minor women characters are allowed to tell their own stories because Fielding sympathizes with them and believes that women should have the authority to describe their own experience. This stance ignores the fact that women who do tell their own stories in Fielding's novels experience "punitively severe" punishments for the amorous adventures they relate. Thus it seems more likely that Fielding allows these female characters to tell their own stories in order to demonstrate the immorality of women's tales, and in order to undermine their authority to write—because, he implies, they typically choose to write immoral stories.

31. See also Mona Scheuermann who similarly argues that, "Sophia's greatest [charm], as defined by Allworthy, is that she will not have an opinion in the company of men" (97).

32. *The Novel as Family Romance*, 71.

33. Gary Gautier discusses "Marriage and Family in Fielding's Fiction," and concludes that "Fielding's representation remains conservative, despite complexities in its gender politics" (*Studies in the Novel* 27 (Summer 1995): 111–28).

34. "Controlling the Text," 329.

35. In this way, as Zionkowski and Richetti argue, he reveals his desire to elevate one class of men and authors above all others.

36. See Nancy Armstrong's *Desire and Domestic Fiction*, wherein she argues that, in general, authors attempt to sever the language of politics from the domestic space of the novel.

Chapter 4: Writing Men Reading in *The Female Quixote*

1. Miriam Rossiter Small, *Charlotte Ramsay Lennox: An Eighteenth-Century Lady of Letters*, Yale Studies in English, no. 85 (New Haven: Yale University Press, 1935), 13; Philippe Sejourne, *The Mystery of Charlotte Lennox: First Novelist of Colonial America (1727?–1804)* Publications des Annales de La Faculté des Lettres, Aix-en-Provence, Nouvelle série, no. 62 (Editions Ophrys, 1967), 11.

2. Tuchman argues that "The novel was a lowly genre" (45) until 1840 primarily because it was considered a female genre: "[Literati] were not sneering at the profit; rather they were expressing disdain based on class and gender" (Tuchman 28). Moreover, she describes the rise of male novelists as a nineteenth-century phenomenon, because it was not until after 1840 that male writers saw the novel as an important genre. Before 1840, she notes, women fared well because men had not fully perceived the social and economic value of women's endeavors and so they had not yet set the standards and established the practices that would formally exclude women from novel writing (215). According to Tuchman, "in the late nineteenth century men used their control of major literary institutions to transform the high-culture novel into a male preserve" (5).

3. Small 228. Rather than focus on women's critical appraisal of Lennox within the journals or letters of her peers, her biographers, for instance, call our attention to her contemporaries' personal responses to her. In discussing eighteenth-century women's critical appraisal of Lennox, one of her biographers, Sejourne, refers to Hester Thrale Piozzi's diary. There, Piozzi wrote "though her books are generally approved, nobody likes her" (quoted in Sejourne, 24). Sejourne also cites an anonymous letter that asserts that some women were "offended by [Lennox's] personal uncleanliness" (25). These early scholars suggest that an ulterior motive for women's dislike of Lennox was that she was a man's woman. They point, for instance, to the infamous incident recounted in Boswell's *Life of Johnson* where Johnson placed a laurel "which initiated her into the fraternity of male letters" on her head (Laurie Langbauer, *Women and Romance: The Consolations of Gender in the English Novel* [Ithaca: Cornell University Press, 1990], 82). While many women may have disliked Lennox personally, however, women such as Bluestocking Elizabeth Carter recognized her genius as an author.

4. See, for example, Deborah Ross, "Mirror, Mirror: The Didactic Dilemma of *The Female Quixote*, *SEL: Studies in English Literature, 1500–1900* 27 (1987): 455–73; James J. Lynch, "Romance and Realism in Charlotte Lennox's *The Female Quixote*," *Essays in Literature* 14 (1987): 51–63; and Langbauer.

5. See also Lawrence Stone, *The Family, Sex and Marriage in England 1500–1800*, abridged edition (New York: Harper and Row, 1977), who asserts that: "women's education played a part in leading to demands for greater freedom of choice in mate-selection and a greater share in family decision making . . . On the other hand, it presupposed a growing number of women wholly withdrawn from productive work and with it a great deal of enforced leisure on their hands. There is no doubt whatever that large numbers of bourgeois and even lower-middle-class wives were now being educated like their social superiors for a life of leisure, and were being withdrawn from useful economic employment in their

husbands' businesses" (233). While women's education during this period might have led to their having more authority within the home, it also educated them away from the productive forces of economic labor and to a life of increased leisure. Single and widowed women were very limited as to the kinds of employment they could seek if they had no male relatives to support them. See also the chapter titled, "Women's Education and Women's Rationality," in Alice Browne's *The Eighteenth-Century Feminist Mind* (Brighton: The Harvester Press, 1987), a historical account of eighteenth-century feminism, and Jane Spencer, *The Rise of the Woman Novelist*.

6. *Nobody's Story*, 153–54.

7. Sejourne, 19.

8. Doody, "Shakespeare's Novels."

9. Charlotte Lennox, *The Female Quixote or The Adventures of Arabella*, ed. Margaret Dalziel, (New York and Oxford: Oxford University Press, 1989), 130. Further references will be cited parenthetically in the text.

In light of characters' and authors' obsession with the romance, Clara Reeve's claim that "at the time it first appeared, the taste for those Romances was extinct . . . that [*The Female Quixote*] came thirty or forty years too late" (*The Progress of Romance and The History of Charoba, Queen of Aegypt* [1785. Reprint. New York: The Facsimile Text Society: 1930], II: 6) seems somewhat inaccurate.

10. Laurie Langbauer, for example, examines female authors' responses to, and the consequence of, the yoking of the terms "women" and "romance" in her book.

11. I borrow Barthes' description of productive reading as an activity of reading which leads to the development of literary judgment. Remember too—as Henry Fielding points out in *Tom Jones*—the word "critic" is derived from the Greek word for judgment. To judge well is to be a good critic; to speak of one's ability to judge is to speak of his or her ability to be a critic.

12. For more on the belief in the reformative function and nature of critical discourse during this period, see Eagleton's *The Function of Criticism*.

13. Fielding's narrator's attitude toward "raillery" is very similar to that of Arabella, e.g., "tho' there may be some Faults justly assigned in the Work . . . it will favour rather the Malice of a Slanderer, than of the Judgment of a true Critic, to pass a sever Sentence upon the whole, merely on account of some vicious part (*Tom Jones*, XI: I).

14. In *Bearing the Word*, Homans uses psycholinguistic theory to define and explain two different language systems: the literal and the figural. Homans suggests that women's place in language "from the perspective of an androcentric literary tradition (and the psycholinguistic theory it generates) is with the literal, the silent object of representation, the dead mother, the absent referent" (32). She sees women's novels as articulating the ambivalence which arises from the cultural myths which define women's place in language within the literal, and their desire to "reproduce the nonsymbolic language they shared with the mother . . . a literal language that looks like (or even really is, given that these writers acknowledge their appropriation) an embrace of the very position to which male theory condemns the feminine." Homans further asserts: "[There] are moments [in a novel] . . . in which there is an implicit contradiction between [its] continuous representation of female experience and the text's seeming suddenly to become aware that the implication of such representation is, from the perspective of the symbolic order, the silence and objectification of women. In a literary culture dominated by the symbolic order and its values, the word that women writers and

their female characters most often bear is the word of their own exclusion from linguistic practice, even if they take up this bearing in the (unconscious) hope of bearing their inclusion in another linguistic practice" (32–33).

15. Both Landes and Elshtain remind us that the bourgeois public sphere is constituted by language.

16. Desire is a critical force in the shaping of an ideology of reading. My discussion of the desires that motivate characters' readings owes much to the work of Roland Barthes. For Barthes, there are "three ways by which the image of reading can capture the reading subject. According to the first mode, the reader has a fetishist relation with the text being read. . . . According to the second mode . . . the reader is drawn onward *through* the book's length by a force always more or less disguised, belonging to the order of suspense: the book is gradually abolished, and it is in this impatient, impassioned erosion that the delectation lies. . . . Then there is a third adventure of reading . . . : that of Writing; reading is a conductor of the Desire to write. . . . In this perspective, reading is a veritable production: no longer of interior images, of projections, of hallucinations, but literally of work: the (consumed) product is reversed into production, into promise, into desire for production, and the chain of desires begins to unroll, each reading being worth the writing it engenders, to infinity . . ." (*The Rustle of Language*, 40–41). See also *The Pleasure of the Text* and *Criticism and Truth* for a further discussion of Barthes' theory of the erotics of reading. See Patricia Meyer Spacks, who argues that Lennox's novel develops a "complex thematic of plot . . . as a dynamic of desire" (*Desire and Truth: Functions of Plot in Eighteenth-Century Novels* [Chicago and London: The University of Chicago Press, 1990], 12). Ultimately, she asserts, "There is no way for Arabella to win: controlling social facts limit plot's possibilities" (33).

17. As noted above, most readings of Lennox's novel focus on the issues of women and romance, particularly in terms of women's desire to read that particular genre. In the past, a number of critics have also conflated Lennox's persona as an author with that of her heroine. For example, Langbauer believes that Arabella's problem is that she reads the romance as an accurate representation of reality. She then ruefully asserts that Lennox ultimately loses control of her novel because, like Arabella, she cannot herself avoid reproducing romance. Katherine Sobba Green similarly asserts that, "from the purview of reader-response theory," Arabella's quixotism is "an identificatory model taken too far" (*The Courtship Novel 1740–1820: A Feminized Genre* [Lexington: The University Press of Kentucky, 1991], 47), but fortunately she does not take her own identificatory model too far. Instead, Green looks for the ways in which courtship novels subvert patriarchy and uncover "the insufficiencies of masculinist representations of women" (7). To that end, she reads Lennox's novel "as an important confluence of gender and genre; its valorization of the courtship plot was an empowering strategy both for the identifactory readers who had new prerogatives of choice in marriage and for the 'women of honor' who were to write women's histories in the future (53). Most recently, Catherine Gallagher argues that Arabella's problem is that she fails to recognize the fictionality of romance, and that as an author, Lennox skillfully "broadcast her dispossession [as an author] and thereby invited the investment of time, labor, and money" in such works as *The Female Quixote* (202). Gallagher's reading is a provocative and often a persuasive one, but I think it overlooks Lennox's authorial assertion of critical authority.

18. Again, Margaret Homans' psychoanalytic theory of gendered discourse provides an interesting context within which to examine the conflict which exists be-

tween the two symbol systems that influence male and female experience, and culture's need to suppress and repress that system most closely associated with women.

19. Barthes, *The Rustle of Language*, 39.

20. Ibid.

21. In discussing the repression of desire, Roland Barthes discusses two sorts of Libraries: the public and the domestic. Within the realm of the domestic, there are those books-as-objects "of a desire or an immediate (without mediation) demand. Domestic (and not public) space deprives the book of any function of social, cultural institutional *appearance*. Of course the book-at-home is not a pure fragment of desire: it is (generally) traversed by a mediation which has nothing particularly clean about it: money; we have had to buy it" (*The Rustle of Language*, 38). Like Barthes, Arabella's male relatives expect that the library left behind by Arabella's mother will have no function within the social, cultural milieu. They consciously perceive her books as pure "fragments of desire," but again, like Barthes, they understand on some level that these romances have an economic aspect to them.

22. Quoted in Ross, 470.

23. In Margaret Homans' terms, this is another way that women "bear the word" of their exclusion from language.

24. The Countess's education, could be better than that of many men, but it probably does not equal that of the learned divine. And this could be another reason why she cannot reform Arabella. As Kathleen Duke notes in her dissertation, "Women's Education and the Eighteenth-Century British Novel," (Ph.D. diss, University of Arkansas, 1980): "During the eighteenth century, public opinion identified learning and learned men with the university education from which women were officially barred. . . . The truly learned, classically educated woman remained an anachronism throughout the eighteenth century" (35).

25. Many critics are disturbed by the Countess's abrupt departure from the novel—they note that this very singular character would have been the ideal instrument "for saving the heroine from her folly" but it is possible to read this not as a retreat from a feminist assertion of female power, but as an affirmation on Lennox's part of the role that the Countess sees herself filling in society. One reason that the Countess serves as an example of a good woman is because the illness of her mother sparks the Countess's dutiful behavior. Her education and learning have made it possible for her to be a better caretaker. The Countess reinforces the overtly stated philosophy of Haywood's *The Female Spectator*, which argues that education will not train women to usurp male power, it will only help them become better wives and mothers.

26. To further substantiate this point, Johnson's criticism of the romance cited in this chapter reveals a male anxiety that romance discourse, in its power to persuade men that there is a reality outside that of the world of economics and politics, can inhibit a man's ability to perform properly within that socio-economic world.

Leland Warren argues similarly, "If Arabella must resort to a ready-made fantasy to find a discourse through which she can shape her life, eighteenth-century women were similarly driven toward isolating modes of speaking by being denied access to the language of public affairs. And the confused motives for the male-dominated world's forcing women toward inert discourse is reflected in the actions of the various male characters in the novel who, intentionally or not, help maintain Arabella's delirium. Finally, this male ambivalence suggests that for the eighteenth century, female discourse was forced to represent an aspect of human speech that was simultaneously desired and despised." What distinguishes Warren's argument from mine, however, is that Warren assumes, like those individuals whom Spencer describes, that the language of emotions has no reality: "Female conversation fascinates because in reaching toward the condition of pure art it offers glimpses of a world free from the confusions of reality." While Warren may feel that patriarchy is responsible for women's exclusion from the public realm, he apparently feels that the damage has already been done, and that there is nothing much to do about it. He states that because women have been excluded from society, they speak a language which "must be set apart. Otherwise . . . women's ways with words might seduce all speech to the condition of fantasy to which it naturally threatens to sink anyway" ("Of the Conversation of Women: *The Female Quixote* and the Dream of Perfection," *Studies in Eighteenth-Century Culture* 11 [1982]: 368).

27. See Johnson's *The Rambler*, vol. 3, *The Yale Edition of Works of Samuel Johnson* ed. by W. J. Bale and Albrecht B. Shauss. (New Haven and London: Yale University Press, 1970), no. 4.

28. Ross, 470.

29. *Seductive Forms*, 208.

30. *Women and Romance*, 82.

CHAPTER 5. FRIENDSHIP, EQUALITY, AND INTERPRETATION IN *THE CRY*

1. While a number of sources say that Jane Collier collaborated with Sarah Fielding on this narrative (see, for example, Eaves and Kimpel, *SR*; Battestin, *HF*; Battestin and Probyn, introduction to *Correspondence*; and Carolyn Woodward, "Sarah Fielding," *Encyclopedia of British Women Writers*, ed. Paul Schleuter and June Schleuter [New York: Garland, 1988], 171–73), there is, as Woodward points out, no incontrovertible evidence that she did ("Who Wrote *The Cry*?: A Fable for Our Times," *Eighteenth-Century Fiction* 9 (October 1996): 91–97. *The Cry*'s introduction and the prefatory remarks to each of its volumes suggest a collaborative effort by their use of the pronoun "we." Linda Bree notes that "the similarities between [Sarah Fielding's] previous work and Jane Collier's [also] provide support that they wrote *The Cry* together" (*Sarah Fielding* [New York: Twayne Publishers, 1996], 16). Given *The Cry*'s attempts to elevate principles of collaboration and community, I will speak, then, of the narrative as though Collier did play a significant role in its creation. For a reading of *The Cry* that emphasizes its feminist and communal rhetoric, see also Woodward's "Feminine Virtue, Ladylike Disguise, and Womanly Community: Sarah Fielding and the Female I AM at Mid Century," *Transactions of the Samuel Johnson Society of the Northwest* 16 (1985): 57–71.

2. My argument with regard to Sarah Fielding's quest for literary authority and attitudes toward patriarchal literary culture differs widely from that of critics such as Jane Spencer. Spencer characterizes Sarah Fielding as writing only for male approval: "Delighted to find an argument that made intellectual study acceptable in them, and a champion of their sex like Richardson to promote it, these women novelists of the mid-century [like S. Fielding] sought to keep masculine approval by disclaiming any intention to overturn the sexual hierarchy" (94).

Sometimes the authority of female writers is actually undercut by well-intentioned scholars who appropriate their novels for their own theoretical purposes. In an article whose function it is to test the "adequacy of [Northrop Frye's] literary theory," for instance, J. Paul Hunter uses his reading of *The Cry* to reveal one of the more problematic aspects of Frye's search for literary archetypes: "here is a novel that, whatever its limitations, takes its strength not from its similarity to other books or from its representation of archetypal people and situations but from its informed cultural historicism, a quality that has to be read in its own highly individualized and time-bound terms" ("Novels and History and Northrop Frye," *Eighteenth-Century Studies* 24, no. 2 [Winter 1990–91]: 237). Hunter here uses the Fielding-Collier work to establish the authority of his own theoretical position, rather than to argue that *The Cry* deserves critical attention because of its "informed cultural historicism."

3. Sarah Fielding [with Jane Collier], *The Cry: A New Dramatic Fable*, (1754); intro. Mary Anne Schofield (Delmar, N.Y.: Scholars' Facsimiles and Reprints, 1986) I, 8. As I noted above, while the edition of *The Cry* that I use lists only Fielding as the author, I will follow Woodward's lead and assume it was written with the help of Jane Collier. Further volume and page references to this work appear parenthetically in the text.

4. Their theory foreshadows that of Georg Lukács who similarly suggests that drama, better than other literary forms, gives voice to multiple perspectives (*The Theory of the Novel*, trans. Anna Bostock [Cambridge: MIT Press, 1971], 45). See also Mikhail Bakhtin, who argues that the *novel* reveals best these qualities (*The Dialogic Imagination: Four Essays*, trans. Michael Holquist [Austin: University of Texas Press, 1981]). For this reason among others, *The Cry* may be read as a provocative hybrid of drama and novel.

5. Portia may be said to "write aloud," to use what Barthes describes as a form of vocal writing which allows for the corporeal exteriorization of discourse. Roland Barthes discusses "vocalized writing" in *The Pleasure of the Text*: "Writing aloud is carried by the grain of the voice—an erotic mixture of timbre and language: "writing aloud searches for (in a perspective of bliss) . . . the pulsational incidents, the language lined with flesh, a text where we can hear the grain of the throat, the patina of consonants, the voluptuousness of vowels, a whole carnal stereophony: the articulation of the body, the tongue—to succeed in shifting the signified a great distance and in throwing so to speak, the anonymous body of the actor into my ear: it granulates, it crackles, it caresses, it grates, it cuts, it comes: that is bliss" (66).

6. See Carol Gilligan's *In a Different Voice* (Cambridge: Harvard University Press, 1982), and *Mapping the Moral Domain* (ed. Carol Gilligan, Janie Victoria Ward, and Jill McLean Taylor, with Betty Bardige [Cambridge: Harvard University Press, 1988]. Both volumes discuss the moral development of middle-class women and how their morality influences these women's negotiation of the network of human relationships.

7. Bree also writes that for many scholars "the most significant thing about [Sarah Fielding] was her relationship to one of the two great canonical novelists of the eighteenth century (and, indeed, that the second most significant thing about her was her relationship to the other: she was a close friend of Samuel Richardson)" (vii).

8. Battestin and Probyn, xxii.

9. See Battestin, *HF*; Battestin and Probyn; and Woodward, "Who Wrote *The Cry*?"

10. *The Monthly Review* 8 (April 1753): 274.

Mary Anne Schofield published her facsimile edition in 1986, itself an unaffordable text for many scholars. Among less conservative readings, Deborah Downs-Miers looks at the ways Sarah Fielding's fictions subvert patriarchal order in "Springing the Trap: Subtexts and Subversions," *Fetter'd or Free: British Women Novelists 1670–1815*. ed. Mary Anne Schofield and Cecilia Macheski (Athens: Ohio University Press, 1986), 308–23. She argues: "It is the liminality of women, the suspension of their consciousness between being-object and becoming-subject, a psychological basis of their cultural marginality, which constitutes the real subject of Fielding's work. This liminality also provides the structure and methodology for Fielding's work. She knows women speak in a subtext, often placing their real meanings and intentions into a variety of what I call 'parenthetical forms,' forms not prescribed by the limits of the rules" (309).

27. *David Simple*, 5.

28. I attempt here to show, that is, how Donoghue's argument with regard to male authors might be usefully applied to female authors.

29. Battestin writes "Apprehensive that [Richardson] might consider this friendly gesture an impertinence, she apologized for her 'vanity in daring but touch the hem of [Clarissa's] garment' " (*HF*, 445). See also Eaves and Kimpel, *SR*. One might note that even though Sarah Fielding did not put her name on the pamphlet, she made sure that Richardson knew that she wrote it. Despite the pamphlet's relative lack of popularity, it apparently had a substantial impact on the person to whom it was primarily addressed—Richardson himself. Peter Sabor argues, "Many of the notes that Richardson added to the second and third editions of *Clarissa*, as well as the greatly expanded preface and postscript, answer criticism made in *Remarks on Clarissa*, in much the same way that Sarah Fielding has answered them herself" (*Remarks*, vi). The pamphlet begins in the form of a direct address to the author of *Clarissa*, but it soon becomes, like much of the literary criticism written by women of the eighteenth century, a novelistic dialogue amongst a number of characters. Further references to this work appear parenthetically in the text.

30. While similarly pointing to Fielding's self-deprecatory stance, Laura L. Runge also notes Fielding's appropriation of the Spectator trope when she asserts that Fielding's subversive pose as epistolary novelist-critic "emphasizes the role of spectator with a tangential relationship to knowledge that authorizes the ability to judge without prejudice" (148).

31. Section X, *The Works of Henry Fielding, Esq.*, ed. and with a biographical essay by Leslie Stephen, vol. 7 (London: Smith, Elder, & Co., 1882): 264.

32. The authors themselves use the pronoun "they" when speaking of the Cry to denote that while the Cry often speaks as a single unit, within that unit there are a multitude of individual voices. For the sake of clarity, however, I will, instead, use the pronoun "it."

33. See Terry Lovell, *Consuming Fictions*, (London and New York: Verso, 1987). In this book on late-eighteenth-century readers, Lovell notes: "Interpersonal relations are ubiquitous and cannot be confined to the private sphere. They are negotiated in public as well. There are intermediate zones which developed necessarily at the time of separation from public to private. Each sphere had its public and private faces. To use Goffman's dramaturgical metaphor, there was a backstage to the public and a frontstage to the private." This seems an apt description of how Fielding and Collier make use of the theatre in *The Cry*.

34. *The Female Spectator*, I: v, 263.

35. See, for example, Terry Eagleton's *Function of Literary Criticism* where he

discusses the attempt of Addison and Steele to radically dissociate politics and knowledge in what he refers to as "cultural" rather than strictly "literary" criticism (17). As an example of twentieth-century attempts to focus on the moral rather than the political, William Warner discusses the humanistic response to Richardson in both his book on *Clarissa* and in "Reading Rape." In the latter, he responds to criticism about the ways in which he himself ignored the political in his literary analysis of Clarissa and Lovelace. Wayne Booth serves as a useful example of "moral" criticism in terms of *Tom Jones* (*The Rhetoric of Fiction* [Chicago: University of Chicago Press, 1983]); Miriam Rossiter Small is another example of a scholar who focuses on the moral rather than the political in her discussions of Charlotte Lennox.

36. Preface, *The Works of Henry Fielding, Esq.*, vol. 7, 153.

37. *The Monthly Review* 4 (January 1751), 229.

38. Louis Althusser discusses the educational system as the most powerful state apparatus for repression in his important essay, "Ideology and Ideological State Apparatuses (Notes Toward an Investigation) (January–April 1969)," *Lenin and Philosophy and other Essays*, trans. Ben Brewster (New York: Monthly Review Press, 1971): "I believe that the ideological State apparatus which has been installed in the dominant position in mature capitalist formations as a result of a violent political and ideological class struggle against the old dominant ideological State apparatus, is the educational ideological apparatus" (152). He states further: "The School takes children from every class at infant-school age, and then for years, the years in which the child is most 'vulnerable,' squeezed between the family State apparatus and the educational State apparatus, it drums into them, whether it uses new or old methods, a certain amount of 'know how' wrapped in the ruling ideology . . . or simply the ruling ideology in its pure state (ethics, civic instruction, philosophy)" (155). Collier and Fielding seem particularly astute in their criticism of education, and cognizant of the fact that in order to affect change in the belief system of a society, one must first seek to change those institutions—those State apparatuses, to use Althusser's term—which most profoundly affect the subject in culture.

39. Fielding's and Collier's conception of language seems very close to that of certain twentieth-century feminist psycholinguists: "We learn who we are through the acquisition of language. . . . Using language, we internalize the laws of the world, especially those that reflect the patriarchal powers. We are, then divided within ourselves through the use of language, which guarantees the presence of alienating forces within the individual" (Jane Gallop and Carolyn Burke, "Psychoanalysis and Feminism in France," *The Future of Difference*, ed. Hester Eisenstein and Alice Jardine [New Brunswick, N.J.: Rutgers University Press, 1980], 109).

40. Barthes, *The Rustle of Language*, 41.

41. See Fielding's prefaces to *David Simple* and *Familiar Letters between the principal characters in David Simple and some others, to which is added a vision* (London: A. Millar, 1747), for example. With regard to Henry's scorn for Richardson's lack of a classical education, Eaves and Kimpel point to *Shamela*, noting that it provides evidence that, "[h]e also, as an educated man, disapproved of Richardson's detailed realism and of his 'lowness' and thus can be regarded as a reactionary classicist who failed to see the freshness of Pamela" (*SR*, 128–29).

42. I here paraphrase Josette Feral's discussion of women creating a new language with which to subvert patriarchy; see "The Powers of Difference" in *The Future of Difference*, ed. Hester Eisenstein and Alice Jardine (New Brunswick: Rutgers University Press, 1980), 93.

43. *Joseph Andrews*, ed. Martin C. Battestin (Middletown, Conn.: Wesleyan University Press, 1967).

44. In *The Origins of the English Novel 1600–1740*, Michael McKeon discusses the Baconian conception of Scripture: "The reliance of Protestant thought on the figurative language of the Bible as the one true sense and 'literal' Word of God is profoundly analogous to the new philosophical argument that in nature's book was to be found the register and signature of divine intent" (75). Portia literalizes Scripture through her actions. Interestingly, McKeon talks of the religious crisis of the late seventeenth century, when, after the Restoration, dissenters repudiated Scripture "according to the standards of objective truth and historicity," and called it fiction: 'To speak the truth, the first time that I gave it a Reading, which was dispatch'd in a very little time, I took it for an ill-concerted Romance, to which however I gave the name of Sacred Stories" (79). McKeon's discussion gives one reason why men, particularly educated men, were not reading the Bible. It also raises the possibility that women were given it to read, because like other romances, the Bible would divert a woman's attention from the economic and political arenas.

45. "For ye are all children of God by faith in Jesus Christ. / For as many of you have been baptized into Christ have put on Christ. / There is neither Jew nor Greek, there is neither bond nor free, there is neither male nor female: for ye are all one in Christ Jesus" (3 Galatians: 26–28).

46. I suspect that concluding the narrative with Portia as the Savior figure may be one reason why Richardson "felt the ending was poorly managed"; another is that by Portia's reform of the story of Clarissa to one in which the female heroine reforms the rakish plotter and then marries him, Fielding and Collier contradict, in no small way, Richardson's assertion that "a reformed rake does not make a good husband." The man who bristled at others' suggestions that he change the ending to *Clarissa* offered to publish a second edition of *The Cry* if Fielding would revise hers. Since no second edition exists, she apparently refused.

47. *The Monthly Review* 10 (April 1754), 282.

48. To the Reverend Leonard Chappelow, 15 March 1795, *Piozzi Letters*, vol. 2, 249.

49. See especially the Introduction to, and chapter 5 of, *The Fame Machine*.

Chapter 6. Privacy, Privilege, and "Poaching" in *Mansfield Park*

1. In discussing "the quarrel between 'criticisim' and 'scholarship' " in the nineteenth century," Eagleton sighs, "the dispute ... is for the most part a domestic one, conducted within an institution which permits the critic's voice to be 'disinterested' to the precise extent that it is effectively inaudible to the society as a whole" (*The Function of Criticism*, 66).

2. Ibid., 58.

3. See for example, James Thompson, "Jane Austen," *The Columbia History of the British Novel*, ed. John Richetti, et al. (New York: Columbia University Press, 1994): 275–99.

4. Austen had read and thought highly of Lennox's *The Female Quixote*. See R. W. Chapman, ed., *Jane Austen's Letters to her Sister Cassandra and Others*

(Oxford: Clarendon Press, 1932), 173. All subsequent citations will refer to *Jane Austen's Letters* and the page number.

5. Ibid., 443.

6. See, for example, two of the essays in Janet Todd, ed., *Jane Austen: New Perspectives*, Women and Literature Series, no. 3. (New York: Holmes & Meier, 1983): Nina Auerbach's "Jane Austen's Dangerous Charm: Feeling as one Ought about Fanny Price," 208–23, and Marylea Meyersohn's "What Fanny Knew: A Quiet Auditor of the Whole," 224–30. Hereafter textual references to either of these two essays will cite the author and page number.

7. Since the Enlightenment, Michel de Certeau argues, reading in school has always been understood as a passive act of consumption for all but the specialist critic. He defines consumption as an act of appropriation, an act wherein the consumer assimilates what she takes in, rather than becoming similar to it. Operating under this assumption, ordinary readers can disrupt the proper power relations that the educational system prescribes between specialist critics/teachers and themselves as students. When they do, they are, in de Certeau's terms, poachers: "travellers [who] move across lands belonging to someone else, like nomads poaching their way across fields they did not write, despoiling the wealth of Egypt to enjoy it themselves" (*The Practice of Everyday Life*, trans. Steven Rendall [Berkeley, Los Angeles and London: The University of California Press, 1984], 174).

8. Jan Fergus, *Jane Austen: A Literary Life* (Houndsmills and London, The Macmillan Press, Ltd., 1991), ix. All subsequent citations will refer to author's name and page.

9. Ibid., 22.

10. *Jane Austen's Letters*, 299–300. Quoted in Fergus, 139.

11. Fergus, 140.

12. Ibid., 141.

13. Ibid., 145.

14. Deborah Kaplan, *Jane Austen Among Women*, (Baltimore and London: The Johns Hopkins University Press, 1992), 103. Subsequent citations to this text will refer to author's name and page number.

15. Ibid., 100.

16. Ibid., 103.

17. Ibid., 103.

18. de Certeau, 173.

19. See *Jane Austen's Letters*, 453.

20. Fergus, 145.

21. See also Laura G. Mooneyham, *Romance, Language and Education in Jane Austen's Novels* (New York, St. Martin's Press, 1988), 86.

22. Tony Tanner, *Jane Austen* (Cambridge, Mass.: Harvard University Press, 1986), 157.

23. *The Oxford Illustrated Jane Austen*, ed. R. W. Chapman, vol. 3, *Mansfield Park*, third edition (1934; reprint, Oxford and New York: Oxford University Press, 1988), 113. Further references will be cited parenthetically in the text and will begin with the abbreviation *MP*.

24. *The Function of Criticism*, 40.

25. Ibid., 51.

26. de Certeau, 176.

27. de Certeau, 169.

28. Tanner, 157.

29. Jill Dolan, *The Feminist Spectator* (Ann Arbor: UMI, 1988), 23.

30. de Certeau, 169.

31. Auerbach, 208. For this reason, Fanny is considered to be one of Austen's most problematic characters. In *Jane Austen's Novels: The Art of Clarity* (New Haven and London: Yale University Press, 1992), Roger Gard notes that Fanny "provokes feelings in critics that range from constrained and dutiful pity and admiration to positive repulsion" (123). See also John Halperin, *The Life of Jane Austen*, (Baltimore: Johns Hopkins University Press, 1989).

32. Meyersohn, 224.

33. de Certeau, 172.

34. One reason their union is initially considered to be impossible is because they are first cousins. See Misty G. Anderson, who examines the danger of incest in *Mansfield Park* in "'The Different Sorts of Friendship': Desire in *Mansfield Park*," *Jane Austen and Discourses of Feminism*, ed. Devoney Looser (New York: St. Martin's Press, 1995): 167–84.

35. de Certeau, xiii.

36. *The Emergence of the American University* (Chicago and London: The University of Chicago Press, 1965), 25. See also Patricia Albjerg Graham, "Expansion and Exclusion: A History of Women in Higher Education," *Signs* 3: 759–73.

37. Graff, *Professing Literature: An Institutional History* (Chicago and London: The University of Chicago Press, 1987), 23.

38. In *The Ordering of the Arts in Eighteenth-Century England*, Lipking discusses antecedent texts for Samuel Johnson's *Lives of the Poets*; one of them is Mrs. Elizabeth Cooper's *The Muses Library* (1737). Lipking calls Mrs. Cooper's anthology of English poetry with introductory sketches "trivial," and notes, "There is plenty to object to in Mrs. Cooper. She obviously believes . . . that her own age has achieved a perfection in verse which makes even the best of past ages seem a little quaint; and she overexploits the charming feminine breathlessness that flirts through her pages" ([Princeton: Princeton University Press, 1970], 419). Quotations like these illustrate the need for critics to be more aware of the ways in which they may respond differently to texts depending on the gender of the author, and the consequent need to examine the ways they themselves use the language of desire in their criticism.

39. *The Function of Criticism*, 67. See also McCrea's *Addison and Steele are Dead*. There McCrea argues for an English department professional who acknowledges the interrelationship between life as a professional and his life as an ordinary person, and who will likewise see criticism as a discourse that negotiates the relation between all manifestations of private and public in the human experience. He attributes Addison and Steele's loss of status in English departments, in part, to its current denizen's desire to keep "their academic and personal lives . . . separate" (223). McCrea interprets the discourse of *The Spectator* as a personalized one.

Works Cited

Adburgham, Allison. *Women in Print: Writing Women and Women's Magazines from the Restoration to the Accession of Victoria*. London: George Allen and Unwin Ltd., 1972.

Addison, Joseph and Richard Steele. *The Spectator*. Edited by Donald F. Bond. 5 vols. New York: Oxford University Press, 1965.

Althusser, Louis. "Ideology and Ideological State Apparatuses (Notes Toward an Investigation) (January-April 1969)." In *Lenin and Philosophy and other Essays*, translated by Ben Brewster, 127–86. New York: Monthly Review Press, 1971.

Anderson, Misty G. " 'The Different Sorts of Friendship': Desire in *Mansfield Park*." In *Jane Austen and Discourses of Feminism*, edited by Devoney Looser, 167–83. New York: St. Martin's Press, 1995.

Armstrong, Nancy. *Desire and Domestic Fiction: A Political History of the Novel*. New York: Oxford University Press, 1987.

———. "The Rise of the Domestic Woman." In *The Ideology of Conduct: Essays in Literature and the History of Sexuality*, edited by Nancy Armstrong and Leonard Tennenhouse, 96–141. New York: Methuen Press, 1987.

———, and Leonard Tennenhouse. Introduction to *The Ideology of Conduct: Essays in Literature and the History of Sexuality*, edited by Nancy Armstrong and Leonard Tennenhouse, 1–24. New York: Methuen Press, 1987.

Auerbach, Nina. "Jane Austen's Dangerous Charm: Feeling as one Ought about Fanny Price." In *Jane Austen: New Perspectives*, Women and Literature Series, edited by Janet Todd, no. 3. New York: Holmes & Meier, 1983. 208–223.

Austen, Jane. *The Oxford Illustrated Jane Austen*. Volume 3, *Mansfield Park*, edited by R. W. Chapman. 3rd ed. 1934. Reprint, Oxford and New York: Oxford University Press, 1988.

Bakhtin, Mikhail. *The Dialogic Imagination: Four Essays*. Translated by Michael Holquist. Austin: University of Texas Press, 1981.

Balderston, Katharine C., ed. *Thraliana: The Diary of Mrs. Hester Lynch Thrale (Later Mrs Piozzi) 1776 1800*. Vol. 1: 1776–1784. 2nd ed. London: Oxford University Press, 1951.

Ballaster, Ros. *Seductive Forms: Women's Amatory Fiction from 1684 to 1740*. Oxford: Clarendon Press, 1992.

Barker, Gerard. "*David Simple*: The Novel of Sensibility in Embryo." *Modern Language Studies* 12, no. 2 (Spring 1982): 69–80.

Barthes, Roland. *Criticism and Truth*. Translated and edited by Katrine Pilcher Keuneman. Minneapolis: University of Minnesota Press, 1987.

———. *The Pleasure of the Text*. Translated by Richard Miller. New York: Hill and Wang, 1975.

———. *The Rustle of Language*. Translated by Richard Howard. New York: Hill and Wang, 1986.

Bartolomeo, Joseph F. *A New Species of Criticism: Eighteenth-Century Discourse on the Novel*. Newark: Delaware University Press, 1994.

Battestin, Martin C. "Fielding and 'The Dreadful sin of Incest.' " *Novel* 13 (1979): 6–18.

———, with Ruth R. Battestin. *Henry Fielding: A Life*. New York: Routledge Press, 1989.

———, and Clive T. Probyn, eds. *The Correspondence of Henry and Sarah Fielding*. Oxford: Clarendon, Press, 1993.

Bean, Brenda. "Sight and Self-Disclosure: Richardson's Revision of Swift's 'The Lady's Dressing Room.' " *Eighteenth-Century Life* 14 (February 1990): 1–23.

Beasley, Jerry. "Women and Early Fiction." *Studies in the Novel* 19, no. 3 (Fall 1987): 239–44.

Behn, Aphra. Preface to *The Lucky Chance*. In *The Other Eighteenth-Century*, edited by Robert Uphaus and Gretchen M. Foster. East Lansing, Mi.: Colleagues Press, 1991. 63–65.

Bender, John. *Imagining the Penitentiary: Fiction and the Architecture of Mind in Eighteenth-Century England*. Chicago and London: The University of Chicago Press, 1987.

Bloom, Edward A. and Lillian D. Bloom, eds. *The Piozzi Letters: Correspondence of Hester Lynch Piozzi, 1784–1821 (formerly Mrs. Thrale)*. Vol. 2, 1792–1798. Newark: University of Delaware Press, 1991.

Booth, Wayne C. *The Rhetoric of Fiction*. Chicago: University of Chicago Press, 1983.

Botica, Allan Richard. "Audience, Playhouse and Play in Restoration Theatre 1660–1710." Ph.D. diss., University of Oxford, 1985.

Bree, Linda. *Sarah Fielding*. New York: Twayne Publishers, 1996.

Brown, Laura. *English Dramatic Form, 1660–1760: An Essay in Generic History*. New Haven: Yale University Press, 1981.

Browne, Alice. *The Eighteenth-Century Feminist Mind*. Brighton: The Harvester Press, 1987.

Burrows, J. F. and A. J. Hassall. "*Anna Boleyn* and the Authenticity of Fielding's Feminine Narratives." *Eighteenth-Century Studies* 21, no. 4 (Summer 1988): 427–53.

Butter, Janet. "The Garden: Early Symbol of Clarissa's Complicity." *Studies in English Literature* 24, no. 3 (1984): 527–44.

Campbell, Jill. *Natural Masques: Gender and Identity in Fielding's Plays and Novels*. Stanford, Calif.: Stanford University Press, 1995.

Carlton, Peter J. "The Mitigated Truth: Tom Jones's Double Heroism." *Studies in the Novel* 19, no. 4 (Winter, 1987): 397–409.

Carroll, John, ed. *Selected Letters of Samuel Richardson*. London: Oxford University Press, 1964.

Castle, Terry. *Clarissa's Ciphers: Meaning and Disruption in Richardson's "Clarissa."* Ithaca: Cornell University Press, 1982.

Chapman, R. W., ed. *Jane Austen's Letters to her Sister Cassandra and Others*. Oxford: Clarendon Press, 1932.

Chibka, Robert L. "Taking 'The Serious' Seriously: The Introductory Chapters of

Tom Jones." *The Eighteenth Century: Theory and Interpretation* 31, no. 1 (Spring 1990): 23–45.

Cook, Elizabeth Heckendorn. *Epistolary Bodies: Gender and Genre in the Eighteenth-Century Republic of Letters*. Stanford, Calif.: Stanford University Press, 1996.

Cornett, Judy D. "The Treachery of Perception: Evidence and Experience in *Clarissa*." *University of Cincinnati Law Review* 63 (1994): 165–93.

Cottom, Daniel. *The Civilized Imagination: A Study of Ann Radcliffe, Jane Austen and Sir Walter Scott*. Cambridge: Cambridge University Press, 1985.

Cunningham, Robert Newton. *Peter Anthony Motteux 1663–1718: A Biographical and Critical Study*. London: Basil Blackwell, 1933.

DeCerteau, Michel. *The Practice of Everyday Life*. Translated by Steven Rendall. Berkeley, Los Angeles and London: The University of California Press, 1984.

Dolan, Jill. *The Feminist Spectator*. Ann Arbor: UMI, 1988.

Donoghue, Frank. *The Fame Machine: Book Reviewing and Eighteenth-Century Literary Careers*. Stanford: Stanford University Press, 1996.

Doody, Margaret Anne. "Shakespeare's Novels: Charlotte Lennox Illustrated." *Studies in the Novel* 19, no. 3 (Fall 1987): 296–310.

———, and Florian Stuber. "*Clarissa* Censored." *Modern Language Studies* 18, no. 1 (Winter 1988): 74–88.

Downs-Miers, Deborah. "Springing the Trap: Subtexts and Subversions." In *Fetter'd or Free: British Women Novelists 1670–1815*, edited by Mary Anne Schofield and Cecilia Macheski. Athens: Ohio University Press, 1986. 308–23.

Duke, Kathleen. "Women's Education and the Eighteenth-Century British Novel." Ph.D. diss., University of Arkansas, 1980.

Eagleton, Terry. *The Function of Criticism*. New York: Verso Press, 1984.

———. *The Rape of Clarissa: Writing, Sexuality and Class Struggle in Samuel Richardson*. New York: Oxford University Press, 1982.

Eaves, T. C. Duncan, and Ben D. Kimpel. *Samuel Richardson: A Biography*. New York: Oxford University Press, 1971.

Elshtain, Jean Bethke. *Public Man, Private Woman: Women in Social and Political Thought*. Princeton: Princeton University Press, 1981.

Erickson, Robert A. *Mother Midnight: Birth, Sex, and Fate in Eighteenth-Century Fiction*. New York: AMS Press, 1986.

Ezell, Margaret J.M. *Writing Women's Literary History*. Baltimore: The Johns Hopkins University Press, 1993.

Feather, John. *A History of British Publishing*. New York: Routledge, 1988.

Feral, Josette. "The Powers of Difference." In *The Future of Difference*, edited by Hester Eisenstein and Alice Jardine, 88–94. New Brunswick, N.J.: Rutgers University Press, 1980.

Fergus, Jan. *Jane Austen: A Literary Life*. Houndsmills and London: The Macmillan Press Ltd., 1991.

Fetterley, Judith. *The Resisting Reader: A Feminist Approach to American Fiction*. Bloomington: Indiana University Press, 1978.

Fielding, Henry. *An apology for the life of Mrs. Shamela Andrews*. Edited by Sheridan W. Baker, Jr. Berkeley: University of California Press, 1953.

———. "Articles from *The Champion.*" Vol. 5 of *The Works of Henry Fielding, Esq.* 10 Vols. Edited by Leslie Stephen. London: Smith & Elder & Co., 1882.

———. *The Covent Garden Journal.* Edited by Gerard Edward Jensen. 2 vols. New York: Russell & Russell, Inc., 1964.

———. "An Inquiry into the Causes of the Late Increase in Robbers, etc." In Vol. 7 of *The Works of Henry Fielding, Esq.* Edited by Leslie Stephen. London: Smith, Elder, & Co., 1882.

———. *The Jacobite Journal and Related Writings* Edited by Martin C. Battestin. Middletown, Conn.: Wesleyan University Press, 1975.

———. *Joseph Andrews.* Edited by Martin C. Battestin. Middletown, Conn.: Wesleyan University Press, 1967.

———. *The History of Tom Jones, A Foundling.* Ed. Martin Battestin. Middletown, Conn.: Wesleyan University Press, 1975.

Fielding, Sarah. *The Adventures of David Simple: Containing an Account of His Travels Through the Cities of London and Westminster in the Search of a Real Friend.* Edited by Malcolm Kelsall. New York: Oxford University Press, 1969.

———. *The Countess of Delwyn.* London: A. Millar, 1759.

———. *Familiar Letters between the principal characters in David Simple and some others, to which is added a vision.* London: Millar, 1747.

———. *The Governess: or, Little female academy.* 1749. Reprint, New York and London: Pandora Press, 1987.

———. *Lives of Cleopatra and Octavia.* Lewisburg, Penna.: Bucknell University Press; London: Associated University Presses, 1994.

———. *Remarks on "Clarissa."* Augustan Reprints Series, nos. 231–32. 1749. Reprint, Los Angeles: William Andrews Clark Memorial Library, 1985.

———, [with Jane Collier]. *The Cry: A New Dramatic Fable.* Delmar, N.Y.: Scholars' Facsimiles and Reprints, 1986.

Flynn, Carol Houlihan. *Samuel Richardson: A Man of Letters.* Princeton: Princeton University Press, 1982.

Foucault, Michel. *The History of Sexuality.* Vol. 1. Translated by Robert Hurley. New York: Pantheon Press, 1980.

———. "What is an Author?" In *The Foucault Reader*, edited by Paul Rabinow, 101–120. New York: Pantheon Books, 1984.

Gallop, Jane and Carolyn Burke. "Psychoanalysis and Feminism in France." In *The Future of Difference.* Edited by Hester Eisenstein and Alice Jardine, 106–22. New Brunswick, N.J.: Rutgers University Press, 1980.

Gallagher, Catherine. *Nobody's Story: The Vanishing Acts of Women Writers in the Marketplace, 1670–1820.* Berkeley and Los Angeles: University of California Press, 1994.

Gard, Roger. *Jane Austen's Novels: The Art of Clarity.* New Haven and London: Yale University Press, 1992.

Gautier, Gary. "Marriage and Family in Fielding's Fiction." *Studies in the Novel* 27 (Summer 1995): 111–28.

[Gildon, Charles]. *A Comparison between the Two Stages.* 1702. Reprint, New York: Garland Press, 1973.

Gilligan, Carol. *In A Different Voice: Psychological Theory and Women's Development.* Cambridge: Harvard University Press, 1982.

———, Janie Victoria Ward, and Jill McLean Taylor, eds. *Mapping the Moral Domain*. Cambridge: Harvard University Press, 1988.

Gillis, Christina Marsden. *The Paradox of Privacy: Epistolary Form in "Clarissa."* Gainesville: The University of Florida Press, 1984.

Graff, Gerald. *Professing Literature: An Institutional History*. Chicago and London: The University of Chicago Press, 1987.

Graham, Patrica Albjerg. "Expansion and Exclusion: A History of Women in Higher Education." *Signs* 3 (1978): 759–73.

Green, Katherine Sobba. *The Courtship Novel 1740–1820: A Feminized Genre*. Lexington: The University Press of Kentucky, 1991.

Green, Susan. "A Cultural Reading of Charlotte Lennox's *Shakspear Illustrated*." In *Cultural Readings of Restoration and Eighteenth-Century English Theater*, edited by J. Douglas Canfield and Deborah C. Payne. Athens and London: The University of Georgia Press, 1995.

Griffin, Dustin. *Literary Patronage in England, 1650–1800*. Cambridge and New York: Cambridge University Press, 1996.

Gwilliam, Tassie. *Samuel Richardson's Fictions of Gender*. Stanford: Stanford University Press, 1993.

Habermas, Jurgen. *The Transformation of the Public Sphere*. Translated by Thomas Burger. Cambridge: MIT Press, 1989.

Halperin, John. *The Life of Jane Austen*. Baltimore: The Johns Hopkins University Press, 1989.

Haney-Peritz, Janice. "Engendering the Exemplary Daughter: The Deployment of Sexuality in Richardson's *Clarissa*." In *Daughters and Fathers*, edited by Lynda E. Boose and Betty S. Flowers, 181–207. Baltimore and London: The Johns Hopkins University Press, 1989.

Haywood, Eliza. *The Female Spectator 1744–46*. 4 vols. London: A. Millar, W. Law and R. Cates, 1744–46.

Homans, Margaret. *Bearing the Word: Language and Female Experience in Nineteenth-Century Women's Writing*. Chicago: University of Chicago Press, 1986.

Hudson, Nicholas. "Signs, Interpretations, and the Collapse of Meaning in *Tom Jones* and *Amelia*." *English Studies in Canada* 16 (March 1990): 17–34.

Hume, Robert D. *The Development of English Drama in the Late Seventeenth Century*. Oxford: Oxford University Press, 1976.

Hunter, J. Paul. *Before Novels*. New York: Norton, 1991.

———, "Novels and History and Northrop Frye." *Eighteenth-Century Studies* 24, no. 2 (Winter 1990–91): 225–41.

———. "The World as Stage and Closet." In *British Theatre and the Other Arts*, edited by Shirley Strum Kenny, 271–87. Washington: The Folger Shakespeare Library, 1984.

Jacob, Giles. *The Poetical Register: or, the Lives and Characters of the English Dramatic Poets*. 1719. Reprint, New York: Garland Press, 1970.

Johnson, Glen M. "Richardson's Editor in *Clarissa*." *Journal of Narrative Technique* 10, no. 2 (Spring 1980): 99–114.

Johnson, Samuel. *The Rambler*. Vol. 3, *The Yale Edition of Works of Samuel Johnson*. Edited by W. J. Bate and Albrecht B. Strauss. New Haven and London: Yale University Press, 1969.

Kaplan, Deborah. *Jane Austen Among Women*. Baltimore and London: The Johns Hopkins University Press, 1992.

Kernan, Alvin. *Printing Technology, Letters and Samuel Johnson*. Princeton: Princeton University Press, 1987.

Ketcham, Michael G. *Transparent Designs: Reading, Performance and Form in the Spectator Papers*. Athens: University of Georgia Press, 1985.

Keymer, Tom. *Richardson's "Clarissa" and the Eighteenth-Century Reader*. Cambridge: Cambridge University Press, 1993.

Landes, Joan B. *Women and the Public Sphere in the Age of the French Revolution*. Ithaca, N.Y. and London: Cornell University Press, 1988.

Langbauer, Laurie. *Women and Romance: The Consolations of Gender in the English Novel*. Ithaca: Cornell University Press, 1990.

Lennox, Charlotte. *The Female Quixote or The Adventures of Arabella*. Edited by Margaret Dalziel. New York and Oxford: Oxford University Press, 1989.

———. *Shakspear Illustrated, or the novels and histories on which the plays of Shakspear are founded*. London: A. Millar, 1753.

Lenta, Margaret. "Comedy, Tragedy, and Feminism: The Novels of Richardson and Fielding." *English Studies in Africa* 26, no. 1 (1983): 13–25.

Lipking, Lawrence. *The Ordering of the Arts in Eighteenth-Century England*. Princeton: Princeton University Press, 1970.

Loesberg, Jonathan. "Allegory and Narrative in *Clarissa*." *Novel* 15, no. 1 (1981): 35–59.

London, April. "Controlling the Text: Women in Tom Jones." *Studies in the Novel* 19, no. 3 (Fall 1987): 323–33.

———. "Sarah Fielding." In *Dictionary of Literary Biography: British Novelists 1660–1800*. Vol. 37. Edited by Martin Battestin, 199–202. Detroit: Bruccoli, 1985.

Lovell, Terry. *Consuming Fiction*. London and New York: Verso, 1987.

Lukacs, Georg. *The Theory of the Novel*. Translated by Anna Bostock. Cambridge: MIT Press, 1971.

Lynch, James J. "Romance and Realism in Charlotte Lennox's *The Feamle Quixote*." *Essays in Literature* 14 (1987): 51–63.

Lyons, Paddy and Fidelis Morgan, eds. *Female Playwrights of the Restoration: Five Comedies*. London: J. M. Dent & Sons, Ltd.; Rutland, Vt.: Charles E. Tuttle Co., Inc., 1991.

Manley, Mary Delarivier. *Secret memoirs and manners of several persons of quality, of both sexes, from the New Atalantis, an island in the Mediteranean*. Edited by Rosalind Ballaster. New York: New York University Press, 1992.

Maurer, Shawn Lisa. " 'As Sacred as Friendship, as Pleasurable as Love': Father-Son Relationships in the Tatler." In *History, Gender & Eighteenth-Century Literature*. Edited by Beth Fowkes Tobin, 14–38. Athens, Ga. and London: The University of Georgia Press, 1994.

———. "Reforming Men: Gender, Sexuality and Class in the Early Periodical Essay." Ph.D. diss., University of Michigan, 1991.

McCarthy, William. "The Repression of Hester Lynch Piozzi: or, How We Forgot a Revolution in Authorship." *Modern Language Studies* 18, no. 1 (Winter 1988): 99–111.

McCrea, Brian. *Addison and Steele are Dead: The English Department, Its Canon, and the Professionalization of Literary Criticism.* Newark: University of Delaware Press, 1990.

McKee, Patricia. *Heroic Commitment in Richardson, Eliot, and James.* Princeton: Princeton University Press, 1986.

McKeon, Michael. *The Origins of the English Novel 1600–1740.* Baltimore: The Johns Hopkins University Press, 1987.

Meyersohn, Marylea. "What Fanny Knew: A Quiet Auditor of the Whole." In *Jane Austen: New Perspectives.* Women & Literature Series, edited by Janet Todd, no. 3. New York: Holmes & Meier, 1983. 224–30.

Milhous, Judith. *Thomas Betterton and the Management of Lincoln's Inn Fields, 1695–1708.* Carbondale: Southern Illinois University Press, 1979.

Mooneyham, Laura G. *Romance, Language and Education in Jane Austen's Novels.* New York: St. Martin's Press, 1988.

Morgan, Fidelis, ed. Introduction to *The Female Tatler*, vii–xi. London: J. M. Dent & Sons, Ltd; Rutland, Vt.: Charles E. Tuttle Co., Inc., 1992.

Motteux, Peter. *The Gentleman's Journal, or the monthly miscellany.* London: R. Baldwin, 1691–93.

Myers, Mitzi. "Reform or Ruin: A Revolution in Female Manners." In *Studies in Eighteenth-Century Culture,* edited by Harry C. Payne, vol. 11, 199–216. Madison: University of Wisconsin Press, 1982.

Nestor, Deborah J. "Representing Domestic Difficulties: Eliza Haywood and the Critique of Bourgeois Ideology." *Prose Studies* 16, no. 2 (August 1993): 1–26.

Novak, Maximillian. Introduction to *Educating the Audience: Addison, Steele, and Eighteenth-Century Culture,* edited by Edward A. and Lillian D. Bloom, and Edmund Leites. Los Angeles: William Andrews Clark Memorial Library, University of California, 1984.

Nussbaum, Felicity and Laura Brown. "Revising Critical Practices: An Introductory Essay." In *The New 18th Century: Theory, Politics, English Literature,* edited by Felicity Nussbaum and Laura Brown, 1–22. New York: Methuen Press, 1987.

Payne, Deborah C. " 'And Poets shall by Patron-Princes Live': Aphra Behn and Patronage." In *Curtain Calls: British and American Women and the Theater, 1660–1820,* edited by Mary Anne Schofield and Cecilia Macheski, 105–19. Athens, Ohio: Ohio University Press, 1991.

Pepys, Samuel. *The Diary of Samuel Pepys: A New and Complete Transcription.* Edited by Robert Latham and William Matthews. 10 vols. Berkeley: University of California Press, 1970.

Perry, Ruth. "Bluestockings in Utopia." In *History, Gender & Eighteenth-Century Literature,* edited by Beth Fowkes Tobin, 159–78. Athens and London: The University of Georgia Press, 1994.

———. *Women, Letters and The Novel.* New York: AMS Press, 1980.

———. "The Veil of Chastity: Mary Astell's Feminism." In *Sexuality in Eighteenth-Century Britain,* edited by Paul-Gabriel Bouce, 141–58. New York: Barnes & Noble, 1982.

Pettit, Alexander. "Wit, Satire, and Comedy: *Clarissa* and the Problem of Literary Precedent." *Studies of the Literary Imagination* 28 (Spring 1995): 35–54.

Pocock, J. G. A. *Virtue, Commerce, and History: Essays on Political Thought and*

History, Chiefly in the Eighteenth Century. Cambridge: Cambridge University Press, 1985.

Preston, John. *The Created Self: The Reader's Role in Eighteenth-Century Fiction*. New York: Barnes & Noble, 1970.

Reeve, Clara. *The Progress of Romance and The History of Charoba, Queen of Aegypt*, 1785. Reprint, New York: The Facsimile Text Society: 1930.

Richardson, Samuel. *Clarissa, or The History of a Young Lady*. Edited by Angus Ross. New York: Penguin, 1985.

———. *The Apprentice's Vade Mecum*. Introduction by Alan Dugald McKillop. 1734. Reprint, Los Angeles: William Andrews Clark Library, University of California, 1975.

Richetti, John J. "Class Struggle Without Class: Novelists and Magistrates." *The Eighteenth Century: Theory and Interpretation* 32.3 (Autumn 1991): 203–218.

———. "The Old Order and the New Novel of the Mid-Eighteenth Century: Narrative Authority in Fielding and Smollett." *Eighteenth-Century Fiction* 2.3 (April 1990): 183–196.

———. "Voice and Gender in Eighteenth-Century Fiction: Haywood to Burney." *Studies in the Novel* 19.3 (Fall, 1987): 263–271.

Rogers, Katharine. "Sensitive Feminism vs. Conventional Sympathy: Richardson and Fielding on Women." *Novel* 9 (1976): 256–270.

Rose, Mark. *Authors and Owners: The Invention of Copyright*. Cambridge, MA and London: Harvard University Press, 1993.

———. "The Author in Court: *Pope v. Curll* (1741)." *The Construction of Authorship: Textual Appropriation in Law and Literature*. Ed. Martha Woodmansee and Peter Jaszi. Durham and London: Duke University Press, 1994. 211–229.

Ross, Deborah. "Mirror, Mirror: The Didactic Dilemma of *The Female Quixote*. *SEL: Studies in English Literature, 1500–1900* 27 (1987): 455–473.

Ross, Marlon B. "Authority and Authenticity: Scribbling Authors and the Genius of Print in Eighteenth-Century England." In *The Construction of Authorship: Textual Appropriation in Law and Literature*, edited by Martha Woodmansee and Peter Jaszi, 231–57. Durham, N.C. and London: Duke University Press, 1994.

Runge, Laura L. *Gender and Language in British Literary Criticism, 1660–1790*. Cambridge: Cambridge University Press, 1997.

Scheuermann, Mona. *Her Bread to Earn: Women, Money, and Society*. Lexington: University Press of Kentucky, 1993.

Schofield, Mary Anne. *Eliza Haywood*. Boston: Twayne Publishers, 1985.

Sejourne, Philippe. *The Mystery of Charlotte Lennox: First Novelist of Colonial America (1727?–1804)*. Publications des Annales de La Faculté des Lettres, Aix-en-Provence. Nouvelle Serie, 62. Editions Ophrys, 1967.

Shaftesbury, Anthony Ashley Cooper, Third Earl. "From 'Soliloquy: or Advice to an Author.'" In *Eighteenth-Century Critical Essays*, edited by Scott Elledge, vol. 1, 176–213. Ithaca: Cornell University Press, 1961.

Shevelow, Kathryn. *Women and Print Culture: The Construction of Femininity in the Early Periodical*. London and New York: Routledge Press, 1989.

Small, Miriam Rossiter. *Charlotte Ramsay Lennox: An Eighteenth-Century Lady of Letters*. Yale Studies in English, Vol. LXXXV. New Haven: Yale University Press, 1935.

Smallwood, Angela J. *Fielding and the Woman Question: The Novels of Henry Fielding and Feminist Debate 1700–1750*. New York: St. Martin's Press, 1989.

Snow, Malinda. "The Judgment of Evidence in *Tom Jones*." *South Atlantic Review* 48, no. 2 (May 1983): 21–36.

Spacks, Patricia Meyer. *Desire and Truth: Functions of Plot in Eighteenth-Century Novels*. Chicago and London: The University of Chicago Press, 1990.

Spencer, Jane. *The Rise of the Woman Novelist: From Aphra Behn to Jane Austen*. New York: Basil, 1986.

Stone, Lawrence. *The Family, Sex and Marriage in England 1500–1800*. Abr. ed. New York: Harper and Row, 1977.

Straub, Kristina. *Divided Fictions: Fanny Burney and Feminine Strategy*. Lexington: The University Press of Kentucky, 1987.

Stuber, Florian. "On Fathers and Authority in *Clarissa*." *Studies in English Literature* 25, no. 3 (1985): 557–74.

Tanner, Tony. *Jane Austen*. Cambridge: Harvard University Press, 1986.

Thompson, James. "Jane Austen." *The Columbia History of the British Novel*. Edited by John Richetti et al. New York: Columbia University Press, 1994. 275–99.

Tobin, Beth Fowkes. "Arthur Young, Agriculture, and the Construction of the New Economic Man." In *History, Gender and Eighteenth-Century Literature*, edited by Beth Fowkes Tobin, 179–97. Athens, Ga. and London: The University of Georgia Press, 1994.

Todd, Janet. *The Sign of Angellica: Women, Writing and Fiction 1660–1800*. New York: Columbia University Press, 1989.

———, ed. *Bibliography of Women and Literature*. New York: Holmes & Meier, 1989.

Tuchman, Gaye, with Nine E. Fortin. *Edging Women Out: Victorian Novelists, Publishers, and Social Change*. New Haven: Yale University Press, 1989.

Turner, Cheryl. *Living by the Pen: Women Writers in the Eighteenth Century*. London and New York: Routledge Press, 1992.

Van Boheemen, Christine. *The Novel as Family Romance: Language, Gender, and Authority from Fielding to Joyce*. Ithaca: Cornell University Press, 1987.

Veysey, Laurence. *The Emergence of the American University*. Chicago and London: University of Chicago Press, 1965.

Warner, William. "The Elevation of the Novel in England: Hegemony and Literary History." *ELH: English Literary History* 59, no. 3 (Fall 1992): 577–96.

———. *Reading "Clarissa": The Struggles of Interpretation*. New Haven: Yale University Press, 1979.

———. "Reading Rape: Marxist-Feminist Figurations of the Literal." *Diacritics* 13, no. 4 (Winter 1983): 12–32.

Warren, Leland. "Of the Conversation of Women: *The Female Quixote* and the Dream of Perfection." *Studies in Eighteenth-Century Culture* 11 (1982): 367–80.

Watt, Ian. *The Rise of the Novel*. Berkeley: The University of California Press, 1957.

Woodward, Carolyn. " 'Feminine Virtue, Ladylike Disguise,' Women of Community: Sarah Fielding and the Female I at Mid-Century." *Transactions of the Samuel Johnson Society of the Northwest* 15 (1984): 57–71.

———. "Sarah Fielding." In *Encyclopedia of British Women Writers*, edited by Paul Schleuter and June Schleuter, 171–73. New York: Garland, 1988.

———. "Who Wrote *The Cry*?: A Fable for Our Times." *Eighteenth-Century Fiction* 9 (October 1996): 91–97.

Zimmerman, Everett. "*A Tale of a Tub* and *Clarissa*: A Battling of Books." In *Critical Essays on Jonathan Swift*, edited by Frank Palmeri, 143–63. New York: G. K. Hall & Co., 1993.

Zionkowski, Linda. "Territorial Disputes in the Republic of Letters: Canon Formation and the Literary Profession." *The Eighteenth Century: Theory and Interpretation* 31, no. 1 (Spring 1990): 3–22.

Zomchick, John P. "'A Penetration which Nothing Can Deceive': Gender and Juridical Discourse in Some Eighteenth-Century Narratives." *SEL: Studies in English Literature, 1500–1900.* 29, no. 3 (Summer 1989): 535–61.

Index

"An Inquiry into the Causes of the Late Increase in Robbers, etc." (*The Works of Henry Fielding*), 116, 119, 177n.31, 178n.36
A comparison between the Two Stages ([Gildon]), 23–24
Adburgham, Alison, 157n.47
Addison, Joseph, and Richard Steele, 11, 14, 18, 20–29, 30, 37, 41, 44, 45, 49–50, 85, 118, 139, 143, 148, 154n., 178n.35. *See also specific works by title*
Adventures of David Simple, The (S. Fielding), 112, 113, 114–115, 175n.12, 176n.24, 177n.27
Allworthy (Tom Jones), 36, 71–73, 75, 76, 78, 79, 85–86, 87, 134
Althusser, Louis, 178n.38
Anderson, Misty G., 181n.34
Anna Howe (*Clarissa*), 45–47, 52, 54, 55, 99
Apprentice's Vade Mecum, The (Richardson), 57, 163n.39
Arabella (*The Female Quixote*), 36, 89, 92–109, 132, 134, 150
Arietta (*The Spectator*), 22–25, 46, 93
Armstrong, Nancy, 34, 157n.53, 169n.36; 154n.17; and Leonard Tennenhouse, 154n.17, 167n.16
Art of Ingeniously Tormenting, The (Collier), 111
Auerbach, Nina, 144, 180n.6, 181n.31
Austen, Jane, 11, 12, 34, 134–48, 150, 151. *See also specific works by title*
authority: critical, 11–12, 14–17, 19, 21, 37, 38, 43–45, 47, 56, 87, 91–92, 118, 122, 134, 135, 136, 140, 145; cultural, 21, 27, 30, 39, 44, 62, 64, 65, 66, 68, 75, 76, 77, 88, 139, 141–42, 143; literary, 110, 112–13, 139, 143, 148; moral, 12, 30, parental, 51, patriarchal, 56, 99–101, 114, 142, 146; readerly, 12, 53, 145, 147; women's, as readers, spectators, and writers, 22–23, 29–35, 44, 82, 97–100, 110–33, 151
author(s): amateur, 45–46, 88; and class, 66; /Critic, 70, 135; and gender, 134, 135, 137; and competition, 34–35, 63, 80–81, 87, 90–92, 137; professional, 136, and reviewers, 74, 116–17, 137–39; and their readers, 64, 65, 70, 136–37, 138; as moral exemplars, 30, 62, 129, 132, 139, 141, 147. *See also* women
Authors and Owners (Rose), 158n.1, 164n.45, 167n.18
authorship, 12–14, 38, 65, 66, 67, 77, 112, 115

Bakhtin, Mikhail, 174n.4
Ballaster, Ros, 33–34, 107, 155n.30, 156n.40, 157n.52, 173n.29
Barker, Gerald, 175n.13
Barthes, Roland, 162n.29, 170n.11, 157n.56, 162n.30, 171n.16, 172nn.19 and 20, 174n.5, 178n.40
Bartolomeo, Joseph, 166n.10
Battestin, Martin C., 80, 90, 113, 165n.5, 168n.28; with Ruth Battestin, 160n.21, 166n.7, 167n.25, 173n.1, 177n.29; and Clive T. Probyn, 165n.5, 173n.1, 174n.8, 176n.19
Bean, Brenda, 164n.43
Beasley, Jerry, 175n.13
Before Novels (Hunter), 13, 156n.38
Behn, Aphra, 24, 25–26, 89, 153n.9, 156n.41, 175n.13
Belford (*Clarissa*), 41, 48, 49, 55–62, 130, 134
Bender, John, 166n.11

192

INDEX 193

Betty Thoughtless (Haywood), 34
Bible, 14, 37, 40, 57–58, 129–32, 134, 164 n.40, 179 n.44. *See also* Scriptures
Blifil (*Tom Jones*), 64, 70–77, 78, 84
Bloom, Edward A. and Lillian, 167 n.25, 154 n.10, 176 nn.21 and 25, 179 n.48
body, the, and reading, 52–55, 57, 61, 97–102, 119, 127–28. *See also* desire and reading, erotics of
Booth, Wayne, 166 n.13, 178 n.35
Boswell, James, 169 n.3
Botica, Allan Richard, 154 n.21
Bradshaigh, Lady, 159 n.12, 161 n.24, 165 n.2
Bree, Linda, 173 n.1, 174 n.7, 175 n.11, 176 n.18
Brown, Laura, and Felicity Nussbaum, 153 n. 3
Browne, Alice, 170 n.5
Burrows, J. F. and A. J. Hassall, 168 n.30
Butter, Janet, 162 n.31

Campbell, Jill, 74, 166 n.13, 168 n.27
canon, literary, 11, 12–13, 65, 89, 135, 137, 151
Carlton, Peter J., 79, 167 n.23
Carroll, John, 159 nn.12 and 13, 160 nn.16 and 20, 161 nn.23 and 24, 162 n.28, 165 nn.2 and 6
Castle, Terry, 162 nn.31 and 33, 163 n.34
Centlivre, Susannah, 155 n.31
Cervantes, Miguel de, 89, 107
Champion, The (H. Fielding), 74
Chapman, R. W., 179 n.4, 180 n.4, 180 nn.4 and 23
Chapone, Sarah, 50, 161 n.23
Chibka, Robert, 166 n.13
Cibber, Colley, 44, 74, 116
Civilized Imagination, The (Cottom), 155 nn.25 and 26, 156 n.42
Clarissa (character), 35, 41, 42, 44–62, 80, 100, 129, 131, 132
Clarissa (Richardson), 35, 38–62, 63, 66, 67, 80, 84, 89, 99, 106, 115, 129, 132, 134
clergyman, as symbolic critic, 36, 106–7, 134–35, 140–43, 146–47, 149, 150. *See also* Learned divine, the
Collier, Jane, 13, 110, 111–12, 116, 120, 151; and Sarah Fielding, 11, 12, 34, 37, 109, 110–33, 134, 150, 173 n.1, 176 n.26. *See also specific works by title*
Cook, Elizabeth Heckendorn, 41, 159 n.9, 163 n.35, 164 n.46, 165 n.47
copyright law, 35, 38–40, 66
Cornett, Judy, 161 n.25, 167 n.19
Correspondence of Henry and Sarah Fielding, The (Battestin and Probyn) 165 n.5, 173 n.1, 174 n.8, 176 n.19
Cottom, Daniel, 21, 155 nn.25 and 26, 156 n.42
Countess of Dellwyn, The (S. Fielding), 176 n.
Covent Garden Journal, The (H. Fielding) ,74
critic(s): author(s)-as, 70; definition of, 12, 68, 70, 88, 124; editor(s)-as-, 40–62, 12, 55; hacks, 11, 37, 66, 74, 91, 93, 94; ideal, 12, 37, 68, 106, 134; judge(s)-as-, 68, 91; male, 23–24, 25, 36, 41, 43, 44, 70, 71, 92–93, 142–43; novelist/, 13; as pedagogue, 129–33, 134, 135, 142; professional, 12, 35, 60, 69, 70, 117; representations of, 21, 23, 30, 41, 91–97; role of, 21, 40–41; spectator/, 15, 41; twentieth-century, 13, 22, 30, 42, 64, 65, 66, 135, 139, 147–51; women as, 12, 42, 43, 44, 61, 82–83, 84–85, 94–97, 107–09, 110–33, 139–40, 143–51. *see also* readers, spectators and women
critical practice, 14, 16, 38, 41, 65, 66, 73–74, 91–97, 111, 115–16, 117
criticism: and novelists, 11, 34, 70, 148; definition of, 65, 70, 88, 128–29; education and literary, 22, 69, 134–36, ideology of, 13, 143, 150–51; history of, 11, 65, 115, 134–35; literary, 66, 71, 73, 87, 110; novel-as-, 11, 33; moral, 103–6, 126, 129–33; political, 35–36, 71, 73–77, 87, 109, 117–18, 140; professional, 11, 64, 66; and women, 25, 66, 89–92, 94–97, 107–9, 110–33, 148–51. *See also* critical practice

Criticism and Truth (Barthes), 157n.56
Cry, the (character), 37, 116–17, 122–25, 131, 133
Cry, the: A New Dramatic Fable (S. Fielding, with Collier), 34, 36, 109, 110–33, 149, 176n.26
Cunningham, Robert Newton, 154n.13
Curll, Edward, 35, 39
Cylinda (*The Cry*), 150

David Simple: Volume the Last (S. Fielding), 111, 114, 178n.41
de Certeau, Michel, 136, 140, 180n.7, 181nn.30 and 35
desire (see also reading, erotics of): for critical language, 52, 84; and reading, 52–56, 72, 73, 76, 81–82, 85; sexual, and reading, 35, 52–53, 56, 81, 85, 98–101
Desire and Domestic Fiction (Armstrong), 157n., 169n.36
Diary of Samuel Pepys, The, 19–20, 154nn.19 and 20
discourse: aesthetic, or, of taste, 21–22, critical, 14, 41, 136, 137, 150; cultural, 23, 26, 32; feminine, 12, 22, 23, 29, 45–46; moral/immoral, 36, 48, 52, 53, 59–60, 76, 77, 79, 91; of power, 76, 149; public/private, 17–20, 29–33, 45–46, 49–50, 76, 134, 150; of romance, 36, 46, 50, 53–54, 92–102; of sexuality, 35
Dolan, Jill, 181n.29
Don Quixote (Cervantes), 89, 107
Donoghue, Frank, 11, 112, 133, 152n.4, 167n.17, 175nn.14 and 15, 177n.28, 179n.49
Doody, Margaret Anne, 91, 153n.9, 160n.18, 170n.8
Downs-Miers, Deborah, 177n.26
Drama, 15, 34, 46, 48–49, 52, 82, 92, 142, 144–45; as metaphor of critical practice, 110–33. See also Theater
Duke, Kathleen, 172n.24

Eagleton, Terry, 14, 21, 22, 29, 42, 135, 140, 141, 149, 152n. 2, 155nn. 26 and 28, 156n.45, 158n.6, 160n.15, 163n.34, 170n.12, 177n.35, 179n.1, 180n.24, 181n.39

Eaves, T. C. and Ben D. Kimpel, 113–14, 158n.5, 164n.42, 165n.2, 167n.25, 173n.1, 176n.23, 177n.29, 178n.41
Edmund Bertram (*Mansfield Park*), 136, 140–43, 145–46, 148, 150
Educating the Audience (Bloom and Bloom), 154n.10
education: and class, 120–22; interpretation, 16, 17, 19, 57; literary criticism, 18, 66, 71, 73, 75, 79, 81, 134–48; role of, in development of a private sensibility, 16–17, 19, 21–22, 120; and the romance, 95–96, 98–99; and the spectator/reader personae, 12, 16; women's, 17, 18, 23, 34, 40, 50, 81–84, 90, 103–4, 120–23, 126–28
Elshtain, Jean Bethke, 154n.15, 171n.15
Emergence of the American University, The (Vesey), 181n.36
Epistolary Bodies (Cook), 159n.9, 163n.35, 164n.46,
Erickson, Richard, 59, 164n.44
Ezell, Margaret J. M., 153n.5

Faerie Queene, The (Spenser), 117
Fame Machine, The, (Donoghue), 112, 152n.4, 175n.14, 179n.49
Fanny Price (*Mansfield Park*), 34, 37, 136, 139–40, 142–48, 151
Feather, John, 158n.5
Female Quixote, The (Lennox), 36, 89, 91–109, 110, 132
Female Spectator, The (Haywood), 12, 14, 29, 30–33, 37, 40, 46, 114, 119, 157n.48, 172n.25, 177n.34
Female Spectator, The (character), 18, 30–33, 37, 69–70, 136, 140, 143
Female Tatler, The (Manley?), 155n.31
Feral, Josette, 178n.42
Fergus, Jan, 136–37, 139, 180n.8
Fetterley, Judith, 156n.46
Fielding-as-Narrator (*Tom Jones*), 36, 69, 78, 79, 83, 87, 88, 130
Fielding, Henry, 11–13, 35, 36, 42, 44, 62, 63–64, 64–88, 89, 90, 109, 110, 112, 113, 114–15, 116, 119, 124, 132, 148, 149–50, 153n.6, 170n.13, 176n.23, 177n.31, 178n.36,

179n.43; and Sarah Fielding, 80–81, 83; and Richardson, 63, 77, 80. *See also specific works by title*
Fielding, Sarah, 11–13, 34, 44, 67, and Jane Collier, 11, 12, 111, 34, 36–37, 109, 110–33, 134, 150, 173n.1, 176n.26; and Henry Fielding, 80–81, 83; and Richardson, 80, 109, 112–14, 115–16, 120, 153n.9, 160n.21, 175n.12, 176n.24, 177nn. 27 and 29. *See also specific works by title*
Flynn, Carol Houlihan, 162n.31
Foucault, Michel, 34, 157n.57, 159n.10, 163n.38
Function of Criticism, The (Eagleton), 135, 149, 152n. 2, 155nn. 26 and 28, 156n.45, 170n.12, 177n.35, 179n.1, 180n.24, 181n.39

Gallagher, Catherine, 12, 39, 90, 157n.51, 158nn.3, 4, and 8, 170n.6, 171n.17
Gallop, Jane, and Carolyn Burke, 178n.39
Gard, Roger, 181n.31
Gautier, Gary, 168n.33
Gentleman's Journal, The (Motteux), 14, 20, 154n.11
[Gildon, Charles], 155nn. 32 and 34, 156n.39
Gilligan, Carol, 174n.6
Gillis, Christina Marsden, 161n.26
Goldsmith, Oliver, 175n.14
Governess, The (S. Fielding), 113, 114, 160n.21
Graff, Gerald, 149, 181n.37
Graham, Patricia Albjerg, 181n.36
Green, Katherine Sobba, 171n.17
Green, Susan, 153n.9
Griffin, Dustin, 176n.19
Gwilliam, Tassie, 163n.35, 165n.47

Habermas, Jurgen, 156n.35, 161n.27
Haney-Peritz, Janice, 34, 157n.54, 160n.16, 163n.37, 165n.47, 168n.26
Hardwicke, Lord Chancellor, 39, 43, 67, 68–69, 160n.19
Haywood, Eliza, 11, 12, 14, 18, 29–42, 46, 50, 109, 114, 119, 140, 157nn. 47 and 48, 172n.25, 175n.13, 177n.34. *See also specific works by title*
Henry Fielding (Battestin, with Battestin), 63–64, 74, 80, 160n.21, 166n.7, 167n.25, 173n.1, 177n.29
History of British Publishing, A (Feather), 158n.5
History of Cleopatra and Octavia, The (S. Fielding), 112, 176n.24
History of Sexuality, The (Foucault), 157n.57, 163n.38
Homans, Margaret, 163n.36, 170n.14, 171n.18, 172n.23
Hudson, Nicholas, 166n.11
Hume, Robert D., 154n.21
Hunter, J. P., 13, 153n.8, 154n.18, 156n.38, 174n.2

Ibrahim (Pix), 24
Imagining the Penitentiary (Bender), 166n.11
interiority, 18, 21, 50. *See also* sensibility, private
interpretation: definition of, 124; and gender, 17, 29–34, 41–45, 121–28, 135; literary 12, 140; and the Lord Chancellor, 43, 68–69, 70, 87, 88; juridical, 66, 70, 72; of evidence, 70–74; moral, 30, 80

Jacob, Giles, 155n.33
Jacobite's Journal, The (H. Fielding), 74
Jane Austen's Letters (Chapman), 179n.4
Jane Austen: A Literary Life (Fergus), 180n.8
Johnson, Glen M., 40, 158n.7, 164n.41
Johnson, Samuel, 93–94, 106, 108, 134, 172n.26, 173n.27
Jonson, Ben, 124–25, 168n.25
Joseph Andrews (H. Fielding), 63, 74, 113
judgment: aesthetic, 11, 20–22, 27, 31–32, 40, 43, 59–61, 115, 141–42; critical, 12, 38, 41, 42, 52, 53, 55, 56, 61, 62, 93–96, 103, 137, 142, legal, 65, 66, 69, 70–73, literary, 41, 44, 45, 52, 66, 91, 93, 102; moral/immoral, 41, 54, 55, 61, 64, 69–73, 75–77,

115, 120, 125–26, 132, 145, 146; rules of, 38

Kaplan, Deborah, 138, 180n.14
Kelsall, Malcolm, 112, 113, 175n.12, 176n.20
Kernan, Alvin, 158n.5, 166n.12
Ketcham, Michael C., 154n.23
Keymer, Tom, 164n.44

Landes, Joan B., 23, 155n.35, 171n.15
Langbauer, Laurie, 169nn.3 and 4, 170n.10, 171n.17, 173n.30
law, 35, 70, 102; and its relationship to literature, 38–41, 64, 66, 118–19; of criticism, 22, 66, 138; patriarchal, 100–102, 106, 118
learned divine, the (character): in *The Female Quixote*, 36, 106–9; as a model critic, 36, 134, 150
legal system, practices of, 38–41, 65, 66, 70–77; and rights of ownership, 38–40, 43, 58, 61–62
Lennox, Charlotte, 11–13, 34, 36, 89, 90–91, 91–109, 110, 132, 134–35, 147, 149, 150, 153n.9, 176n.20. *See also specific works by title*
Lenta, Margaret, 166n.14
Lipking, Lawrence, 181n.38
literacy: 16–17, 22, 50, 119, 149, 151; cultural, 22, 50; ideology of 15, kinds of, 14; print, 15, 22
literary marketplace, 15, 22, 38–39, 65; women and, 136–39
Loesberg, Jonathan, 164n.46
London, April, 86, 160n.21,166n.14, 168n.34
Lost Lover, The (Manley), 23
Lovelace (*Clarissa*), 35, 41, 44, 46–62, 80, 115
Lovell, Terry, 177n.33
Lukács, Georg, 174n.4
Lynch, James J., 169n.4
Lyons, Paddy, and Fidelis Morgan, 156n.37

Manley, Mary de la Rivière, 23, 24, 155n.31, 175n.13
Mansfield Park (Austen), 11–13, 34, 37, 135–36, 139–48

Maurer, Shawn Lisa, 155n.29, 156n.44
McCarthy, William, 168n.25
McCrea, Brian, 152n.1, 181n.39
McKee, Patricia, 163n.34
McKeon, Michael, 13, 153n.6, 164n.40
Memoirs of Socrates (S. Fielding), 112
Meyersohn, Marylea, 145, 180n.6
Milhous, Judith, 154n.21, 156n.36
Monthly Review, The, 112, 119, 120, 132, 133, 174n.10, 175n.14, 176nn. 15, 16, and 17, 178n.37, 179n.47
Mooneyham, Laura, 180n.21
Mother Midnight (Erickson), 164n.44
Motteux, Peter, 14, 16–17, 20, 78, 154n.11. *See also specific works by title*
Mr. Glanville (*The Female Quixote*), 93–97, 99–104, 106–7
Mr. Spectator (character), 18, 20–29, 30–33, 35, 36, 37, 38, 41, 54, 69, 78, 88, 106, 139
Myers, Mitzi, 12, 152n. 5

Nestor, Deborah, 157n.50
"Noble Statuary, The" (Motteux), 16–17, 78
Nobody's Story (Gallagher), 157n.51, 170n.6, 171n.17
Novak, Maximillian, 154n.10
novel: history of, 39, 65; rise of, 13, 63
novelist-critic, 13, 70. *See also* author/critic

Origins of the English Novel, The (McKeon), 13, 153n.6
Oxford Illustrated Jane Austen, The (Chapman), 180n.23

Pamela (Richardson), 38, 40, 63, 80
Payne, Deborah, 20, 154n.22
Pepys, Samuel 18–19, 20, 154nn.19 and 20
periodicals, 11–33, 40, 44, 65–66, 94, 117
Perry, Ruth, 12, 152n. 5
Pettit, Alexander, 161n.22
Piozzi Letters, The (Bloom and Bloom), 176nn.21 and 25, 179n.48
Pix, Mary, 24

Pleasure of the Text, The (Barthes), 157n.56, 162n.30, 174n.5
poaching, 136, 140, 143–44
Pocock, J.G.A., 157n.51
Pope v. Curll, 35, 67, 68, 160n.19
Pope, Alexander, 35, 39
Portia (*The Cry*), 37, 115–33, 134, 150
Practice of Everyday Life, The (de Certeau), 180n.7, 181nn.30 and 35
Preston, John, 165n.46
Pride and Prejudice (Austen), 137
print culture, 12, 13, 17–18, 41, 64, 69, 80
privacy, 18, 19, 21, 27–29, 41, 52, 84, 127, 138–39, 142, 144–48
public/private, 13–33, 40–42, 44–46, 48–52, 58, 61–62, 64, 66, 67–70, 71, 78, 80, 84, 86, 87–88, 96, 99–100, 105–9, 120–21, 134–36, 138–39, 150–51
publishing industry, 38–41, 65, 112–13, 132. See also literary marketplace

Radcliffe, Ann, 89
Rambler, The (Johnson), 93, 134, 173n.27
Rape of Clarissa, The (Eagleton), 158n.6, 160n.15, 163n.34
reader(s): amateur/professional, 11–12, 14, 15, 30, 35–36, 37, 46, 48, 49–50, 87, 88, 136; and writer(s), the relationship between, 42–45, 57, 67–68, 85, 135, 136; elitist, 65–66; ideal, 68; moral, 43, 53, 125, 147; privatized, 11, 27, 36; representations of, 34; spectator, 12, 40–41, 50, 51–53, 58, 68; women as, 40, 48, 50, 51–53, 80–87, 95–100, 103–9, 110–33. See also critic(s) *and* women
reading: and class, 15–17, 19–22, 27–29, 43, 67, 83, 93–97, 106–7, 109, 119–20, 139; erotics of, 52–53, 77–86, 98–101, 127–28; practices, 134
Reeve, Clara, 153n.9, 170n.9
reformation: aesthetic, 59–61, 105, 142, 147; of immoral discourse, 52, 59–61, 128–29; literary, 35, 38–39, 133; of manners, 41, 51, 58, 62, 100, 103–7, 129–33, 147, 150
Remarks on "Clarissa" (S. Fielding), 44, 67, 115–16, 177n.29

Resisting Reader, The (Fetterley), 157n.46
Richardson, Samuel, 11–13, 34, 38–62, 65, 66, 67, 74, 90, 91, 93, 96, 106, 110, 113, 148, 149–50, 153n.9, 176n.23; as editor and printer, 39–40; and Sarah Fielding, 80–81; and Henry Fielding, 63, 77, 80–81. See also specific works by title
Richetti, John, 65, 164n.46, 166n.8, 168n.35
Rise of the Novel, The (Watt), 13
Rise of the Woman Novelist, The (Spencer), 153n.6
Rogers, Katharine, 65, 166n.14
romance, 50, 53, 80–81, 91–109, 126–29, 131, 134
Rose, Mark, 39, 67, 68, 158n. 1, 164n.45, 167nn. 15 and 18
Ross, Deborah, 169n.4, 172n.22, 173n.28
Ross, Marlon B., 161n.26
Royal Mischief, The (Manley), 23, 24
Runge, Laura L., 153n.9
Rustle of Language, The (Barthes), 171n.16, 172nn.19 and 20, 178n.40

Sabor, Peter, 161n.22, 167n.21, 177n.29
Samuel Richardson: A Biography (Eaves and Kimpel), 113–14, 158n.5, 164n.42, 165n.2, 167n.25, 173n.1, 176n.23, 177n.29, 178n.41
Scheuermann, Mona, 160n.17, 168n.31
Schofield, Mary Anne, 157n.47, 174n.3, 177n.26; and Cecilia Macheski, 154n.22, 177n.26
Seductive Forms (Ballaster), 157n.52, 173n. 29
Sejourne, Philippe, 169n.1, 170n.7
Selected Letters of Samuel Richardson (Carroll), 159nn.12 and 13, 160nn.16 and 20, 161nn.23 and 24, 162n.28, 165nn.2 and 6
sensibility: aesthetic, 27, 38, 141–42, 143, 144, 147; critical, 85; private, 16, 27–28, 31, 36, 41, 45, 50–51, 54, 58, 70, 75, 128, 138, 143–48; refined, 47

sexuality, 34, 52–53. *See also* reading, erotics of
Shaftesbury, third earl, 83, 168 n.29
Shakespeare, William, 32, 34, 108, 118–19, 125
Shakspear Illustrated (Lennox), 108
Shamela (H. Fielding), 63
Shevelow, Kathryn, 22, 29, 155 n.29, 156 n.42, 157 n.49
Sir George (*The Female Quixote*), 91–94, 96–97, 101–2, 106
Small, Miriam Rossiter, 90, 169 nn.1 and 3, 178 n.35
Smallwood, Angela, 166 n.14
Snow, Malinda, 166 n.11
Sophia (*Tom Jones*), 36, 68, 70, 75, 76, 80, 82, 83–87, 132
Spacks, Patricia Meyer, 171 n.16
spectator(s): /critic(s), 15, 20, 30, 70; as editor(s), 58, 59–60, female, 13, 25–26, 84–85, 143–44, 145; /judge(s), 77; /reader(s), 12, 40–41, 50, 51–53, 58, 68; literate, 57, trope, 30, 77, 140, 145
Spectator, The (Addison and Steele), 11, 14, 20–29, 35, 44, 118, 143, 155 nn. 23 and 24, 156 n.42
Spencer, Jane, 153 n.6, 170 n.5, 173 n.2, 176 n.26
Spenser, Edmund, 117
Stage Licensing Act of 1737, 74, 90
Sterne, Laurence, 175 n.14
Stone, Lawrence, 169 n.5
Stuber, Florian, 160 n.18, 163 n.37
Swift, Jonathan, 59–60, 117, 164 n.43

Tanner, Tony, 144, 180 n.22
Tenny, Tabitha Gilman, 89
Theater, and spectators, 19 21, 25 26, 32, 111, 115, 117–18. *See also* Drama
Thompson, James, 179 n.3
Thrale, Hester Lynch (Piozzi), 113, 133, 167 n.25, 169 n.3
Tobin, Beth Fowkes, 156 n.44

Todd, Janet, 152 n. 5
Tom Jones (character). See *Tom Jones*
Tom Jones (H. Fielding), 35, 64–88, 132, 170 n.13, 176 n.23
Tuchman, Gaye, 169 n.2
Turner, Cheryl, 12, 153 nn.5, 6, and 7, 159 n.14

Una (*The Cry*), 117, 124, 126

Van Boheemen, Christine, 85, 166 n.14, 168 n.32
Veysey, Laurence, 149

Walpole, Horace, 90
Walpole, Robert, 74, 118
Warner, William Beatty, 163 n.34, 165 n.46, 175 n.13, 178 n.35
Warren, Leland, 172 n.26
Watt, Ian, 13, 153 n.6
women: and the private sphere, 66, 84, 86–87, 99–100, 103–4, 138–39; as moral guardians, 40, 66; critics, 26, 32–34, 36–37, 82, 96, 147, 148–51; in print culture, 66, 89–91, 107–9, 139; and privacy, 84; readers, 17, 18, 20, 26–27, 41–44, 46–47, 67, 80–87, 136, 138, 142–44, 145, 146–48; spectators, 25–26, 32–33, 82; writers, 22–25, 33–34, 36–37, 89–91, 107–9, 134, 135, 136, 138. *See also* Critics, Public/Private, *and* Readers
Women and Print Culture (Shevelow), 155 n.29
Women and Romance (Langbauer), 173 n.30
Woodward, Carolyn, 173 n.1, 174 nn.3 and 9, 176 n.17

Young, Edward, 90, 113

Zimmermann, Everett, 158 n. 7, 164 n.41
Zionkowski, Linda, 11, 65, 152 n.3, 159 n.14, 166 n.8, 168 n.35
Zomchick, John, 165 n.1, 166 n.11